ON THE EDGE OF POLITICS

Contributions in Political Science
Series Editor: Bernard K. Johnpoll

ON THE EDGE OF POLITICS

The Roots of Jewish Political Thought in America

WILLIAM S. BERLIN

CONTRIBUTIONS IN
POLITICAL SCIENCE, NUMBER 14

GREENWOOD PRESS
Westport, Connecticut • London, England

Library of Congress Cataloging in Publication Data

Berlin, William S.
  On the edge of politics.

  (Contributions in political science; no. 14
ISSN 0147-1066)
  Bibliography: p.
  Includes index.
  1. Jews in the United States—Politics and
government. 2. Political Science—United States—
History. 3. United States—Politics and government.
I. Title. II. Series.
E184.J5B49   301.45'19'24073   78-4018
ISBN 0-313-20422-5

Library of Congress Catalog Card Number: 78-4018
ISBN: 0-313-20422-5
ISSN: 0147-1066

First published in 1978

Greenwood Press, Inc.
51 Riverside Avenue, Westport, Connecticut 06880

Printed in the United States of America

10 9 8 7 6 5 4 3 2 1

To My Parents

CONTENTS

ACKNOWLEDGMENTS

Acknowledgments are confining. There are many people who have helped in the creation of this book—more than I can fairly acknowledge, more than I truly know. Friends and family who have helped me over the years in large and small ways have lent support to this effort. This book, in other words, has been part of my life, and my life has depended on many people. In addition, these words can hardly express the nature of my debts or the extent of my gratitude.

This book has profited from the comments and criticism of a number of individuals. David Leverenz, Gordon Schochet, and Dennis Bathory made many useful suggestions. Bernard Johnpoll made some excellent recommendations regarding two chapters which subsequently underwent revision. Mary Matro journeyed through the entire text, searching out lapses in style and grammar. Wilson Carey McWilliams helped me in countless ways, going beyond the intellectual content of this study into those invisible areas which may need no acknowledgment.

Others who have helped me in this endeavor include Harriette Podhoretz, Lary May, Marilyn Rye, and John Lee. Roberta Weber typed the manuscript with skill and generosity.

Finally, I wish to thank those to whom this book is dedicated, my parents, for helping in their way to make it all possible.

William S. Berlin

About the Author

William S. Berlin is assistant professor of political science at
Montclair State College in New Jersey.

ON THE EDGE
OF POLITICS

INTRODUCTION

Assimilation has been both a personal and political drama in the American experience. Immigrant confessions, in the form of autobiography, bear witness to the anxieties and ambitions of those who have wished to become Americans. Citizenship, a legal and political condition, has implied to many a condition of the psyche as well: the right attitude, the correct belief, the appropriate aspiration. Gilbert K. Chesterton, with this in mind, compared America, albeit favorably, to the Spanish Inquisition: America seeks to convert immigrants to a creed based on equality and freedom.[1]

At our best moments this has meant that ideas are to be taken seriously, infusing citizenship with an intellectual vitality almost inseparable from practical action. The democratic creed becomes, in truth, a kind of "civil religion," subject to exposition and critical interpretation. Perhaps, too, just as the content of religious belief has become simplified and divorced from action, so has the intellectual life of the democratic creed slowed apace. Ideas, as Louis Hartz suggests, assume an irrational governance, hardening into dogma of unconscious formulas. Belief, in this case, becomes something of a public posture, a defense against the fear of exclusion, rather than an expression of commitment.[2]

For many immigrants who journeyed to America the tensions of assimilation were experienced at first as practical rather than intellectual problems. One needed to learn a new language, find a job, pursue a trade, and adapt to certain transactional aspects of the new culture. The pull of the Old World might be satisfied in neighborhood and family life, in ethnic association, and religious congregation. There might seem to be two worlds, particularly for the later immigrants—the modern American world and the old-fashioned neighborhood. Yet the two realms were neither equal nor respectfully coexistent. The conflict between generations showed that these realms produced frictions that went beyond practical adjustments to a new environment.[3]

These tensions, however painful, were ones most settlers were willing to endure. The very decision to emigrate—choosing a new homeland and separating from kin—prefigured the problems of adaptation and generational conflict. Beyond this, America offered not only the romance of achievement, but real benefits to achieve. Many immigrants might feel caught in the middle, between old loyalties and new aspirations, but it was a captivity many would not surrender, once they had tasted its fruits.

Inevitably, the dilemma of "Americanization" involved political conceptions, too, although little conscious theory developed around it. In the least, becoming an American implied the comprehension of certain political norms, however distant or complex. It involved some conception of the polity, even an unconscious or inaccurate one. Older Americans, wary of foreign influence, were sensitive to this fact. Thomas Jefferson feared large waves of immigration because newcomers often were reared in cultures with inferior political ideas and dangerous attitudes.[4] Similarly, the progressives' zeal to Americanize through the schools paid ideas a kind of negative tribute while denigating the beliefs of the immigrants. Many newcomers came to understand that acceptance in America required the adaptation of older attitudes about politics to those of the American creed. Sometimes, as we shall see, this adaptation was less thorough and more complex than it may have seemed.

This book is based on some simple assumptions embedded in the foregoing discussion. Immigrants who came to America did not arrive tabula rasa, despite their desire to Americanize and the glow of the new culture. They carried in their baggage attitudes and experience which neither a new environment nor a desire to forget could entirely erase. The maintenance of old ways and ideas was both a conscious and unconscious problem. Some who professed to forget had better memories than they realized. For others, the opposite might be the case. Ethnic associations, for example, while maintaining a measure of Old World culture, often were less painful ways of learning New World values.[5]

For Jews, the tension between old and new was probably even more complicated than it was for other immigrants. It was more acute because Judaism had implied separation from the nations of the world. In Europe, Jews had lived in their own communities, generally excluded by Christian society, a vulnerable people apparently dependent on the whims of worldly power. But Jewish separation was at root more profound and also more positive. Viewing themselves as the people who had accepted God's covenant, Jews were to be before God "a kingdom of priests, and a holy nation," who fashioned their lives to the service of Torah.[6] In order to serve the Lord faithfully, they needed to separate from those who did not accept the terms of God's covenant.[7]

Thus the Jews have been a people of history who have seen their existence as a refutation of ordinary history. The observant Jew each day recalls and reviews the Exodus, the authority of Moses and David, and the destruction of the Temple. The separation of the Jews, therefore, helped preserve the ancient moral demands inherent in the covenant. Moreover, since the covenant demanded communal responsibility along with distinctive rituals, behavior, and dress, an exclusive communal life was an absolute necessity.[8]

The immigrant Jew then was more likely to be conscious of his past and conscious of a distinct identity than were other newcomers. Jewish experience had fostered alienation from the ways of the Gentiles, but it also encouraged an awareness of a unique history and tradition. Much of this experience had been expressed in written and oral traditions which the Jew was commanded to study. Loyalty to family, people, and history demanded a sense of detachment. The immigrant Jew, in certain respects, may have wanted to remain a stranger.

Yet just as Jews might be more attached to their religion and culture than were other immigrants, so might they be more attracted to modern America.[9] For one thing, many of the Jews who left Europe were not the most highly religious. As with most other immigrants, it was the more adventurous and least settled who first endeavored to make the change. The Orthodox Jews, in fact, were probably among the last to journey in the years surrounding both World War I and World War II.[10] The Enlightenment, which had touched Eastern European Jewish culture by the dusk of the nineteenth century, often resulted in a ticket to America.[11]

More significant, the United States was unlike other nations to which Jews had dispersed. Jews had been welcomed elsewhere, usually for economic reasons, but America was a nation which in certain ways was akin to the Jewish spirit. The Puritans, who had etched much of the American tradition, considered themselves a "chosen people," the "new Israelites," and looked upon the Old Testament with a piety similar to that of the Jews.[12]

For Americans, a nomadic people descended from immigrants, the Exodus, the promised land, and an underlying sense of homelessness might also have special meaning. The belief in a transcending moral law, the sense of mission through example, and the idea of the Kingdom of God—these were all agreeable to the Jewish tradition. If a Jew must separate because the external world is ungodly and cold, what does he do in a nation which aspires to higher values and extends an open hand?

Thus for Jews the tensions of settlement could be fit into the wider dilemma of separation versus participation.[13] How can a traditionally distinct people live in a nation whose traditions of citizenship involve participation? How could the American creed and the Judaic tradition be reconciled?

The purpose of this book is to discover and describe some of the political aspects of the Jewish adaptation to America. I assume that the question of "separation versus participation" was expressed in ideas about politics and citizenship, in an image of America, and the place of the Jew within it. I assume that the past was important, as a conscious or unconscious influence, as a demand on present and future. Specifically, I am concerned with the degree to which older political ideas were maintained or modified in the American environment. Thus I shall try to suggest some directions which Jews have taken in America.

I have used a deliberately liberal interpretation of what it means to be a Jew. Hence the subjects are diverse: although they share a self-consciousness as Jews, their religious beliefs vary considerably. While traditional, Orthodox Jewish communities reflect the most genuine form of the religion, even these communities have included a wide variety of believers, practitioners, and dissenters.[14] The American Jewish population has probably widened the variety but narrowed the core. Although Orthodoxy has always been at the heart of Judaism, in America it is embraced by a small minority among those who describe themselves as Jewish. Undoubtedly many Americans who consider themselves ethnic Jews may have little or no conscious religious belief.[15]

Instead of concentrating on the rigorously orthodox or, on the other extreme, liberally selecting from among those who have Jewish names, I have opted for a middle road. The individuals covered in this book write about Jews, are concerned about Jews, and think of themselves as Jews. Almost all are concerned with the Jewish question—the position of the Jews in modern society. In some cases, their concept of Judaism (or Jewishness) seems diluted or false. In other cases, atheistic Jews may have standards and values which seem ironically traditional.[16] It is important to include both extremes since some modification of tradition surely has occurred. If American Jews represent a departure from tradition, it is nevertheless significant to trace the path of their wanderings to discern whether it is an exit or a detour.

Although religious belief is essential to Jewish identity, it will not limit our scope to the minority who practice all the laws of Torah. While the essence of Judaism springs from Orthodoxy, this does not disqualify those who deny this discipline, nor does it exclude those whose rebellion is measured in respect to these standards. Also, in practical terms it is obvious that there has been a distinct Jewish culture whose adherents, even if they are atheists or agnostics, can trace their roots to what Franz Kafka described as "a community conditioned by faith."[17]

The criteria employed here, however, do except a number of immigrants who were identified as Jewish. Many labor leaders and socialists rarely wrote of themselves as Jews, preferring to identify with secular movements or beliefs. Samuel Gompers and Emma Goldman, for example, avowed little concern for Jewish issues, although we can assume that their Jewish backgrounds guided them in perhaps unconscious ways. Analysis of this type of individual, while it is tempting and often fruitful, has generally been avoided.[18]

This work focuses on a variety of individuals, mostly immigrants, in an attempt to isolate and then integrate three aspects of their thought:

1. Their concept of Jewish identity. Their general thoughts or impressions regarding Jews and politics.
2. Their conception of America, notably American politics.
3. Their view of the role of the Jew within America, as Jew and American citizen.

In some cases, it is not possible to satisfy this neat typology, and certain leaps of analysis have to be attempted, hopefully with enough successful landings to have justified the effort. Most immigrants, for example, were not active participants in political life, but some did express or intimate attitudes relevant to the issues under investigation.

Essentially this work is a modest foray into the rather unexplored domain of political adaptation and assimilation. It is modest, among other reasons, because it deals with a limited number of individuals who either wrote in English, or whose works were translated from Yiddish. My lack of Yiddish thus inhibits any inclination I might feel toward the lure of sweeping generalization. However, since this book does concentrate on those who were attracted to American life, this deficiency is mitigated by the fact that those who wrote in English were probably most expressive of the tensions and issues of Americanization.

The first two chapters establish both a theoretical and a historical background, although in different settings. In Chapter 1, I try to synthesize traditional Jewish attitudes toward politics with an emphasis on the pre-American Diaspora experience. In Chapter 2, the political thought of German Jews in America is analyzed, taking Louis Brandeis as an example. Since German Jews were dominant among American Jewry until this century, and also were increasingly active in American politics by the late nineteenth century, this focus would seem appropriate. The remainder of the book deals primarily with Jewish immigrants and first-generation Americans from Eastern Europe and Russia. Brief biographical summaries of those who are studied appear at the end of the text.

CHAPTER
1
JUDAISM AND POLITICS

Much has been made of the lack of political experience of modern Jewry. The innocence of German Jews in the years between general emancipation and the rise of Hitler has correctly been compared to the political insensitivity of all of Western European Jewry in the nineteenth century.[1] Even those Jews who were intimate with power, men such as the Rothschilds in France and Austria or Bleichroeder in Germany, generally attained political influence as a result of their financial standing, not because they had defined political ambitions. Their reluctance to engage in politics reflected an attitude somewhat similar to that of their poorer and more religious brethren. The central authority was generally tolerant, sometimes friendly, and occasionally even dependent for financial support. Thus as long as one's way of life was not seriously threatened, it was prudent to cooperate.

Even those individual Jews who were attracted to political life as a mark of their civic equality reflected the restraints of their general background. Often they were the sons of wealthy businessmen and financiers whose knowledge of Judaism and ties to other Jews were minimal. Men such as Disraeli and Rathenau, probably the most prominent political figures of this type, were hardly men of policy. Other assimilative Jews were active in liberal politics, notably in Germany and Austria where their inexperience became manifest during the rise of political anti-Semitism in the late nineteenth century.[2]

Others delved into scholarship, sometimes diverting their interest in power towards intellectual analysis and disputation.

The major reaction to the alleged passivity and political inexperience of the Jew has, of course, been Zionism. The creation of a Jewish State (or, more accurately, a state made up of Jews) was the goal of mostly secular Jews who found the path to assimilation blocked or too difficult. Zionism has sought to "normalize" the Jew—by returning him to the land of the Fathers, to an agricultural economy, in an environment where power is held by Jews alone.

While Israel is a critical symbol for modern Jews, it is important to remember the simple truth that most Jews live in America, not in Israel. More important, Israel is not without its critics among contemporary Jewry.[3] Zionism, in fact, garnered only moderate support before World War II. To the Orthodox, for example, Zionism has often represented an avoidance of the demands of Diaspora: God dispersed the Jews among the nations as a punishment for their sins; the return to Zion must be a return to righteousness, a messianic return. For Reform Jews, on the other hand, the creation of a Jewish State has implied a secular danger, a threat to those Jews who wish to assimilate in other nations.

The Holocaust experience, coupled with the besieged position of Israel since its inception, has coalesced nearly universal Jewish support for Israel, even among groups that were formerly reluctant. However, the creation of a "normal" Jewish State has not ended the argument as to the proper Jewish attitude toward power. Philip Roth, for example, has expressed concern over the admiration shown for Israeli military prowess, seeing it as antithetical to traditional Jewish attitudes concerning power.[4] Similarly, Michael Selzer, in a number of works, has attacked the misguided fascination with politics he perceives among contemporary Jews.[5] The persistence of this type of criticism, in fact, gives us some hint as to the enduring strength of certain older attitudes toward political life which Jewish life has fostered.

These older attitudes, viewed today mostly in their relationship to passivity and inexperience, derived in the main from the unique position of the Jews, as well as from Judaism itself. Thus the religion of the Jews to a great degree molded the Jewish experience, although surely anti-Semitism played its part in reinforcing the need for an exclusive group existence. It is an indisputable fact that Jews were generally barred from political participation in Christian society. However, it is equally as indisputable that, for the most part, this exclusion was welcomed by Jewish leaders, since it matched a moral predilection within the religion and culture: Jews should not participate in Gentile politics.[6]

The Diaspora experience taught the Jews that communal autonomy would best be served by cooperating with external political authority. Surrounded in most places by unpredictably hostile populations, the Jews perceived that higher authorities, usually secular, were more reliable for protection, and that the common people were to be distrusted. The price was often an economic service, which, as time went on, might draw the Jewish community into closer, and possibly more dangerous contact with the local Gentile world. As Hannah Arendt has shown, this situation was endorsed by many Jews into the nineteenth century:

> This prejudice, which expressed a definite historical truth but no longer corresponded to new circumstances, was as deeply rooted in and as unconsciously shared by the vast majority of Jews as corresponding prejudices about Jews were commonly accepted by Gentiles.[7]

Arendt indicates, too, that wealthy and enlightened Jews in Germany, for example, often allied with the state because they were politically aloof rather than politically involved. The state, at one time economically reliant on Jewish financiers, became the protector of their neutrality. As anti-Semitism became a genuine political issue by the late nineteenth century, many of these Jews were either unaware or unprepared to confront the issue. Political aloofness, in Arendt's view, led to political catastrophe.

Jews, she argues, "had no political tradition or experience," and consequently have entered the modern era lacking in the art of politics. Arendt traces this abstinence to the "very nature of Jewish history," and sees in it a unique paradox. Jewish culture has nourished a concern with the world, along with a distinct world view, yet has taught the eschewal of political action.

> Jewish history offers the extraordinary spectacle of a people . . . which began its history with a well-defined concept of history and an almost conscious resolution to achieve a well-circumscribed plan on earth and then, without giving up this concept, avoided all political action for two thousand years.[8]

However, Arendt's analysis of this phenomenon tends to reject other aspects of the Jewish experience which did touch on political life. No doubt it is true that Jews had avoided political action outside their own communities. Still, the existence of long-standing Jewish settlements, as well as the endurance of the Jews as a separate people, suggest that political traditions were not absent. The maintenance of the group and the organization of the community, for example, demand some form of political activity, however indirect. In addition, and this is but the other side of Arendt's perspective, religion and experience fostered attitudes about external politics. Jewish political traditions may have ill prepared modern Jews for Western political life, but this is irrelevant to the fact that these traditions did exist.

Reliance on high authority was viewed as a necessary condition for the maintenance of communal autonomy and separatism. Distance from the state also derived from the same source: the desire to separate from the ways of the nations. To repeat, Jewish political inexperience and aversion to political power were not primarily the results of Jewish suffering. Nor were they mere defensive reactions to the hostility of the non-Jewish world. Ghetto walls have two sides, and it was only when Jews decided to seek integration in an apparently secular culture that this aspect of their background became a "Jewish problem."[9] Before this, alienation from the state was an aspect of the role of Judaism in the Disaspora.

Jewish thought and communal life contain distinct, if elusive, traditions concerning politics. The Jewish communities of Eastern Europe were permitted a great degree of autonomy and self-government within the protective sphere of the state. While admittedly this self-government was never complete, and had waned considerably in the nineteenth century, the Jewish immigrant to the United States probably came from a background which, in certain ways, was much more participatory than that of his Christian counterparts from Eastern Europe. Perhaps alone among the traditional communities of Eastern Europe, the "shtetl" (town or village) endeavored to balance individual achievement with group obligation, equality with status, and popular participation with respect for authority. Salo Baron, in his major work on the subject, has described the Jewish community as "a sort of little state, interterritorial and non-political, but none-the-less quasi-totalitarian."[10]

It is curious that Baron, who goes on to describe, in encyclopedic fashion, the election of communal officers, sanctions and punishments, the powers of various officials, and the decision-making process itself, persists in calling the Jewish community "nonpolitical." Surely, the traditional Jewish community was nonpolitical in the sense that it exerted minute influence on affairs beyond its boundaries. However this should not obscure the existence of political life within these communities. The needs of the community induced political practices which were often obscured by the predominance of religion and the absence of normal police power. It is perhaps more apt to say that political life had a form rather different from that of the modern era.

For the religious Jew, community is both a virtue and a necessity. As noted earlier, God's covenant required a commitment from Jews as a *people*. Salvation for the Jew is not guaranteed by being a member of the "chosen people"; rather it is practically dependent on being of a people who continually choose God and obey His commandments. (Thus, according to the Talmud, a non-Jew who obeys the Torah has special standing before God.) One cannot, however, fulfill the Torah in private, nor as an ascetic. A minimum of ten Jewish males is necessary for worship in the synagogue. This requirement in itself demands concentration of settlement. The commandments to charity, loving thy neighbor, caring for "the stranger, the fatherless, and the widow," and seeking social justice—these all demand community and involvement.[11] Furthermore, the requirements of a religion which ordains special foods and eating habits, distinctive physical appearance, rules and rituals which structure experience, and social divorce from nonbelievers make community an absolute necessity for emotional support alone.

Children of God obey his rules, fear his judgment, and trust in his mercy. In Judaism, God is ubiquitous yet beyond, personal yet majestic, near yet far. He is the sole ruler of the world, even though most of the world is unappreciative of his sovereignty. Part of the Jewish mission is to assert the immediacy of God, as "king of the world," by reducing all earthly power to its proper perspective and by constantly emphasizing human weakness. Political authority in Jewish thought, although important in establishing order and molding the community to the service of God, is entirely secondary to the reality of divine authority. "Ye shall not be afraid of the face of any man," and "Thou shalt have no other gods before me," are related commandments in this regard.[12]

It is important to note, however, that opposition to earthly authority outside the Jewish community was not considered a primary injunction. The daily prayer service, in fact, contained (and still contains) a prayer for the welfare of the government. This authority was necessary, as indicated earlier, to maintain the integrity of the Jewish community. Given the weakness and the dependence of the community, along with the need to maintain separateness, submission to higher authority was not considered a transgression of the commandments. Obedience paid to a distant government, in truth, allowed the community to ignore its sovereignty in most important respects. Moreover, being and remaining a Jew was in itself seen as a stubborn denial of the world and its gods. Participation in external politics always involved the temptations of power, the corruption of man, and the possible betrayal of one's people. As one modern Jewish writer has observed: "Judaism forbids us to enter the struggle for power as a means of redressing those iniquities to which it sensitizes us. . . ."[13] Power itself is viewed as a danger, since it easily deludes people into aggrandizing their own handiwork, a handiwork too often associated with violence.

For the traditional Jew, the state was alien, usually distant and usually tolerated. It was alien not only because it was in the hands of non-Jews, but because it was a dangerous aggregate of power. Politics, the attempt to shape and direct human affairs through human authority, becomes too easily a rival to the rulership of God in the world. Any state, in this view, although necessary, is based on a myth or tends toward one—the denial of God's sovereignty. Moreover, any religion which is associated with a state substitutes political for spiritual power and betrays the religious burden. Genuine religion demands a responsibility and commitment which most men seek to avoid. Politicized religion eases this commitment by joining faith to government protection or the will of the majority.[14]

The Jew learned also, from religion and experience, that the "evil inclination" has dominated history, and that suffering and error are assigned to human destiny. Hence even for many who have strayed from religion the teaching of Ecclesiastes still rules: One must approach the vanity of this world with patience, if not resignation. For many Jews, religious or otherwise, this has led to a detached apoliticality, an inwardness and reliance on family and friends as the true and lasting measures of human action. "You'd do better to marry," the Jewish uncle counsels his socialist niece. "Then you will have children and your own rebels on your hands."15 Family life thus becomes the microcosm of politics, where the world's dramas are contained in an intimate setting.

The Bible makes it clear too that excessive reliance on political authority is not only an affront to God ("They have rejected me, that I should not reign over them"16), but a danger to the community as well. The desire of the Jews for a king, it is warned, will breed war, military aggrandizement, interference with family life, and widespread injustice. In addition, the desire for a leader who will "go out before us, and fight our battles" implies a lessening of communal obligations and participation.17

It is also significant that the reign of Saul—a man fallible, like the rest—does not alter the popular nature of the covenant. God judges both kings and people, but in the end the quality of the people is more important. A king must walk with God in spite of the waywardness of his people. Yet if the people obey and fear God, so too will their leaders walk with them:

> Now therefore behold the king whom ye have chosen, and whom ye have desired! and, behold, the Lord hath set a king over you. If ye will fear the Lord, and serve him, and obey his voice, and not rebel against the commandment of the Lord, then shall both ye and also the king that reigneth over you continue following the Lord your God: But if ye will not obey the voice of the Lord, but rebel against the commandment of the Lord, then shall the hand of the Lord be against you, as it was against your fathers.18

The belief that *all* the people must obey the voice of the Lord challenges political leadership as it demands that each Jew know the Torah and, to some extent, interpret it. Each Jew must strive toward standards which descend from God, and this implies that human authority will be under constant criticism. It also means that in any community, public opinion is likely to be a powerful force, sometimes overriding the wishes of established leaders. Most significant, however, is the prepotency of the covenant over political authority. Keeping the commandments is the overriding obligation, and the kingship, granted grudgingly, and with obvious denigration, is of secondary importance.

Thus both religion and experience taught Jews to be skeptical and critical of political authority. Paradoxically, they also learned to accept it, often in order to remain detached from it. Within the Jewish community, power was also viewed with reserve, limited as it was by a loyalty to higher authorities, both spiritual and secular. Religion stressed the sovereignty of God and political reality underlined the weakness of the Jewish community. In truth, the ability of Diaspora Jews to dilute the dangers of power within the community was related to the weakness of the community in its larger environment. Its ultimate dependence and vulnerability discouraged political ambition and undercut any tendencies to aggrandize leaders of local government. Experience reinforced skepticism about power while it heightened the reality, repeated in daily prayer, that "His is the power and the government."

Communal government was generally directed toward the carrying out of Mosaic law. Government was necessary to administer religious and social commitments: the education of the young, burial of the dead, tax collection, the dispensation of charity, the purification and sale of meat, etc. The community often had a plethora of public officials including an elected council, tax assessors, lay judges, along with special supervisors of the synagogue, communal schools, charities, weights and measures, streets, social relations (sexual morality, mingling with Gentiles), auditors of accounts, and "defenders of the articles" of the constitution.[19]

All of these posts were elective, although in some cases wealth and heredity could help obtain an office. The main political body was the plenary assembly whose membership, as in the days of old, consisted of male heads of households. This body usually gathered irregularly in the synagogue, where meetings were informal, often raucous affairs marked by prolonged argument and debate. Procedure was not very important and majority rule, while it was respected, was not always followed. The proximity, or identity, of political and religious matters was symbolized by the use of the synagogue for debate, and the prayer service for dissent. The unhappy citizen, frustrated by his fellow Jews in the communal assembly, could take his petition to God by interrupting the prayers before the weekly reading of the Torah.

While a governing apparatus was necessary to maintain civil order, the foundation of this order, along with the roots of communal authority, lay in religion. The tasks of political organization derived from holy writ. The Torah includes a wide variety of social concerns, and the words of the prophets, although frequently unheeded, were clear reminders of the need for justice in the world. Yet the Old Testament contains many things, sometimes confusing and contradictory, and it is often difficult to discern the right path. The world and the self, it was assumed, are prone to "the evil inclination" which diverts man from true freedom, which is with God. Obeying the Lord is often a matter of wisdom and judgment: judging the world and oneself by the teachings of Scripture, and judging Scripture itself for the truths embedded within. Thus the common good is never perfectly clear. Human effort and judgment are required to continue God's revelation; to keep the community and individual on the path of righteousness.

The supremacy of the written law meant that a decision which, in another community might be more obviously political, tended in Jewish life to be judicial, and made by a religious authority. Questions of group survival, it is true, or of the relationship of the community to the state, might overrule the commandments of Torah. Too, these issues were often negotiated by "court Jews," privileged individuals who had special access to high authority.[20] However, religious authorities were sometimes influential in these decisions or in their implementation.

The rabbi, the judge, and the teacher were the critical Judaic figures who carried political influence. They were superseded, in the older biblical tradition, at least, by the prophet—one who freely expresses the will of God to the world. Moses, who was both priest and prophet, was told by his father-in-law to appoint judges, over whom he would remain the highest judge. As such, he would exemplify the varied qualities of religious and political authority.

> You shall represent the people before God, and bring their cases to God; and you shall teach them the statutes and the decisions and make them know the way in which they must walk and what they must do.[21]

The judge must be a surrogate of God, deciding in His name, and hopefully with insights into divine wisdom. At the same time, he must teach the law (in itself a teaching), therefore preparing men for that future time when all will recognize the truth of God's revelation. Those who lead and judge the people must be teachers, as God Himself is a teacher.[22] The best judgment, moreover, is one which is free of physical coercion. Isaac Bashevis Singer remembered his father's "Beth Din" (rabbinical court) as an institution which, at its best, rested on good will and ultimate trust in divine power. Unlike political institutions which are based on force, the Beth Din, in Singer's view, was directly related to the weakness of the Jewish community.

> The Beth Din could exist only among a people with a deep faith and humility, and it reached its apex among the Jews when they were completely bereft of worldly power and influence. . . .[23]

Judge, sage, and elder had significant political influence since their knowledge and experience gave direction to the community, usually through interpretation of the law. This influence, however profound, was usually informal, and always variable. Most communities in the Diaspora attempted to prevent the concentration of power in the hands of the rabbinate. The community usually appointed the rabbi, but often his tenure was uncertain. Many communities encouraged "a large-scale turnover, which prevented rabbis from taking root in a community. . . ."[24] Checks on his power also came from the communal bureaucracy, those officials previously cited, who were involved in economic, welfare, and educational activities. In many cases, a wealthy oligarchy might rival or supersede the spiritual leadership. Finally, the rabbi was rarely the sole judicial authority. Litigants could consult lay elders, rabbis from other villages or regions, or sometimes higher courts.

The influence of the rabbi or sage depended on his learning and holiness. A great scholar and teacher might attract followers from many miles away. His words would be relayed to remote communities where lesser men led religious services and wielded less authority. In some instances his teachings might be codified in writing, a form of legislation that would endure beyond death. In Hasidic communities, especially, the influence of the "tzaddik" (the learned and good man) could be enormous.[25] But the tendency to glorify a man was always challenged within the religion. The first commandment is a powerful reminder that a man's primary obligation is to God, in whose eyes men are basically equal.

The insecurity of this world, the mutability of life which was Job's painful lesson, imply also a certain flexibility to human institutions and aims. In the Old Testament, in fact, political institutions rise and fall, and are often swept away by the voice of the prophet, who, in truth, is the great human legislator. When the prophet leads it is because he can transcend the normal political realm. Similarly, the judge, sage, and teacher, while politically influential, often sought to go beyond the worldly area of politics.

If the Jewish community reflected vaguely defined realms of authority, it was because it considered the true authority to be the Lord, and every Jew was equally expected to obey His law. Mosaic law is not particularly concerned with political structure, although it does stress the need to recognize a virtuous leader. The uncertainty of the Jewish position in the world, the possibility that tomorrow might bring destruction or dissolution of the immediate community, instructed the Jew that reliance on human institutions could not be complete. Consequently, self and family became preservers of tradition and bearers of a "portable law." Politics was submerged, perhaps even sublimated, in diverse realms, none fixed with precision, since the world was a priori insecure.

In sum, the Diaspora experience had confirmed in Jews a distance from the formal government, while it had accustomed them to a local politics subordinated to religious faith and group survival. In the local realm, political power was diluted by external realities and the predominance of religion. Here, too, it blended with other roles, thus encouraging an approach to political life that involved criticism, teaching, judicial legalism, and, at times, spiritual leadership. Moreover, the position of the Jews taught them to see political institutions as fluid and perishable, and to enhance familial and social organizations as mainsprings of group survival.

In the absence of land and state, the condition of the Jews for most of their history, it was these approaches to political life which were most dominant. Some Jews, it is true, came to America from immediate backgrounds that were seemingly more conducive to political activity.[26] Yet they constituted a small minority of the great mass of Jewish immigrants who were closer to traditional attitudes. As we shall see, some of those who appeared more inclined to political activism also retained the customary approach to political power.

CHAPTER
2
LOUIS BRANDEIS: THE LIBERAL AS JEW

Jewish immigration to the United States can be divided into three distinct segments. The first Jews came primarily from Spain and Portugal, sometimes settling in Holland or Brazil before voyaging to America. Their numbers were quite small and usually limited to settlements along the Atlantic coast. Nevertheless, their religious orthodoxy and pride in cultural differences fostered a sense of distinctiveness which lingers to this day.[1]

These early Sephardic communities were easily outnumbered by the influx of German Jews in the nineteenth century. While the Spanish Jews remained a kind of distant social elite within American Jewry, the Germans quickly made a significant impact on economic and religious activities in the new land. Starting as itinerant traders and merchants, many were able to amass large fortunes in an era of widespread economic development. Investment banking and large-scale merchandizing, for example, produced the wealth of families such as the Schiffs, Lehmans, Seligmans, Strauses, Altmans, and Belmonts, among many others.[2] In religious affairs, as well, the German Jews were extremely important, being mainly responsible for the emergence of Reform and Conservative Judaism. Thus when the largest wave of Jewish immigration, from the Russian and Austrian Empires, began in the late nineteenth century, Jewish life in America had a definite German accent.

Predictably, relations between Germans and East European Jews were often strained. The East Europeans were both traditional and poor. They were concentrated in squalid neighborhoods, an obvious people whose peculiarities stood out in sharp relief. They lacked social acceptability and decorum and, worse, their neighborhoods spawned criminals who threatened to stigmatize the entire Jewish population. More emotional and spiritual, the newcomers often clashed with the comfortable and respectable German "uptowners" who treated them with a rather cold benevolence.[3]

The tension between these two groups was not original to America. In Germany, assimilated Jews pressured the German government and their own religious leaders to restrict the migration of "oriental" Jews to German soil.[4] The medievalism of the East Europeans was in one sense a reminder of how far their brethren had moved from traditional Judaism. The Enlightenment had spread to German Jewry by the early eighteenth century, and those who chose America in the next century often came from secular backgrounds. Many had professional training in the Old World, some were political refugees (the "forty-eighters"), and the many who still adhered to Judaism practiced a religion whose fundamentals had been radically challenged.

Jewish emancipation and civil rights had been declared in Prussia by the middle of the eighteenth century. A minority of Jews, led by Moses Mendelssohn and his disciple David Friedlander, had welcomed emancipation, seeing it as coupled with progressive adaptation to German society. They shared with German liberals the belief that faith was essentially a personal matter with limited public manifestations, although the inner conflict in this position was difficult to hide. "Special nationality, special food laws, special education," Friedlander wrote, "—all this has to give way to the full acceptance of the state and the fulfillment of the duties of citizenship—except the faith of Israel and its ritual manifestations."[5]

German liberals and Jewish enlighteners agreed that social conditions were mainly responsible for the particularity of the Jews. Freeing the individual Jew, they believed, would lead eventually to the decline of archaic religious behavior. What many Jewish liberals failed to perceive, or purposefully avoided, was the equation of emancipation with conversion which many German humanists often implicitly assumed. Wilhelm von Humboldt, for example, advised a strategy of "divide and convert":

If you will endeavor to loosen the links between the individual Jewish churches and do not foster a single orthodoxy among the Jews, but rather further schisms through a natural and justifiable tolerance, the Jewish hierarchy will fall apart itself. Individuals will come to realize that theirs is only a ceremonial order but not really a religion, and they will turn toward the Christian faith, driven by the innate desire for a higher belief. . . .[6]

Increasingly Judaism in Germany lost some of its characteristic attributes, both ritual and spiritual. The basis for the Reform movement was laid by such German rabbis as Abraham Geiger and Samuel Holdheim who, questioning the Mosaic revelation, argued that Judaism was predominantly a creed. In the nineteenth century, supernatural religion was reduced even further through the work of the "historical school." Persuaded by the romantic emphasis on the "Volk," many Jewish scholars developed the idea that religion was the *expression* of a people and its history. Anchoring religion to the affairs of men, these scholars were only to encourage reformers who argued that all values and practices were rooted in time and human needs, and therefore open to questioning.[7]

In the United States a similar pattern emerged. While many German Jews remained with Orthodoxy, liberal elements quickly gained considerable influence. Under the leadership of such men as Isaac Mayer Wise and David Einhorn, Reform Judaism developed as a movement aiming at social and political equality, the uplifting of the Jew, and the general diffusion of Jewish values. According to Wise, the Jew "lacks the consciousness of manhood in himself. . . . The Jew must become an American in order to gain the proud self-consciousness of the free-born man."[8] Jews who had submitted to Old World authority could expand to full potential in America. Moreover, one could retain the essence of identity and tradition through proselytizing in the New World, by teaching Judaic values. Although Wise retained a belief in revelation and the "mission of Israel," many other Reform Jews did not. For many religion became ethics, or ethical culture, and the moral law replaced the Mosaic law as a fundamental guide.[9]

In pursuing the Jewish "mission" in America, many German Jews came to equate the moral law with the basic tenets of liberal democracy. Naomi Wiener Cohen has remarked that Oscar Straus "would merely have broadened the concept of the Jewish law to include the

Magna Carta, the Declaration of Independence, and the Declaration of the Rights of Man."[10] Their identification was more with the older liberalism of the Founding Fathers than with the egoistic liberalism of Herbert Spencer. They were individualists, but they stressed duties along with individual rights.

Their identification with an earlier America seemed to spring from various sources. One was a desire to show that Jews had been a part of America from its period of birth, if not from before. Oscar Straus, in his *Origin of Republican Form of Government in the United States of America*, and in numerous lectures, reminded his audiences that biblical Israel provided a "democratic model" for the earliest Americans. Modern American republicanism, he wrote, "is the nearest approach to the ideals of the prophets of Israel that ever has been incorporated in the form of a State."[11] Straus, in fact, went so far as to subsidize research into the allegedly Jewish origins of Christopher Columbus, presumably to cement even further the Jews' relationship to America, and to ease any underlying insecurity about their position.

A more important source of identification, however, was philosophical. Essentially the men of "our crowd" shared the assumptions of an enlightened liberalism which had reformed their religion and dignified their citizenship, and whose spirit they felt in the pulse of America. Like the Founders, they could accept religion as a private affair, where it might serve as cause and inspiration, compatible with American ideals and good citizenship. Religion became an individual preference, clannishness became a Jewish trait which would eventually expand into feelings of universal brotherhood, and fellow Jews became coreligionists.[12] To many—men like Jacob Schiff and Louis Marshall, for example—religion *was* important, and it was well that its private inspiration seemed to match the public spirit. Public expressions of American Jews as a group, on the other hand, were seen as improper and dangerous.

Louis Marshall, who for years headed the American Jewish Committee, insisted that Jews should organize only for religious or philanthropic purposes (despite the fact that the charter of the Committee clearly implied political activities).[13] Political organization was considered dangerous because it might suggest to some that Jews had "interests different from those of other American citizens."[14] Similarly, Zionism might invite the charge of divided loyalty. Hence, when the

American Jewish Committee did act politically to protect Jewish interests, its actions were invariably portrayed as responses to a threat to the American creed. Although this equation was motivated to some extent by their insecurity as Jews in America, these leaders were seriously committed to an American creed, and some, like Marshall, sought to apply it to other minorities.[15]

When these men did act politically, they usually acted as *individuals*, as men of personal influence. Group efforts and mass organization lacked dignity in their eyes. Such activities also threatened to make Jews too obvious, potentially triggering an anti-Semetic reaction which these men saw lurking behind their somewhat abstract faith in American opinion.

The old liberalism, with its emphasis on the individual citizen and the secular, but morally inspired, public sphere, matched well with the background and condition of the German-Jewish elite. Civil and political rights for Jews were relatively recent in European life and most Jews had scant political experience in the modern nation-state. One political mode that had endured since the Middle Ages was that of the "court Jew," the wealthy notable who has special privilege and influence with men of power.[16] Individual influence, used discreetly and wisely, might protect the interests of the broad mass of Jews. This was the political approach which men such as Schiff, Marshall, Straus, and even Brandeis found most congenial.

Attracted to the freedom of America, imbued with ambitions which needed an open environment in which to thrive, German Jews found the new land a fertile soil for individual achievement. Its culture might seem inferior, but America was perceived as an open, active nation, large enough to tolerate differences. As with most immigrant groups, love of country had a more personal meaning. In addition, German Jews tended to be educated, historically minded, and concerned with public issues. Thus patriotism and ambition sometimes merged in a desire to serve in some public capacity.

By the close of the nineteenth century descendants of German-American Jews began to find their way into public life.[17] Most were Republicans, attracted to the party of Lincoln and liberalism. During the ensuing decades progressive idealism was a powerful lure which attracted reform-minded sons of immigrants who had "made it" in America. A considerable number achieved some prominence in national affairs—such men as Henry Morgenthau, Oscar Straus, Herbert Lehman, Louis Marshall, Eugene Meyer, Robert Moses, Walter Lippmann, Walter Weyl, Cyrus Adler, and Julian Mack, among others. Clearly the most outstanding of this group was Louis D. Brandeis, the "people's attorney," and the first Jew to serve on the United States Supreme Court.

COMPANIONSHIP WITHOUT COMMITMENTS

At the start of World War I, Louis Brandeis was probably the most prominent Jew in American political life.[18] Even before his appointment to the Supreme Court, Brandeis had gained stature, and notoriety in some circles, for his role in the Ballinger controversy, in the case against the New Haven Railroad, and in numerous public interest cases. As lawyer and judge he had a significant influence on judicial theory and practice. His relationship with Woodrow Wilson, as policy adviser and counselor, contributed to the development of the "New Freedom" and to the course of modern liberalism. After his sixtieth year, he took on a further cause, the Zionist movement, which held his interest until he died in 1941. He was, in the phrase of an admiring biographer, a "lynchpin" for an assortment of twentieth-century reforms.[19]

Yet words must not be used too loosely. Brandeis, the man *of* politics, must be distinguished from Brandeis, the man *in* politics. Throughout a career which featured controversies that had definite political implications, Brandeis eschewed the consciously political role. He was not a man of strong party loyalties, although he did endorse and sometimes campaigned for political candidates.[20] Like most progressives, he distrusted the political party and probably did not understand it very well. As a crusading attorney, Brandeis saw himself on the side of virtuous ideals and policies, or in service to the public as a whole. Still later, as a justice of the Court, and adviser to presidents, Brandeis could enjoy political influence without the responsibilities of elective office. In these roles, Brandeis paralleled other prominent Jewish-Americans who followed him—Bernard Baruch, Felix Frankfurter, Benjamin Cardozo, Abe Fortas, and Henry Kissinger, to name a few (Walter Lippmann followed a similar path in the field of journalism). His position on the edge of politics was, as al-

ready noted, similar to that of the court Jew who reappears throughout European political history.

We should also inquire into the nature of Brandeis's religious or
ethnic identification. Neither a practicing religious Jew nor a man
with strong ties to his ethnic brethren, Brandeis came to Jewish identification late in life, mainly through Zionism.[21] In spite of his leadership in the Zionist movement, the source of his interest seemed to
originate outside the world of Jews and Judaism. In the controversy
surrounding his appointment to the Court, his religion and background did become a public issue. Yet the fundamentals of his Jewish
identification remained confused, or concealed. In these respects,
Brandeis is certainly not an atypical Jewish-American, nor an atypical
American. It is precisely his representativeness which makes him interesting.

Born a few years before the start of the Civil War, Louis Brandeis
lived until the eve of World War II. He reached maturity during an era
of rampant industrial expansion, and spent much of his active life
grappling with the effects of industrial consolidation. He witnessed
both the emergence of vigorous national government and the subor-
dination of the individual to the principles of organization. Throughout this span, Brandeis preached the virtues of smallness and individuality. His life ended during the New Deal which he both admired and
reproved, and for which he was, to some extent, responsible.

In one sense, Brandeis can be viewed as the model progressive,
spurred into public life by moral outrage at the corruption of government by business and by the violation of American standards of fair
play. Yet Brandeis went further than many progressives, not only in
his activism, but in devising formulas to match his diagnoses of social
ills. He was, by his own admission, a problem solver and social engi-
neer who equated reform with correcting imbalances in society and
men. (His early enchantment with Herbert Hoover reflects their affinity in this regard.) The palliatives he proposed—savings bank life
insurance, government regulation of competition, fair treatment of
women and children employees, unionization of labor, among others
—were basically adjustments for a society whose fundamental premises and goals he warmly accepted. If his activism marked him as a
radical to some industrial titans, his philosophical foundations were
nevertheless tame. He revered the Constitution and its makers and

was satisfied with traditional institutions. He was committed to free enterprise and capitalism, and saw reforms as necessary to save and modify old ways. Like many other progressives, Brandeis was a moderate, if not conservative man.[22]

Brandeis's roots were not unlike those of many of his countrymen. The son of Jewish immigrants from Central Europe, he was able to build upon those polarities of tradition and modernity which so many Americans have struggled to reconcile. He attempted to apply older values when conditions and compromise were ruling them out of the lives of his fellow citizens.

He was born into a family which was both a crucible of Old World romantic liberalism, and a vehicle into a New World of opportunity and advancement. The model of democratic man which Brandeis revered was straight out of his father's generation: the "old" middle class of merchants and shopkeepers, artisans, and professional men. These were men who gathered every evening before dinner to discuss public affairs. Their wives and daughters seasoned their correspondence with quotations from Greek drama and German literature. They brought to America the values of enlightened, bourgeois European Jewry—a respect for culture and education, professional independence, public service through individual endeavor, and a faith in progress. Underlying all was the feeling that religion is best expressed in terms of ethics and conduct, and an enduring respect for history.

The Brandeis home was devoid of formal religion or self-conscious ethnicity. In fact, references in Brandeis's letters indicate that the German heritage was apparently as important as the Jewish in his early years. In her old age, his mother described the religious philosophy which guided her parentage in terms of humanistic ideals and personal altruism. She raised her children without any specific religious belief, emphasizing instead moral conduct and a "kindly spirit." Only "love, virtue, and truth" could form a lasting basis for a child's education and growth. These universal values could withstand the tests of reason, and thus endure permanently in the character of an individual.

> I wanted to give them something that neither could be argued away nor would have to be given up as untenable, namely a pure spirit and the highest ideals as to morals and love. God has blessed my endeavors.[23]

With this type of upbringing Brandeis would feel little religious distinctiveness in a nation dominated by Protestantism. It also may account, in part, for his stern moral views and rigorous sense of duty to the public. However, we may note too that this philosophy (assuming it was practiced as preached) involves perhaps a heavier psychological burden than a religion that could be "argued away." Judaism teaches that the "pure spirit" is never unsullied, that sin is a constant (and hence, to some extent, accepted) companion of rebellious man, and that the "highest ideals" are part of God and are always slightly beyond our reach. One can only be speculative and suggestive in this realm, particularly since Brandeis grew up to be an exceedingly private man, yet these precepts give us some hints as to the foundations of his personality.

The inculcation of a pure spirit and the highest ideals may have been responsible for more than Brandeis's unquestioned sense of duty. In his approach to social and political questions, Brandeis often assumed a consensus on values. The virtue of the Brandeis brief, so it seemed, was precisely that it dealt with *facts*, assuming agreement on traditional values. (In truth, this was not the case, since the facts argued for certain values—compassion, justice, and efficiency—to which the Court had not attended.) Brandeis's contribution to the Court was as the empiricist par excellence. He believed that if all the facts were known, if the public was truly educated, then people would surely agree on the proper course. In regard to labor-management relations, for example, Brandeis argued that "insistence upon discussion—that is, upon ascertainment of facts,—is the most effective and satisfactory method of reaching a proper solution."[24]

Thus the values that could not be argued away in Brandeis were often ascribed to others. Max Lerner was probably correct in describing him as "a social theorist whose 'principles' are nine-tenths submerged in the form of pre-conceptions. . . ."[25] However, these preconceptions remained such—values unquestioned and assumed, pursued with a militant zeal that perhaps masked doubts he refused to acknowledge.

Dean Acheson, who served for a time as Brandeis's law clerk on the Court, once remarked that "if some of his admirers knew him better they would like him less." Brandeis usually kept his "absolutist convictions" under the wraps of stern self-discipline. But Acheson recalled a conversation he witnessed between the justice and a law professor who had great praise for legal relativism:

> The Justice wrapped the mantle of Isaiah around himself, dropped his voice a full octave, jutted his eyebrows forward in a most menacing way, and began to prophesy. Morality was truth; and truth had been revealed to man in an unbroken, continuous, and consistent flow by the great prophets and poets of all time. He quoted Goethe in German and from Euripides via Gilbert Murray. On it went—an impressive, almost frightening, glimpse of an elemental force. . . .[26]

This rigidity often manifested itself in a passion for order and efficiency along with a fear of the emotions. Significantly, while certainly committed to democratic values and the re-creation of the democratic order, Brandeis was often intolerant of personal differences and at times displayed an almost authoritarian concern for loyalty. As a Zionist leader his desire for order and organization was frankly military. He seemed to welcome conflict, ostensibly because it brought out the best in people, and he tended to conceive of political life with a romantic's love for battles and causes. "The best politics," he wrote to Jacob de Haas, "is heavy battalions."[27] In his various reform efforts, but most notably in Zionism, Brandeis displayed a zeal which clearly discouraged dissent. As his rival Louis Lipsky noted years later, "All believers were expected to cooperate."[28]

In his youth, Brandeis had been much moved by Emerson's romantic individualism—by his emphasis on self-reliance, will, and a future "Golden Age."[29] Brandeis, in addition, was an activist, a man who shuttled between Boston and New York, and New York and Washington "endeavoring, both to curb the monopoly, and to free the individual from the thraldom to which this great power has subject so many of our fellow citizens."[30] Freedom involved liberation from dependence, mobilizing and motivating men away from the passivity into which they could easily fall. For Brandeis personally, this meant that he rarely accepted fees for his public work, that his devotion was more to causes than to men, and that activism sometimes represented an end in itself. His was a somewhat separate path, free of commitments which would have compromised his individualism. His major biographer touched on this point, in another context, when he noted that Brandeis occasionally would engender "enmity" because "he . . . let the chips fall where they may."

He was forced inevitably to look beyond the limiting circle of friends, former clients and fellow club members in order to grasp the larger public interest at stake.[31]

Neither an open man nor a philosophical one, Brandeis's deepest beliefs are only suggested by implication. The rigid separation between public and private man is implied by his actions and in his thought. Man has his private work, that which he needs for personal and familial support, or to satisfy personal ambitions. This, however, is a limited realm, although apparently self-sufficient. It is important for a man to have public work, causes outside himself, to which he devotes his superfluous time. He works for the public out of *duty*, not shared needs or emotional commitment.

For Brandeis, man is essentially private, but total immersion in the private sphere involves dangers. The chief peril is an always-latent passivity, easily produced by materialism and the desire for luxuries. Social problem solving was his "luxury," he once explained—a strange way to describe activities which consumed some forty years of his life.[32] All men need "causes," future goals to strive for, which may ennoble them through struggling and sacrifice. Challenges and struggles refine the will and often bring men closer to their finest qualities and deepest beliefs.

The temptations of passivity may also relate to Brandeis's puritanical streak. His friend Norman Hapgood associated it with his abhorrence of material excess as well as his dislike of the movies.[33] More important, it tended to conceal a darker side of Brandeis's vision, which appeared occasionally, particularly in letters to his family. Men must be active and useful to defray in part the painfulness of contemplating the world as it is. Still a young man, he advised his brother-in-law to use his leisure to write on legal topics, instead of devoting it to "unprofitable meditation on the dullness of the times."[34] Brandeis's optimism, his constant striving for future goals, was based in truth on a vision of a society whose essential values had degenerated since his father's time.[35]

The tendencies toward ease and demoralization which disturbed progressives such as Brandeis were associated with both the excesses of the old culture (monopolists, bankers, middle-class men without ideals) and the degeneration of the new immigrant cultures. In the end, if causes failed to move men, Brandeis suggested that tragedy and suffering might. Repelled by an evening of hotel entertainment, he wrote to his brother, quoting Shakespeare, "Man delights me not." He continued, "I guess a heavy batch of adversity wouldn't hurt American morals."[36] A year later, writing of the plight of Jews during the First World War, he somehow managed to sound a note of grisly optimism:

> Great crises bring forth adequate leadership. . . . We may be privileged to witness, blossoming out of the welter of blood in which the world is now submerged, a self-reliant and self-emancipated Jewish people.[37]

Armageddon would bring forth renewal, a new birth. Suffering might be a school for strength, and the end even of tragedy could be a free people. Freedom, once again, was the ultimate ideal: individual freedom balanced by obligations to society. This was the touchstone of Brandeis's social and political efforts, as well as the hallmark of his personal life. Yet, as with so many liberals and progressives, the essence of freedom was negative—liberation from restraints so that the individual, or group, could develop, progress, and perhaps even conquer. This conception of freedom characterized his personal life, and sometimes undercut his relations with those accustomed to easier intimacy.[38] Describing social occasions at the Brandeis home, a family friend wrote perceptively:

> Gatherings of that kind probably gave him a sense of human companionship without commitments, so to speak—companionship which some sort of fear of being touched and opened up, of caution, of desire to remain free, prevented his seeking in the usual more intimate ways.[39]

THE DEMOCRATIC RESTORATION

Man, Louis Brandeis once wrote, is a "wee thing, despite the aids and habiliments with which science, invention, and organization have surrounded him."[40] Despite the fact that it was the creations of modernity which emphasized the smallness of man, Brandeis held to an ardent faith in the ability of science to refashion genuine individuality. His overriding concern was the bigness of modern life, which shadowed individualism, making men as unaware of their potential as it made them overly aware of their limitations.

Brandeis never defined the boundaries of human potential. Nor was he explicit about the inclinations of human nature. He had a liberal's optimism: men could always be better than they are now. To his mother he once wrote:

> But man is strange, at least this one is; he does not enjoy what he has—and he always wants what he does not yet have. That probably is called ambition—the delusion, for which one is always ready to offer a sacrifice.[41]

Alexander Bickel has rightly observed that "the paradox of limited man and his practically limitless potential was . . . at the core of Brandeis's faith. . . ."[42] In small social and economic units man could feel a heightened sense of worth and capability, and perhaps an unlimited potential. As he aged, Brandeis perceived greater value in small political units, too, seeing them as sources of diversity and spiritual values. In Court opinions he urged a wider latitude for state legislation and regulation. He worried to a friend that Tom Johnson should have stayed on as Mayor of Cleveland, "resisting the temptation of a wider political field"—the same temptation to which he had apparently succumbed.[43]

Brandeis's preference for small units was both political and psychological, yet never complete. His own inclinations were for the national arena. Although critical of "excessive nationalism," he fought strongly for a national Zionist organization based on individual, rather than group membership. Typically, he couched his advocacy of the small unit in terms of the efficiency of the larger society. Most important, a sense of unlimited potential and ambition challenges and contradicts the boundaries of the small place. Human ability might in fact be finite, but the hint that men could be like gods was the foundation of progress.

Brandeis's ambivalence on this issue was also reflected in his relatively insignificant concern for the small community. More comfortable with the impersonal society, like many successful Americans, his ties to any one community were attenuated. True, Brandeis as Zionist described America as a nation of nationalities and the Jewish people as a community. Yet, as we shall see again, his notion of community was seriously inconsistent, alternating from an emphasis on atomism to gross generalizations about group identity. This contradiction hinted at a lack of experience or a lack of feeling, and lent support to Paul Freund's comment that "Brandeis' deep sense of attachment to the small community . . . was more a rationally held obligation than an emotional bond."[44]

This mechanistic notion of community was illustrated in his personal life by his efforts to establish the University of Louisville. He assumed the task as another project. Born in Louisville, he saw the university as critical to the life and culture of both city and state. Nevertheless he was in a curious position: directing the project from afar with almost imperious precision, for a community in which he had not lived since he was a teenager, for a city he did not visit during the last fifteen years of his life.[45]

Brandeis shared the progressives' faith in the regulatory powers of the state, a state which should reflect public rather than private interests. Since man had been corrupted by the growth of social and economic institutions (and their adverse political influence), it was now proper for the state to intercede and adjust institutions to the size of men. But this course of action would not nearly suffice. State action, in fact, although often necessary, was not a desirable alternative in his view.

Brandeis distrusted political action and relegated it to a secondary role in his program of reform. Since he saw man primarily from an economic perspective, his proposed reforms dealt mainly with the recreation of economic autonomy. Although legislation might be required to promote these changes, it ought be circumscribed and respectful of essential social forces. These forces, we may note here, are held together by their tension and competition, although the legislature may set "the limits of permissible contest." Brandeis presumed, in this context, at least, that individuals and groups were narrow and self-serving, and that the legislature must place restrictions on their "rights" to aggression and defense. The task of the legislature is to offer "processes of justice" as an alternative to the traditional methods of "trial by combat."[46]

Within this rather grim concept of a "conflict society," the legislature basically reacts, rather than leads, and attempts to deal with social problems through experimentation. But one can hold little faith in legislative remedies. For one thing, Brandeis noted, "remedial institutions are apt to fall under the control of the enemy. . . ."[47] More important, democratic politics are necessarily slow and inefficient. In a letter to Hapgood, Brandeis revealed a weary elitism that went to the heart of his liberalism: "And the fact that our instruments are man with his weaknesses and defects, is at times exasperating."[48]

Like many other progressives, Brandeis was attracted to administration and organization as means to a democratic renaissance. The campaign for a democratic Zion, for example, required strong leadership, disciplined and educated cadres, and efficient organization. For comparable reasons, Brandeis admired the modern administrator, epitomized by Herbert Hoover. Hoover's organizing effort during World War I, he wrote Hapgood, is "the strongest argument for the needlessness of law."[49] Efficient administrators and committed public servants must endeavor to restore conditions in which democratic politics can be tolerated, while man is being constantly improved.

The restoration of democracy depended ultimately on the character of the individual. Democracy, Brandeis believed, is possible "only where the process of perfecting the individual is pursued."[50] The development of the individual required social and economic reforms, but above all, it demanded persistent educational efforts. Intellectuals and university men thus had a large responsibility—to contribute to public life and, at the same time, to uplift it. Intellectuals needed the activism of a cause to make them complete. Similarly, the public required education and economic reforms which would provide greater opportunity for personal development.

Throughout Brandeis's thought and activities there is a contradiction between his emphasis on the individual on the one hand, and his commitment to organization on the other. Nor should we overlook the near-personification of the group which appeared in his Zionist work. He believed that the development of the individual was the supreme concern, yet he had little use for either the costs or the less efficient benefits of individuality. In these respects, the man Brandeis combined an era which glorified the individual with a coming age which would generalize the group. His sensitivity to organization as a political factor, along with his appreciation of the value of publicity and propaganda in a mass society, placed him between the older German-Jewish leaders who worked mainly through personal influence, and the future generation of organizationally minded ethnic leaders.[51]

For Brandeis, the individual and the group could be coordinated by two forces. One was education, to which he referred frequently with a kind of Jeffersonian faith. Education could uplift men, enlightening them as to the real facts of existence, uniting them around a vision of the truth. As many observers have noted, Brandeis saw his role on the Supreme Court as, at least in part, that of an educator—a teacher of his fellow justices, and of the public.[52] In Zionism, too, Brandeis clung to the faith that if the facts were shown to Jewish-Americans, they would naturally support the "cause."[53] Since he held what Acheson described as "absolutist convictions" regarding truth, Brandeis could feel that the proper education would create concord amongst men.

Education, however, was probably insufficient. While Brandeis affirmed a faith in reason, it is unclear as to how much faith he had in people. His stress on education, for example, sometimes seemed more like a faith in training and propaganda, the routine learning of the right material. "The prople have great stuff in them," he once remarked to Acheson in private conversation. "The stuff that our private soldiers showed [in World War I] is in the whole people."[54] Our best qualities, including the achievement of the individual for the sake of the group, appear under challenge or fire. Thus, again, a militant cause, if not a war, might be needed to join Americans to America, and Jews to Zionism.

Typically, the rationale which he suggested for social and political reforms was often efficiency. Originally opposed to women's suffrage, Brandeis came to support it on the grounds of "social efficiency."[55] Efficiency would coordinate the individual to larger societal needs, but if used properly, it would also free the individual by allowing more time for self-development.

Brandeis's concern for efficiency may have satisfied certain deeper needs as well. It is instructive, for example, that Brandeis rarely encouraged or admitted to compassion. Although he was one of the most prominent reformers of his time, there are few references in his writings which even hint at a frankly emotional reaction to social problems.[56] In his address, "The Road to Social Efficiency," he spoke approvingly of "a developing sense of social responsibility" which was replacing an older dependence on relief and "sporadic emotional charity."[57] Efficiency then may have served to neutralize feelings that the culture had classified as suspect in public life.

THE "JEWISH PROBLEM"

Brandeis brought the habits of mind of a problem solver to the question of the Jewish role in America and the world. For him there was a "Jewish problem," and there were specific ways to deal with it.

The problem seems to have become apparent to him in 1912 or shortly thereafter. Until this time Brandeis had made few references to his own Jewish background and no statements at all in respect to larger questions. In fact, in a speech in 1910 he asserted that ethnic or religious issues ought to have a distinctly secondary role in American life. In the spirit of Theodore Roosevelt, Brandeis warned that hyphenated-Americanism was a threat to American unity:

> Habits of living, of thought which tend to keep alive differences of origin or to classify men according to their religious beliefs are inconsistent with the American idea of brotherhood and are disloyal.[58]

The rigidity of this position was to reappear in his attitude towards Zionism. In a few years he was to argue that all good Jews *must* become Zionists.

The apparent conflict between these two positions was resolved by an oft-expressed belief that dedication to American ideals was entirely consistent with Jewish traditions. The Jews as a people exemplified the best traits in the American character—energy, respect for achievement, and democratic values. Moreover, Jewish virtues were particularly relevant to the modern era, an era in which democracy must be revived and restored. Jews, Brandeis asserted, possessed those qualities which twentieth-century reformers sought to encourage in their "struggle" for a new democracy. As we shall see, Brandeis did not believe that these traits were characteristic of all, or even most Jews. However, he liked to pose Jews as a model which other groups could follow.[59]

As Brandeis saw it, the "Jewish problem" was an extension of the problem of liberalism in the twentieth century. Jews came to represent those qualities he perceived in older liberal men. In addition, the Palestinian "experiment" represented a contemporary re-creation of the earlier American experience. Zion was to be a land of immigrants, the voluntary result of Jewish will and effort. Like America, it would be a land of enlightenment and science. Hapgood suggests in this regard that Brandeis's interest in Zionism began when he learned of the discovery of wild wheat in Palestine, and of its possible effects on life in the area. [60]

Brandeis believed that modern liberalism had to be broadened to include group concerns as well as those of the individual. "The movements of the last century have proved that whole peoples have individuality no less marked than that of the single person."[61] In this case, the essential group was the nationality, or the race. The individuality of a people is irrepressible, he urged, and must be expressed in the order of nations. Liberalism had failed to eliminate anti-Jewish prejudice because it had sought to protect individual members of a minority group, rather than seeking to establish group equality. The "Jewish problem" was essentially a matter of securing rights for the Jews as a people or race, so that, freed of artificial limitations, Jews could make their full contribution to the modern world.

A deeper scrutiny of Brandeis's liberal Zionism reveals influences as diverse as John Stuart Mill and Madison Grant. Brandeis utterly avoided the problem of group solidarity by defining the Jewish people as a pure racial group. "The unity of a nationality," he asserted, "is a fact of nature."[62] This assertion also ran contrary to his emphasis on the development of the individual in American life. In effect, Brandeis individualized the group, making unity a practical matter of organization and propaganda. The error of this position, especially in the light of religious laws concerning conversion and intermarriage, should have been obvious. It masks the primary question, which is, as always, "What does it mean to be a Jew?" That Brandeis's answer was racial and negative may be suggested too by his perception of the mainsprings of Jewish consciousness:

> The meaning of the word Jewish in the term Jewish problem must be accepted as co-extensive with the disabilities which it is our problem to remove. It is the non-Jew who creates the disabilities and in so doing gives definition to the term Jew.[63]

Jews, then, while a distinctive racial group, are defined largely by the social attitudes of non-Jews. Denied equal rights and opportunities, Jews have nevertheless learned virtue in the hard school of suffering and rejection. One does not opt to be a Jew; it is a fate to which one is assigned. Yet this also underlines a contradiction: If Jewish identity is the result of non-Jewish attitudes, what distinctive Jewish qualities would be expressed through the settlement of Palestine?

The perspective of the non-Jews of the time was apparently racial, and Brandeis, the man who was something of an ambassador to Jewry, had become well aware of this. His response was to turn racial thinking on its head, arguing that Jews were better than other people, in their potential to be democrats, scientists, and energetic achievers. Brandeis lived through a period in which racial theories not only had popular but intellectual currency. The spirit of solid "Americanism" was equally influential, even before World War I. Brandeis challenged neither of these currents. The key, of course, was the supposed compatibility of Jewish and American traditions. Since such compatibility existed, a dual loyalty need not be a divided one.

In the eyes of the Gentile racist, the similarity among Jews seemed natural and inherent. Again, accepting the assumptions of his detractors, Brandeis urged Jewish unity as an absolute necessity. The improper activities of one Jew reflect on the entire race. In an essay aptly titled, "We Cannot Afford To Do A Mean Thing," Brandeis warned that the individual Jew must realize that all aspects of his behavior need be exemplary.[64] Sinful behavior, moreover, deserved the same harsh punishment to which Jews as a group had been subjected—exclusion and the charge of disloyalty. Thus, in another place, Brandeis asserted that the group had a right to demand from even the "lowliest" Jew the avoidance of behavior which would bring it dishonor. "We may properly brand the guilty as traitor to the race."[65]

His anxiety may have been related to the increasing publicity accorded to Jewish criminals, such as Arnold Rothstein and Herman Rosenthal.[66] These criminals were mostly gangsters and gamblers who had surfaced from the urban slums of the East European Jews. They were a severe embarrassment to middle- and upper-class German Jews who had assiduously sought respectability in American society. Brandeis, perhaps without intention, expressed attitudes typical of this class. He spoke of the demoralization that had set in amongst American Jews, due to the lack of restraint, and the easing of those barriers which had surrounded ghetto life in earlier times. The remedy was basically similar to the goal for democratic man: the inculcation of self-respect, by linking the Jew once again "to the noble past of his race, and by making him realize the possibilities of a no less glorious future."[67]

Thus, despite his laudatory references to Jewish qualities, Brandeis's conception of the contemporary Jew was highly unflattering when viewed in full context. Like other German-Jewish notables, he looked upon Eastern European Jews with distrust, if not contempt. After his break with Chaim Weizmann, Brandeis wrote that "the Easterners—like many Russian Jews in this country—don't know what honesty is. . . ."[68] Similarly, his optimism concerning Jewish development in Palestine rested on an image of the Jew as someone who needed improving:

> In my opinion, our main task must be to make fine men and women in Palestine, and . . . to correct there, so far as possible, those distortions of character and mind which too much commercialism, enforced by separation from the land many centuries, has entailed.[69]

The task demanded not so much a return to Judaism as a turn toward Zionism. The "noble past" was neither the rabbinic nor the prophetic traditions—it was eighteenth-century America. What he proposed was the channeling of energies into nation building: the Jews as pioneers in Palestine.

Brandeis often cited demoralization as the most important object of Zionist activity in America. Jews, like all Americans, needed a cause for which to strive, and Zionism was an ideal choice. Significantly, the Zionist program offered little in regard to the condition of American Jews. Although Brandeis frequently cited slum conditions as a cause of demoralization, he never sought to organize American Jews to·change this reality. American Zionist leaders were either liberal enough to assume that hard work and equal opportunity would suffice, or they were just not concerned with the issue. Thus Brandeis never advocated immigration to Palestine as a solution of the American Jewish problem. To do so he would either have had to confess that his pluralistic view of America was mistaken, or that Jews faced a unique problem.

Brandeis's claim that Zionism would revitalize Jewish life in the United States can only be understood as an aspect of his liberal psychology. Although he professed admiration for Ahad Ha-Am's "cultural Zionism," Brandeis was clearly less concerned with the strength of Diaspora communities than with the rebuilding of Palestine. Furthermore, if American Jews had become morally corrupt, then Zionism offered a cause whose rewards were primarily vicarious and escapist. If Jewish communal life was endangered by the absence of external restraints (although contradictorily, an "eternal anti-Semitism" was often cited as a reason for Zionism), then it would be equally as feasible to attempt to rebuild Jewish communal life from within—to resuscitate what had been lost rather than to demand its modern facsimile.

In Brandeis's view the capacity to grow and develop was inherent in a people, especially the Jews. Jews had been hardened by suffering, their experiences having taught them resilience and faith. Undoubtedly, Brandeis believed that the process of nation building as an external goal would compensate for the decline of tension which had arisen previously from anti-Semitism. A pertinent question, raised only by implication, has to do with the implied differences between German and East European Jews in America. How could he explain the demoralization of the latter, when the Germans had also encountered a lack of restraint in the United States? The newer arrivals apparently lacked the personal discipline and ambition which had characterized the earlier immigrants. They lacked a cause to which they could dedicate their lives. [70] Therefore, while "the desire for full development" is deeply embedded in every people, without an internal character or an external stimulus, people may stagnate or decline.

Most of those in the Brandeis group were descendants of German-Jewish immigrants. They derived in the main from the wealthier section of the Jewish population, and were often the emissaries of a Jewish plutocracy. Their domination of leading Zionist organizations replicated an old practice—the representation of all Jews by wealthy and assimilated notables. Although the Brandeis group saw itself as standing for the democratic principle, by 1921 rank-and-file Zionists came to view them as a distant elite. [71] Since America was not the shtetl, Jewish leaders could not assume a united Jewish following, nor an unknowing Gentile leadership. Solidarity hence became a staccato theme, and social pressure the paramount medium. "Organize, Organize, Organize," Justice Brandeis extolled, "until every Jew in America must stand up and be counted . . . or prove himself . . . of the few who are against their own people." [72]

Solidarity was of equal import because of the need to drape the Zionist movement with the standard of popular sovereignty. Brandeis's conception of sovereignty, as noted earlier, was restrained by hard strands of elitism. If the duty of the mass of American citizenry was mainly to vote, the duty of the mass of American Jewry was to "stand up and be counted." "Members, money, and discipline" were the prime requisites of American Zionism. While all Jews were obviously not Zionists, Brandeis believed that education and organization would inexorably show the way. Revealing the same ambivalence which characterized his progressivism, Brandeis insisted that Zionism be democratic and representative, while through propaganda and organization all Jews would be forced to see that loyalty to both America and to the Jewish race "demands adhesion to the Zionist cause. . . ."[73]

If Jews could be made to see the facts, then the Zionist solution would be readily perceived, solidarity in the mass and complete unity in the ranks would be achieved. The task required missionaries to find those "ready to be converted."[74] Brandeis was convinced that the movement's success depended on the development of a committed vanguard of workers with soldierly virtues. As Zionist leader he ruled with a tone of firm command, often falling into military metaphors to express future plans. Perhaps the proximity of war, the dire plight of European Jews, or his own long-standing desire for battles and causes underlay his approach.

Brandeis was by no means entirely typical of this generation of German-Jewish public men. Where Brandeis's involvement in Jewish affairs was primarily aimed outwards, toward Zionism, others, like Louis Marshall and Jacob Schiff, devoted much of their tremendous energy to the situation of Jews in America. Marshall epitomized the views of the older German-Jewish "establishment." He was opposed to mass organization and politics; he was hostile to any semblance of separatism; and he was, at least in his early years, strongly anti-Zionist. Despite his differences with men such as Brandeis—and these differences tended to melt with time—of far greater significance were the values which these men held in common.

Marshall, Schiff, Straus, and Jesse Seligman were Republicans, and anti-Zionists, at least until World War I. Brandeis was a Zionist, a social reformer, with strong ties to Woodrow Wilson. Yet these dif-

ferences were not as great as they might seem. All these men were reformers in varying degrees (even Schiff supported the workers in the
1916 Cloakmakers' Strike), opposed to party politics, and dedicated
to "good government." Nor were their party affiliations particularly
rigid. Oscar Straus began his career under Cleveland, and ran as a
Progressive Party candidate for governor of New York in 1912, although he was generally a Republican. Schiff, too, a Republican for
much of his life, had ties with the Democrats as well, and supported
Wilson in both of his elections. Brandeis, moreover, was believed to
have been a Republican until his association with Wilson.

Even Zionism, which had stimulated controversy and animosity
within this generation, eventually attracted a convergence of opinion.
All these men were concerned with what Oscar Straus described as
"the brunt and burdens of Russo-Jewish complications and difficulties,"[75] and all sought an alternative to a numerous migration to
America. What alarmed some of them, especially Schiff, was the spectre of *political* Zionism and a Jewish State. This seemed to pose a
threat to the position of the Jews in the West, bringing their loyalty
into potential question, while exposing the Jews to the danger of
power. However, as conditions in Eastern Europe failed to improve,
and as America became a less hospitable alternative, this group of in-
fluentiáls moved to a moderate nonpolitical Zionism. Ultimately, the
positions of Marshall and Schiff were fairly close to that of Brandeis,
whose main concern in Palestine became centered around economic
development.[76]

If these men equated political with personal influence, they remained convinced that civility, moderation, and reasonable argument
lined the path to persuasion. They identified with an older enlightened America and Europe, and they worried that changes were occurring which imperiled those fine balances on which the traditional liberalism had depended. Brandeis tried to counter these changes
through an emphasis on organization and social reform, along with
an attempt to rebuild character through education and inspired
causes. Marshall and Schiff feared that religion was receding too far
from the lives of *all* Americans, leaving a younger generation over-
swayed by popular fads and political movements. If religion could be
reconstituted as a personal and public inspiration, then the old harmony could be retained.[77]

As others have also noted, this generation felt compelled to contain their Jewish concerns within a strict adherence to an American creed.[78] They were exceptionally sensitive to American opinion, and were correspondingly fearful of an anti-Semitism that was not always latent. As men of wealth and position, they had more to lose from social prejudice and were also its more obvious targets.[79] Thus, it is instructive that Brandeis's zeal for Jewish solidarity and loyalty almost replicated the attitude of "100 percent Americanism" toward ethnic minorities.

This call for unity was hardly unique to Brandeis, who was but its most strident herald. In a letter to Chaim Weizmann, Marshall described unity "as the very essence of our lives and thoughts." Unity was necessary to protect Jews, but also to allow them to contribute "to civilization and culture and to the welfare of mankind."[80] In essence, this was the same reasoning Brandeis had offered as the basis for Zionism. In a world where religious community was becoming eroded by modernization and mobility, a concern for ethnic unity tended to become more significant. Ironically, despite their dislike of politics, the concern of these men for Jewish solidarity politicized Jewish affairs to a much greater extent than before.

Hence, it is apparent that during this era Zionism did for some Jews what the state of Israel would do for a later generation. It became an object of service, loyalty, and pride, as well as a source of identity, around which Jews, now less sure of their religious community, could unite. Henrietta Szold, a colleague of Brandeis in the Zionist organization, spoke for many in this respect:

> I became converted to Zionism the very moment I realized that it supplied my bruised, torn, and bloody nation, my distracted nation, with an ideal—an ideal that is balm to the self-inflicted wounds and to the wounds inflicted by others—an ideal that can be embraced by all, no matter what their attitude may be to their Jewish questions.[81]

For Brandeis and his peers the reconciliation of Jewish and American identities would pose little overt problem. Bound to an old creed, they sailed on waters as yet unrocked by depression or the disillusionment of war. Surely these were hard times, and reformers groped for solutions whose urgent necessity belied a frantic desire for a world that seemed to be slipping out of reach. But men such as Brandeis were products of that older world—European and American—which had made them and their fathers fortunate men. For them life was still a ladder of achievement, and as one climbed to greater heights he did not question too hard the soundness of the quest.

Liberalism thus represented more than a reigning national dogma. For Brandeis it was an intellectual and emotional frame, tying him to America as it even defined his marginality. A life of individual commitment and political detachment; an obligation to public service along with private achievement; a life which harmonized personal religion and political creed—was this the path for the Jew in America?

CHAPTER
3
THE IMMIGRANT
EXPERIENCE:
MODERN AMERICA

The massive wave of Jewish immigration which began toward the end of the nineteenth century defies easy generalization in terms of motive or intent. Many Jews were impelled by the fear of physical violence and communal destruction. Yet the brutality and apparent spontaneity of the pogrom crushed more than life and property. For some, the more Russified and politically oriented, it meant the abandonment of revolutionary activity and utopian vision.[1]

However important the physical attack on the Jewish community, we must remember that the pogroms were embedded in a period during which Jewish life was under pressure from other sources as well. For two centuries czarist Russia had been deciding the question of what to do with the Jews. The alternative answers, each attempted in program and policy, included forced assimilation and forced separation. These threats to the Jewish community produced a variety of responses. For many, including the Orthodox religious leadership, czarist intimidation indicated once again God's testing of His people, His determination to make Jewish election a burden which must be carried amongst the unrighteous of mankind. This belief was complemented by the reality that a Jew in Russia was a priori a politically powerless being. Learning to live with intimidation was religious and political wisdom.

Others saw the matter in a different light. The Enlightenment which had dawned upon Moses Mendelssohn in eighteenth-century Berlin began to influence Russian Jewry by the early years of the next century. The universalism of the Enlightenment, its denigration of tradition and religion, eroded the conscious loyalty of many younger Jews to Judaism. While releasing them from spiritual obligations—making them freethinkers—it did not necessarily liberate their enemies. A freethinking Jew was still a Jew, and even a convert found himself in a culture always ripe with hostility. One way of resolving this dilemma lay in the dedication to a program of intellect and action which might convert the entire society to a universalist system. Socialism, anarchism, communism were natural outlets for young Jews who sought assimilation with ambivalence. Assimilation became a distant, perhaps unreachable goal, and more important, it was not defined in Russian terms. Revolutionary activity, although obviously abhorrent to traditional Judaism was nevertheless a way of bringing Russian Jews and Gentiles into conformity with a higher law.[2]

The activities of Jewish radicals epitomized the increased tension within Jewish culture and threatened an increased danger from without. For many of the Orthodox, separation was worth the price of passivity. Since Gentiles were notoriously indiscriminate in regard to Jews, radical action on the part of a minority chanced further suffering for the multitude. This apprehension was not a concern just of the most religious; a wide spectrum lay between the Orthodox and the Jewish radicals. Tension arose typically in generational conflict, as children of the pious began to study Russian, sought the sciences in lieu of the Torah, and abandoned the teachers of their fathers for the wisdom of Marx.

Zionism and Jewish nationalism, which came into prominence during these years, also attempted a kind of resolution to these problems. Zionists argued that only a commitment to independent nationhood could secure either Jewish or Judaic survival. Palestine would be a place where Jews could be Jews as they chose to be, without external intimidation. Zionism was a movement of mainly enlightened Jews who reacted against the persistent anti-Semitism they encountered even in supposedly liberal societies. It attracted Jews who sought independence from the perceived narrowness of their parents.[3] To some of the young, the older generation had erred doubly—in remaining true to traditional Judaism, and in accepting the burden of the Diaspora, living as an accursed people among the nations. In the least, the problem of being a Jew in the modern world could be "worked out" in a hopefully more secure environment.[4]

The image of an earthly Zion was equally as important in marking America as a symbol of aspiration and adventure. An immigrant autobiographer recalled the desperate feelings he had in the Old World, where he was "condemned to inactivity." While his ambitions lay dormant, his boyhood friends had left the narrow limits of his village, seeking grand adventures, "and daily drawing nearer to that magic city of promise, New York."[5] Nor was this young immigrant atypical; America attracted restless souls. The rootless scholar, the revolutionary forced out of Russia for political reasons, the Talmudic student who realizes one day that he no longer believes, the restless father who was a freethinker and ne'er-do-well—these are the types most often reflected in the writings of first-generation immigrants.[6]

Undoubtedly, a large number of Jewish immigrants were the very religious, forced out of Russia by the spectre of violence. Yet there is evidence that the most Orthodox had the least taste for America and rarely considered voluntary emigration.[7] For them the magic of America appeared more like modern paganism than the work of God. In truth, this generation of wanderers was often spoken for by those who had departed from the ways of piety. Moreover, the pace at which many of these immigrants compromised or rejected Jewish Law once in America indicates not only the seduction and demands of the New World, but also the prior weakening of religion in the Old.

Insecurity and estrangement are typical of the immigrant experience. The desire for personal order, for a sense of continuity with the past, usually found some satisfaction in the rapid creation of ethnic neighborhoods and enclaves.[8] For Jews, this problem was somewhat less acute, since insecurity within an alien environment had always been assumed. However, for those who desired to step out, even tentatively, from the traditional community, new problems emerged. America was a temptation, a magnificent ideal which loomed larger than the vast land from which it radiated. Many newcomers would agree with Samuel Gompers: "America is more than a name. America is an ideal. America is the apotheosis of all that is right."[9]

Even for the many whose initiation into America brought disappointment, the new land was still a place of *possibility*. For many this

meant that they had to work, sacrifice, and change in order to reach
the promise of America. Here Jews could benefit from the fruits of
modern society, but here they had to become modern too. They had to
be, in Marcus Ravage's self-descriptive phrase, "Americans in the
Making."[10] Predictably, a sense of transformation, if not conversion,
is a dominant theme in first-generation writing. Thus, a new order became a very real problem to those Jews who strongly embraced American values. What kind of order did America offer? What kind of
order ought it reflect?

Central to this issue is the question of citizenship. How should a Jew
be a member of the American community? What does the polity require, encourage, or deny? To a new arrival, imbued with the possibilities of American freedom, citizenship might be conceived in two
different ways. Citizenship might imply growth and personal enlarge-
ment, the ability to act in ways long suppressed by external restraints.
In America, one could be a free man, unbound by tradition, in a land
where there were few defined limitations. The other view, more typical
of immigrants with previous political interests, was that citizenship
meant a dignified and responsible participation in a lawful community. For those who held fast to this view, America itself might have to
be remade.

The reality of America, of course, often fell far short of the image.
Morris Rosenfeld's sweatshop lamentations testify to the drudgery
which was the fate of the average immigrant.[11] The need to adjust
and survive fixed itself on the newcomer's life, a minatory reminder
that much of the American promise had to be endowed to the future.[12] Survival imposed its own discipline and order, leaving little
time for reflections on citizenship or for political involvement.[13] The
immigrant learned too—or his children learned—that success in
America demanded change, and even greater sacrifice.

Life in America was a revolutionary experience, often threatening
and conservatizing, sometimes hardening people to the ubiquity of
change. Emma Goldman's feelings were hardly unique, if bolder put:
"A new-world was before me, strange and terrifying. . . . Whatever the
new held in store for me I was determined to meet unflinchingly."[14] If
nothing else, America communicated motion and change, the alteration or reversal of older patterns. "All traditions have been upset
here," an older immigrant tells a "greenhorn" in Isaac Bashevis

Singer's novel *The Estate*.[15] In fact, America's primary lesson, especially as the twentieth century developed, might be that permanent order was a thing of the past.

Toleration of change might be practical wisdom for living in America but it was hardly a guide to the good life. Jews, as both Ahad Ha-Am and Erik Erikson have argued, have always been an imitative and adaptive people.[16] Adaptation was made easier by a strong family life and religion which were at the core of the Jewish community. Thus, it should be no surprise that despite important tensions, family instability and mental breakdowns were lowest among Jews as compared to other immigrant groups.[17] Again, Jews learned to tolerate change and external disorder—as a *people*. But in America was the perception of disorder sufficient for those who desired to be part of the new nation? Was it enough for those who desired to live a deeper, fuller life as Jews and Americans?

Beyond this, traditional Judaism had taught that the world, being God's kingdom, always sheltered at least a hidden order or intention. History reflected the Divine will, His love, mercy or punishment, due responses to human fidelity or waywardness. Beyond the appearance of disorder lie deeper realities, reflections of man's moral inclinations and God's rule. But these truths, it was believed, are themselves secondary to the wisdom of the Torah, God's truth for man, which man must act upon and discover.[18]

With this background so close to their experience, some Jews of the immigrant generation sought to dig deeper into the meaning of America. A significant literature has grown out of their encounters with America—mainly autobiographies, some novels, and a few works directly dealing with social and political affairs.[19] It is a literature that must be read—and written about—with some caution. Those who were able to write usually hoped for an American as well as a Jewish immigrant audience. Yiddish words and Jewish customs are often footnoted and explained (sometimes even a glossary might be included). Native Americans are at times specifically addressed, usually to be taught a lesson about immigrant life. Not infrequently these writers had something to prove—the virtues of America, or of themselves, for example. Autobiographies must be read with a filter for sentimentality and personal aggrandisement. Those who wrote, then, were often farther down the road of Americanization or modernization than the average Jew. As such they were scouts on a frontier others might soon travel, although perhaps in different ways.

LOVING AND LEAVING

"A Vilna apartment house," wrote Abraham Cahan,

is different from one in New York. In Vilna, the buildings seem to stand forever. Families seldom move. They draw closer together as the years pass. Each courtyard becomes a little world in itself.[20]

In America, most Jews encountered a mechanized urban environment for the first time. Most migrated from villages and towns of Eastern Europe, acclimating them less to American cities than to neighborhood life within the city. Even European cities, as Cahan implied, sheltered a more traditional way of life.

The immigrant's response to this modern world, as the writers we will discuss exemplify, tended to vary with his ties to traditional Judaism and the Jewish community. Beyond this truism, however, the old culture provided, for some, intellectual perspectives strong enough to resist the feeling of disorder so common to the immigrant in America. These perspectives sometimes coalesced into a critique of modernism, which hinted at a political stance toward America as well.[21]

The American city loomed as a modern, wondrous place, which a traditional mentality might admire but question. Inspired by the vitality and excitement of the new land, Cahan nevertheless found some things in American life "strange, ridiculous, wild, and sometimes even disgusting."[22] Sholom Aleichem, similarly a mature man when he first arrived on her shores, wrote of America through the eyes of a child, a fitting persona for the new land. America liberates childlike passions—curiosity, wonder, and innocent belief, as well as the desire to stray, wander, and gain enormous power. His adults too are enamored with America, and likewise, in a juvenile way.

Aleichem viewed the new world through eyes which may have twinkled but oftentimes disapproved. America champions size, speed, and change ("everybody moves in America"), propelling personal ambition into uncharted domains, undermining the present for future success. Yet change is not progress. As civilization advances ("In America, everybody advances. That is to say, one keeps growing, and every day one gets bigger and bigger . . ."), values seem to get debased and human behavior is frequently on an animal level. The modern subway makes people like the birds and worms, pressed together "like herring in a barrel." "People sit and keep chewing on something, like animals chewing their cud. . . . American people chew gum all their lives long, without stopping."[23]

Debasement is in part the result of amoral freedom. ("In America, everybody spits. America is a free country.") Here freedom is negative and private, expressed in excess or not at all. Harshly critical of American business morality, Aleichem saw advertising as a prime example of the perversion of untutored freedom. In personal affairs, freedom too often meant a narrow individualism, the patron of social irresponsibility. "America's a free country," an immigrant tells a relative still in the Old World. "You're perfectly free to keep your opinions to yourself. . . . Everyone minds his own business as he sees fit, and that's that."[24]

Still, Aleichem was not one to overlook the duality of America, notably the positive values which sometimes inspired personal action. The hope and vitality which this nation generated were good things; what was lacking was guidance and sensible direction. Americans needed a sense of proportion, a constant reminder of human limitations. Delusions of power and progress might lead men to forget their humanity, a special danger for immigrants whose ambitions had been long submerged in the old country.[25]

Most important, Aleichem could appreciate the profound effect America had on the feelings of the immigrant Jew. While his disagreement with America never abated, by the end of his life Aleichem was to portray the immigrant experience in a broader, more sympathetic perspective.[26] The United States was a refuge, despite its failings, and for this the newcomer would ever be grateful. To an immigrant, the image of America was born abroad, a vision of compassion and generosity which lingered to mock and judge the reality he often confronted here. It was, in fact, the visible hope of America—the promise of its traditions—before which modern corruption stood out like a stark silhouette.

At times in Aleichem's works, the promise of justice and compassion shone through, as when an American interferes to defend the boy

Mottel from the fists of his moody brother. If this act reminded Aleichem of the promise of America, he knew also that it symbolized one
of its perils: The new land might court and win the immigrant child.
Mottel's reaction, grateful and ambiguous, could speak for a generation—"Try not to love such a country!" [27]

Another Jewish immigrant, John Cournos, came to see the United
States as the epitome of the modern spirit. Less religious than Aleichem, still a child when he first arrived on these shores, Cournos was
himself more of a modern man. After working as a newspaperman in
Philadelphia, he went on to become a fairly successful novelist and
critic, moving eventually to England where he made his permanent
home.

Cournos expressed a theme which runs sporadically throughout the
works of other immigrant Jewish authors: the return to nature. Nature is often represented as a grand alternative to the grubbiness of
urban life. More significantly, nature is associated with the past, with
one's roots. [28] For Cournos, it was typified by his Russian birthplace,
where he could exist close to life and where he could wander alone in
the woods. America, on the other hand, meant a constant struggle for
money and security, if not survival. [29] Cournos viewed urban society
as a haven of corruption, where industrialism and material ambitions
suppress natural and spiritual qualities.

Cournos, like so many immigrants, was impressed with America's
energy. In his *Autobiography* he complained that this energy is per-
verted into primarily material channels, whereas America's true
greatness inheres in the possibility of harnessing spiritual drives. He
envied a barely remembered brother who remained in Europe for his
energy and worldliness. The material imperative of America inhibits
creative emotional expression. A precursor of contemporary ethnics,
Cournos identified his "passionate nature" with being a Jew: "To
apologize for my folly, then, would be to apologize for my ethnic origins, to apologize for human aspirations." [30]

The activity and bustle of America, along with the heavy demands
placed upon him at an early age, contribute to a picture of a world
basically disordered and insecure. America, and his family as well,
denied him the love and affection necessary for genuine growth. Thus
Cournos, like countless other Jewish writers, frequently portrayed

himself as a Christ figure, eternally suffering on American soil. [31] However, this is a Christ without anger, a paragon which all "great men" attempt to follow. [32]

Given this perspective, Cournos had little feeling for politics, which as an artist, he saw himself above. In fact, Cournos seemed mainly concerned with the private battle. Nor was his emphasis unusual. Russian Jewish immigrants came to an America whose sages were Emerson and Spencer, and many of them came to accept their teachings as a personal code. Mary Antin, Marcus Ravage, along with the main characters in two of the major Jewish novels from this period, all read Spencer with avid curiosity, if not approval. [33] What is interesting about Cournos is both his ambivalence regarding individual competition, and the way he resolved it.

Although suffering seems to single him out, it also toughens and ennobles him. His struggle in the "jungle" of America becomes a source of pride, preparing him for his anxious quest for the recognition he finally achieves—in England. The irony of Cournos's career is that he genuinely accepts that which he seems to deplore—individual competition in a cold, disordered world. Nevertheless, he cannot succeed in America because his spiritual energy is not valued in the American marketplace. For Cournos, London is the setting where he can fulfill American and Jewish values: individual success, intellectual achievement, and emotional expression. When he finally publishes a review in an English journal, however, he compares his achievement with that of an American business tycoon. [34]

In England, Cournos is still the striving individual, with more literary acquaintances than permanent friends. But here he can be more of himself. In England, language and expression earn greater respect (his writing on England is clearly superior to his writing on America), and traditions are still alive. London has what America lacks—"the ghosts of great men." [35]

Britain, however, is no more orderly than America, because for Cournos, the world itself is anarchic. England, in his view, provides more outlets for disorder, especially Hyde Park, which he describes as "a dramatic stage." [36] Here, where there is a "friendly tolerance" for personal expression, the individual can find refuge from the impersonality and competitiveness of modern society. Cournos, himself, does not see it as a refuge, for the same reason that he cannot acknowledge that England is a ground for his competitive strivings.

Hyde Park symbolizes liberal England, a society in which (political) passions can be expressed without doing harm. As in much liberal literature, this condition is constantly imperiled—civil society is always verging on a dangerous anarchy. "There is chaos without—everywhere," he writes, and therefore the individual must maintain a sense of order within.[37] Self control must suffice, angry passions must be suppressed. In describing *The Mask*, his well-received autobiographical novel, Cournos explained that he desired to relate bitter experience without bitterness, "to show the beauty inherent in all tragic things."[38] Hopefully, one can reach a plateau where suffering and fear can be transcended while their reality is denied: they are made into "art." Paradoxically, given Cournos's disaffection with modern America, he remained an unconscious American, repressing real feelings, sacrificing self-expression, while opting for personal moderation:

> Yet I know how foolish it is to feel superior or inferior. One should be beyond both. One should be beyond all labels. One should be just oneself; preferably, a person with balance, whose equilibrium could only be affected from within, not from without. If I could have a motto that I should like to live up to it would be Semper Idem—"always the same."[39]

Cournos, too, could speak for many. Searching for a way to integrate past and present, nature and machine, this "modern Plutarch" would never feel quite at home in America.[40] Aleichem's discomfort, no less deep, was expressed in biting humor, and was supported by the strength of his traditional background (which taught that one need not be overly concerned with not feeling at home in a nation of Gentiles). Besides, Aleichem was part of a wider community, while Cournos, on the other hand, represented himself as the loner seeking a home; seeking, perhaps, a new past as well. For him, Judaism became an "ethnic factor," a separate, submerged realm of the self, needing a friendly world to relieve its tensions.

Indeed, the most perceptive vision of modern America typically comes from those who, like Aleichem, were most at ease with their

Jewish identity. Abraham Joshua Heschel, for example, also equated America with the extremes of modernity, although the new land, to his mind, reflected a great potential for redemption. Heschel was a later immigrant, arriving in the 1930s, after receiving both a rabbinical and modern education in Eastern Europe. Although he usually did not refer directly to America, his critique of the current age clearly embraced his American experience.

Heschel viewed the modern age as a conspiracy against a return to God. We know God through a sense of wonder, a "radical amazement" at commonplace things. God is inherent in the mystery of existence. The modern world denies mystery and human limitations, and liberates evil by avoiding God:

> Yet we finally discovered what prophets and saints have always known: bread and power will not save humanity. There is a passion and drive for cruel deeds which only the awe and fear of God can soothe; there is a suffocating and selfishness in man which only holiness can ventilate.[41]

Modern man does not understand his "dangerous power." Technology and the social sciences deceive us into a faith in self-sufficiency and social reform. God created us free, to choose good or evil, and gave us a law to lead us to Him. For centuries, religion maintained a dialogue which centered around the assumption of human limitations. Now, our desire to be current and fashionable sustains the error of our ego. For Heschel, on the contrary, a Jew without Torah is "obsolete."[42]

Thus the bleakness of our age derives not only from our insensitivity to God and ourselves. Our language and images, our conceptual framework, join to divert us from true paths and eternal questions. Modern man must constantly be reminded that his world, in its denial of God, is essentially false. The world needs a prophetic voice to awaken it, since law and ritual, however important, have little meaning for modern man. Most probably, Heschel saw his own task as pre-prophetic: to restate and reintroduce a "grammar of experience" in which a prophet could arise and speak.[43]

Heschel also found in America a naturalistic interpretation of Judaism which turned God the Father into the "God-idea," and searched Jewish history for its symbolic value.[44] Modern Jewish theology, he believed, was like contemporary philosophy, "where values are a synonym for needs," where individual interests took precedence over the demands of the Almighty. Just as man needs to recognize God's sovereignty, so must he transcend his egotistical interests and commit himself to the divine way.[45]

For Heschel, Torah is God's *way* rather than God's law. Men must act. Traditional Judaism emphasizes *deeds*, right living in the service of God. Holy deeds teach us truths which we can learn only through their performance. "The heart," he writes, "is revealed in the deeds."[46] Good deeds are an invitation to God to join man in partnership. Justice, in this sense, is not an ideal. Rather, it is inherent in the problem of "right living" and good deeds for a community of men.

The quest for justice might lead men to political action, and Heschel's own life bespeaks his sensitivity to this point.[47] He believed that political action, though extremely dangerous in the modern world, teaches men things about themselves and about their fellows. The action itself might educate others as to possibilities for justice and godliness in the world. The divine demand for justice requires that men have social and political concerns. Yet, in truth, this was not Heschel's primary care. Modern man must once again discover God, the true sovereign. Politics, while important, must first be transcended, and then guided by He who is beyond the mystery of existence.[48]

CHRONICLES OF DEGENERATION

Heschel, who arrived later than Cournos and Aleichem, discovered an America in which technology and change had rapidly accelerated. His experience symbolized that of many post-1924 immigrant Jews who were, in general, more religious than those who had come earlier. Their encounter with the New World then might reflect certain polarities immanent in the whole range of Jewish immigration. As they were typically the more Orthodox, so too was America more modern, defined now by realities which, twenty or thirty years before, had been but partially realized.

Here, too, fellow Jews, now secularized and modern, might seem to walk in separate paths. By the third and fourth decades of this century it had become obvious that Jews were no longer untouched by what W. H. Auden saw as a universal ill: "the natural and unconscious community of tradition is rapidly disappearing from the earth."[49] Thus to speak to those who called themselves Jewish, one had to argue in terms of philosophical or universal meaning, or attempt to employ an older rhetoric which rejected the constraints of modern language.

Isaac Bashevis Singer chose the latter route, out of necessity. Arriving in America in the late 1930s, Singer felt that he was too old to learn to write in a new language. More important, Yiddish was "the language of the people I wanted to write about."[50] Singer's characters, like himself, are products of two worlds—traditional Judaism and the world of the Enlightenment. Closer to religious roots, author and characters feel more comfortable with a language in which spiritual expression has not been displaced.

Singer considers most modern Jewish writers to be only superficially Jewish. The genuine Jewish writer must be Judaic, steeped in the Torah and Talmud, thoroughly knowledgeable of Jewish history, and fluent in Hebrew and Yiddish.[51] This Orthodox classification parallels Singer's view of himself as a Yiddish writer:

> The Yiddish writer not only belongs to a minority, but he is a minority within a minority. He is a paradox to his own people.[52]

The man of tradition, the Yiddish writer, although "theoretically dead" in modern Jewish culture, becomes an even greater paradox—a Jew amongst the Jewish people.

For Isaac Bashevis Singer it is difficult to be a Jew in the modern world. While the burden of Judaism was never easy to bear, in past centuries it was supported by communal separatism, family responsibility, and, above all, the rarely challenged authority of God and Torah. Singer is a modern chronicler of the effects of the Enlightenment on Old World Jewry in Europe and the United States. One result of this engagement, in his view, has been the acceptance of worldly, essentially non-Jewish burdens by those who call themselves Jews in modern society.

The son and grandson of rabbis, Singer was reared in what his brother described as "a world that is no more."[53] His formative years were spent both in Warsaw and in provincial shtetls to which his father had been assigned rabbinic appointments. Educated to be a rabbi, he became increasingly attracted to modern science and literature in his early adolescence. His older brother Israel Joshua was the first to wander, abandoning religion for literature and art. I. J. Singer

remained an important influence on his younger brother, Isaac Bashevis, even though his extreme rationalism was never embraced by the
latter. It was his death, in fact, that seemed to release the younger
Singer from a long period of literary drought. [54]

Singer, then, provides a rather unique perspective. Familiar with
both urban and village Jewish life, Orthodoxy and "Haskalah," Poland and America, he is capable of measuring the modern Jew in relation to a way of life with which few today are intimate.

Polish Jewry during the first decades of the twentieth century was
torn between two worlds, neither of which seemed very stable. The
world of the Hasidim and the Orthodox every year was losing more
children to the secularism of the city. Those who sought acceptance
into Polish society soon found, however, that this new world was even
less secure. Others, disillusioned with assimilation, sought a different
form of it in Palestine and America. Anti-Semitism rose in Germany
and Austria in the late nineteenth century and Poland, never averse to
it, soon followed suit.

The external threat was matched by increased dissension within the
Jewish community in Poland. In his novels, Singer's main characters
are almost always loners, men who are distant from the community.
This is true of the pious as well as the lost. Calman Jacoby, a just man,
worships alone in his own prayer house, apart from a Jewish community overly concerned with status and money. Even Singer's rabbis are
often men who, as they grow in wisdom, increase the distance between themselves and their followers. [55] For the pious, it is true, the
community necessarily exists at a lower level of godliness—since it includes so many different kinds of people. Nevertheless, a major theme
in Singer's work is the difficulty of being a Jew in the face of a Jewish
community that is crumbling and degenerating.

If traditional Judaism seemed to be shaken, the world of secularized Jews seemed far less hopeful. Poland itself was hardly a nation,
rather a pawn between Russia and Germany. Jews who sought education and advancement found their paths obstructed on many levels.
Excluded from positions in the government and military, they encountered quotas and hostility in various professions as well. More ex-
posed and less unified than Orthodox Jews, the Jews of the city sometimes turned to messianic political movements to free them from the
new bondage they had chosen. [56]

But for Singer the problem of the secular Jew is more elemental. Is he still a Jew? If not, how does one live a life of meaning in the modern world? A Jew believes and follows the Torah, he lives apart with his own people, he trusts in God and accepts His covenant with its burdens and joys. He seeks not, according to Singer, power over other men. But secular teaching contradicted Scripture, devalued revelation, and challenged the existence of God. Evolutionary theory taught that men evolved from the beasts, yet in Singer's view, too often it reduced people to that level. Singer's typical protagonist, obviously autobiographical, is the Yeshiva boy who has read Spinoza and is never quite the same again. He questions ritual, seeks out answers to the contradictions of the Bible, and searches for some sign or explanation of God's justice. Sometimes he forsakes God altogether, sometimes he quarrels with Him, and sometimes he returns. [57]

Singer suggests that there is a hierarchy of "Jewishness" and that many moderns barely qualify at the lowest level. All Jews ask questions and argue with the Creator, but it is the traditionally pious who are most likely to deal with the "eternal questions." For Singer, doubt and skepticism are not marks of atheism, nor *must* they lead to it (although, in fact, they often do). They are necessities along the road to higher wisdom and piety. Thus there are all sorts of rabbis. A traditional environment produces all sorts of men. But the virtue of this environment is that it encourages a higher wisdom and spirituality among its best sons. Those Jews who have migrated towards modernity are less Jewish for it. If they retain their belief in an always unseen God, if they continue to ask the eternal questions, they remain Jews even though their piety has been diluted by the rejection of ritual and the decline of community. Singer implies that those who have lost God and embrace entirely the world of men are Jews in name only and are capable of anything, even of being Nazis. [58]

The temptations are especially perilous for modern Jews since they are derived from a culture that has encouraged personal commitment to higher beliefs. Political activity is a tremendous danger, since it too easily lures men into a belief in false messiahs, rigid systems, and the delusion that men can be as God. For those who are wise enough to see the limitations of mere worldly commitment, yet are unable to believe in the Almighty, the depth of despair might be especially great. Thus of Asa Heschel, the aimless disciple of Spinoza who is the main character in *The Family Moskat*, Singer writes:

> It occurred to Adele that she had never been able to understand what it was that tortured him. Was it the failure to have had a career? Did his heart long for someone? She was on the point of asking him, but suddenly she knew; he was not a worldly man by his very essence. He was one of those who must serve God or die. He had forsaken God, and because of this he was dead—a living body with a dead soul. She was astonished that this simple truth had eluded her until now.[59]

The Sinful City

It is surely no accident that the devil who tries to corrupt the virtuous town of Frampol is "a gentleman from Cracow." This gentleman is a modern man, a doctor, who seduces honorable townsfolk with the lure of wealth and easier living. Similarly, Yasha, the "magician of Lublin," sinks to his perigee of degradation in Warsaw, the city that has tempted him with the promise of wealth and reputation. In Lublin, a smaller community, Yasha was held "in small esteem."[60]

Cities are places of constant motion, characterized by "hurrying throngs," "a world of trade," and degrading poverty. One character complains that "in Russia people suffered, but I have never met as many maniacs there as in New York City." Singer sees urban life symbolized by "a revolving door . . . swallowing up and disgorging people as though they were caught in some sort of mad dance." The home of the modern mind, the city contains all the contradictions and terrible possibilities of our age:

> I have played with the idea that all of humanity suffers from schizophrenia. Along with the atom, the personality of Homo sapiens has been splitting. When it comes to technology, the brain still functions, but in everything else degeneration has begun. . . . Soon, technology, too, will disintegrate. Buildings will collapse, power plants will stop generating electricity. Generals will drop atom bombs on their own populations. Mad revolutionaries will run in the streets, crying fantastic slogans. I have often thought it would begin in New York. This metropolis has all the symptoms of a mind gone berserk.[61]

Jews may live in their own areas within the city, but the fabric of communal life seems irreparably torn. The neighborhood provides a kind of negative security. It is a place that takes one in and provides some kind of protection from the usually more dangerous Gentile sections. Here remnants of the past are still apparent, faces and forms are reminders of a common history. But the neighborhood is little more than a refuge within. It has few real physical boundaries and, more important, the lives and ambitions of its inhabitants might well transcend the neighborhood streets. It lacks a communal structure, and genuine intimacy is subverted by mobility. Thus Yasha, the magician turned thief, flees to a synagogue for refuge. There he is able to believe once again in the simple prayers, as a long-forgotton devotion returns. Once more in the city street, even in the Jewish quarter, his doubts return and he resents the demands of Judaism. 62

The urban environment is commercial and practical, hostile to the spirit and separate from God. Here external chaos and motion are mirrored in the souls of men. In Singer's novels, the droshky (a Russian carriage) plays an important role: taking passengers through the maze of urban life, it carries them from one state of mind to the next. Contemplation cannot be sustained as time and experience become increasingly fragmented. Of Abram Shapiro, Asa Heschel's initial guide to Warsaw and modern ways, Singer writes: "He loved nothing so much as excitement, days and nights full of motion." 63

While Singer does not sentimentalize the small community—as some of his critics claim—he does see it as a more humane and spiritual environment. 64 The shtetl allows people the security which is required for both contemplation and genuine individuality. Of course, the community can be intimidating, if not immoral. Yet even within a hostile communal environment sources of truth and the possibilities for redemption are more apparent and accessible. In the city it is easy for man to wander lost.

It is instructive in this regard to contrast Singer's urban and village "isolates." As noted earlier, Singer's characters often separate themselves within the small community. Yasha, the magician, returns to God and lives a reclusive life in a hut within his courtyard. Eventually his reputation for piety and wisdom forces him to renew contacts with the village. He is considered a sage, perhaps falsely, and is besieged for advice and blessings. Yasha, like Rabbi Beinish of *Satan in Goray*, Rabbi Jochanan of *The Estate*, and Calman Jacoby of *The Manor*, attempts to separate himself from the world of men and sin, although within a protective community.

This separation is at once a form of self-punishment as well as an attempt to create a wall between the self and worldly temptations. The community, while it provides security, is in each case beset by dissension and a malignant corruption. Singer indicates, however, that extreme separation is both illusory and dangerous for most men. Living within a community always involves responsibilities, whether realized or not. In the case of Yasha, his reputation as an isolate brings the needy to his door. Jacob of *The Slave* also seeks retreat; instead he is thrust into a position of political leadership. Solitude is a danger, too, since it often involves separation from the self along with the world. Yasha's isolation, for example, is founded on a fear of himself, namely the lust for women and power which he has not mastered.[65]

Singer indicates, however, that separation, although it is not the way for most men, is sometimes necessary for others. For Yasha and Jacob the aim of their seclusion is to serve God. In the end, this commitment will ease and conclude their trial. "I believe," Singer has said, "that the Higher powers do not reveal themselves so easily; you have to search for them."[66] Those who seek God may experience revelation. Moreover, Yasha and Jacob are both incomplete men—one unable to discipline his desires, the other, too unaware of them. In each case, seclusion is educational; they must return to the loneliness of adolescence to learn how to be men. Finally, these village isolates reflect Singer's persistent moral theme—they have *chosen* to obey God, they have used their free will.[67]

When Asa Heschel arrives in Warsaw he asks himself, "Is it here I will learn the divine truths?" Singer's answer is quite clear: modern urban man is separate from divine truths, and from truths of nature as well. Urban man does not choose isolation—he is essentially estranged. Beyond this, he is often unaware of his own basic needs. Singer's urban recluses are thoroughly alone, with no community to recognize their fate. Their forays of sociability are utilitarian and temporary. Bessie Popkin, tied to the world through her husband, withdraws from it with his death. Her distrust of the city grows into paranoia, her personal affairs become disorganized and devalued. Losing her door key one evening, unwilling to ask for help, she spends the night on the New York streets, where she learns, at least, that she can survive. "She had almost forgotten that there was a sky, a moon, stars. Years had passed and she never looked up—always down."[68]

The modern city is a fearful and crazy place, fostering a loneliness which can blind one to the always present potential for human communion. As in everything, Singer suggests that there are compensations—even miracles can occur in the city. The cafeteria is a place where the alienated can congregate, sharing some communion over food. Self-consciousness and skeptical observation are vital if people are to retain their sense of God. The urban isolates Singer portrays in positive tones, such as Herman Gombiner and Professor Eibeschutz, are constant questioners and seekers of God. Detached from human relationships, they serve God in their own way, through kindness to animals. Although Singer sees their plight as desperate, he intimates that this might be a necessary way of remaining a Jew under modern conditions.[69]

Cities are founded on mobility and change. Physical and social insecurity encourage a desire for permanence among urban dwellers. For Singer this involves an unfortunate reversal. Human affairs are never permanent: man's estate is not entirely in his own hands. A stable community is a desirable if illusory value in the uncertain lives of men. Without it, the human task is that much harder, and being a Jew is a lonelier quest.

Magicians and Doctors

Singer's vision of the city is consistent with its image in Scripture: it is the home of power and corruption.[70] Here man is deluded by the spectres of both power and impotence, forgetting his own nature, its possibilities and limitations. The city stands as a challenge to God, a conglomerate of power that seduces even good men from their higher tasks. Thus Asa Heschel is suggestive of his Biblical namesake: King Asa, a "builder of cities" who was favored by God. As Asa built and prospered, however, he grew enamored with power, so that in the end he betrayed God by relying on the King of Syria.[71] Similarly, Asa Heschel forsook Judaism for foreign ideas and the ways of the city.

As modern man has forgotten God so has he deified his own works and fantasies. In the contemporary world, Singer infers, political ideologies and psychological fashions have presumed the authority, and

often the fanaticism, which religion once held. As a "hero" of one of
Singer's stories notes, they have become inherent to our age, but-
tressed by the intimidating weight of majority opinion.

> Communism, psychoanalysis, Fascism, and radicalism were the shib-
> boleths of the twentieth century. Oh, well! What could he, Herman
> Gombiner, do in the face of all this? He had no choice, but to observe
> and be silent. [72]

In Singer's view, secular rationalism has itself become an ideology,
hiding the mystery that envelopes the world. Modern movements, political and intellectual, teach falsely when they imply that all is soluble
and comprehensible. Scientists infer that all can be known, neglecting
the problem of first cause, overestimating our knowledge, purposefully overlooking all we do *not* know. On the contrary, Singer writes:

> I reasoned that in the whole chaos there are precise laws. . . . Some-
> where there must be a Knower who knows every thought of each human
> being, who knows the aches of each fly, who knows each comet and
> meteor, each molecule in the most distant galaxy. I spoke to Him. Well,
> Almighty Knower, for you everything is just. You know the whole and
> have all the information . . . and that's why you're so clever. But what
> shall I do with my crumbs of facts? [73]

Despite his interest in the supernatural and his dubiety concerning
modern rationalism, Singer is *not* an irrationalist. Reason itself indicates its own limitations, directing us to the vast unknown and the
mystery which surrounds God. Reason prepares us for the realization
of the Almighty ("I reasoned that in this whole chaos there are precise
laws . . ."). Singer's use of demonology and mysticism in his Old
World stories is at least, in part, suggestive and metaphorical. [74]
While his interest in the mystical is genuine, at times it seems almost
impishly intended to shock us into realizing our blind faith in reason.
The Old World was prepared to accept supernatural explanations
just as we are not. As Singer must know, the appeal of these stories
suggests that we might not be as advanced as we like to believe. "Now
the world is so corrupted," he writes, "that the demons just keep hidden." [75] (This also in an apt description of Singer, the author, whose
judgments are often hidden between the lines of his works. His narration is usually quite reserved, but the text abounds with gentle malice
and critical irony.)

For Singer, the dilemma of modern man is best portrayed in the characters of the doctor and magician. The doctor is often one who has traveled far along contemporary paths. Trained as a scientist, he uses his knowledge to accept a godlike power over human lives. Singer's physicians are typically sensitive and divided souls—men propelled by good intentions, who desire to believe but are dominated by uncertainty (Ezriel Babad of *The Estate* is a good example). Being the most modern of men they are sometimes the most susceptible. Thus, Singer depicts middle-class and educated Jews as being less prepared for Hitler than the rest. Most dangerous, perhaps, is the role attributed by others to the doctor. Frequently he is seen as one who can truly comprehend human life and cure human ills. In the absence of God's sovereignty, the doctor becomes one of the godlike men.

This danger is symbolized even better by the magician—one who, like God, can deal in the unseen. Yasha, "the magician of Lublin," is a bundle of complexity, a man constantly torn by contrary desires. He desires worldly power and fame, yet he is capable of deep religious feeling. He loves and respects his wife, but must always have other women. "He lusted after women, yet hated them as a drunkard hates alcohol." [76] He envies and apes established society but detests its hypocrisy and immorality.

Yasha, encouraged by his admirers, imagines himself with godlike powers, as one who could "unlock all souls." In his fantasies, Yasha sees himself as omnipotent, an emperor of the world and a messiah to his people.

> In his imagination he even led the Jews out of exile, gave them back the land of Israel, rebuilt the temple of Jerusalem. [77]

Singer pointedly juxtaposes Yasha's striving for worldly power with the teachings of Ecclesiastes. Moreover, Yasha is clearly a symbol of the world he wishes to conquer:

> Together with his ambition and lust for life, dwelt a sadness, a sense of the vanity of everything, a guilt that could neither be repaid or forgotten. What was life's purpose if one did not know why one was born, nor why one died? What sense did all the fine words about positivism, industrial reform, and progress make when it was all cancelled out in the grave? [78]

Yasha is an archetypical Singer creation, a man caught in his own trap, deluded by his own magic. Singer implies that Yasha is really a child, a schoolboy who, unable to follow in his pious father's path, takes many paths at once. Unable to accept the responsibility of Jewishness, he loads himself down with destructive worldly burdens. Unable to live with insecurity and mystery, he seeks the power to dominate an alien world. In seeking to conquer the world, Yasha becomes a slave to it, as social codes and the search for status define a new kind of personal orthodoxy.

Lacking a personal conception of God's power, men have great difficulty perceiving the limits of their own. Even without God, Singer believes, the teachings of Orthodoxy are wise: in an uncertain world, know the false, do no evil.[79] Those who seek power over others are themselves enslaved to their lust for dominion. Excessive power invites proportionate abuse:

> When people have extreme power over other people, it's a terrible thing. I always pray to God (and I do pray because I am in my way a religious man), don't give me any power over any other human beings. I have always avoided this kind of power like the plague.[80]

Power, sin, and guilt are unavoidable, arising out of the vagaries of human association. Life is unpredictable, and our knowledge and understanding are necessarily limited. Even when we seek to avoid power and responsibility tricks of fortune may tie us to our brother's fate.[81] For Singer, like Nathaniel Hawthorne, the virtuous man is a humble citizen who carries out his responsibilities to God and community (or in modern society, to those who are close to him).[82] Sometimes these responsibilities include leadership, but the wise man eschews positions of political power. Political leadership, although necessary and possibly virtuous, involves fixed and acknowledged power. Not only does this invite abuse, given human weakness, but it threatens to divert men from the search for the Eternal. As in other respects, Singer remains true to Judaic teachings: The state, worldly power, and political movements represent affronts to divine sovereignty. A Jew ought observe and understand, yet should not seek *positions* of power.

To Singer this attitude is based on more than pure humility. The wise man avoids political power out of a sense of his own shortcomings, but also from a fear of his own potency. Through the pursuit of God men come to appreciate and combat their desire for power. In political life, it is too easy to forget. Thus, even those with good intentions may inevitably abuse their power.[83]

These problems are not confined merely to political life. Singer shows that a moral man may have enormous, if unsought, influence, even beyond his death. The prophets to the Jews, and the Jews (at times) to the world, have stood as witnesses for God and examples for men. To the man of faith, this hope is related to a vision of power which transcends the political. In life, too, the moral man cannot escape the problem of power. Most men want to believe, many will seek to follow, and the good man may find that others want him to lead. Singer's portrayal of the courts of Hasidic rabbis, and the problem of succession, indicate his sensitivity to the political temptations in religious life.[84]

Slavery and Freedom

All people are composed of similar ingredients, yet the combinations are infinitely diverse and defy prediction. Singer emphasizes both individuality and equality: The genuine differences between people are blurred when appraised against the majesty of God. Death, too, is a great equalizer. Holy rabbis suffer temptation and doubt and at death call for their parents like little children. Fools and animals are sometimes closer to eternal truths than the worldly wise.[85] There are only degrees of men, and while these degrees are crucial, they should not blind us to the potential in all men for weakness and strength.

Most people do not understand themselves. Drawn to the earth by physical and social needs, man also has a spiritual nature capable of a higher understanding. Along with our individuality, however, our spiritual nature often goes unrecognized and repressed. An admirable rabbi realizes this truth:

> Man has memories, regrets, resentments. They collect like dust, they
> block him up so he can't recognize the light and life that descends from
> heaven.[86]

Free will contends with human weakness, often yielding to the demands of the senses and the delusions of the mind. "From the moment man is born," Singer has said, "he is compelled, yet at the same time he is given the free will to fight compulsion."[87] Free will is a "rare gift and we get very little of it"—thus, the best people can do is fight compulsion, ascending to higher levels of knowledge and spirit in the process.[88] Only death releases man from travail, perhaps freeing the soul for the genuine life.[89]

The temptation toward extremes is common in Singer's characters, but more so in his women, who appear to be less able to live with doubt. Lust, greed, and pride may easily dominate the personality (again, like Hawthorne, he often concentrates on intellectual pride). For Singer, one of the virtues of the Orthodox tradition is that it teaches moderation and personal discipline. Without restraints, good teaching, and higher guidance the self slides easily into corruption.[90] The "informed heart" also readies us for moments of love, insight, and revelation—unexplained "miracles" that sustain us during our journey through an uncertain world.

Orthodox religion lifts man above the beast and directs him toward God. This is true for Christianity as well as Judaism. Singer describes the peasantry in *The Slave* as wanton and cruel, often no better than the animals with which they live. But these Gentiles are essentially pagan; they do not take Christianity seriously. Singer's Christian characters, such as Felicia of *The Manor* or Mrs. Beechman of "The Letter-Writer" are often morally superior to the secular Jews around them.

For Singer, genuine freedom derives from the attempt to unite one's nature in a striving towards God. This demands the recognition of God's Kingdom and man's subjection, if not slavery. Yasha's decisive moment occurs when he realizes the delusion of his quest for power. Yasha sees the hand of God and reverts to extreme Orthodoxy, separating himself from a world in which he "could no longer breathe."[91] As noted earlier, Yasha's extreme remedy appears to be a necessary antidote to the depth of his illness. Moreover, he has *chosen* to enter the covenant and understands his penance as an act of free will.

Yasha's path is comparable to that of Jacob, the main character of *The Slave* (Yasha, after he returns to Judaism, calls himself "Jacob the Penitent"). Although this novel is set in the seventeenth century, it is in many ways a parable of modern and ancient times. Jacob, fleeing from the Chmielnicki pogroms (referred to as the "holocaust" in the novel), is taken prisoner and sold as a slave to primitive peasants. Here his Judaism must be solitary and he tries to remember the Torah by etching it into stone. While repelled by the culture of his captors, he is infatuated with the sensuous daughter of his owner. His lust for her is at war with his faith, which has been already shaken by the massacres. Unspoken too is Jacob's guilt as a survivor. Not only does he question God but he derides his own failure to save his family, although it is never spelled out in this novel, as it is in Singer's later work, *Enemies*. However, Jacob's abhorrence of meat is related to his images of the slaughter of Jewish children. Indirectly, it seems, Jacob has identified with the aggressor and is punishing himself for it.

Jacob is ransomed from slavery, but the Jewish community to which he returns has been degraded by its suffering. Resentment, backbiting, and a fascination with death pervade the community. (This is quite similar to Singer's description of Hitler refugees in America.) Jacob's freedom then is of little import; superior to slavery, it is hardly an end in itself. Beyond this, Jacob's soul is not free—he still lusts for the forbidden Wanda, and castigates himself for his transgressions with her.

Jacob returns to rescue Wanda and consummate a "covenant of lust." Singer suggests here, as in many other works, that while lust is never sufficient in itself, it could be the basis for deeper communion. Worldly covenants and human commitments are often minor miracles, giving us glimpses of eternal truths. They ransom us from the prison of the self.

It is in his marriage to Wanda that Jacob begins to become a Jew again in the fullest sense. Always a messianic figure to her, Jacob accepts the responsibility of becoming her teacher so as to lead her to the Almighty. Wanda becomes the convert Sarah (as well as Rachel) and Jacob transforms a covenant of lust into a covenant of love and, most important, subjects it to the will of God.[92] Singer makes it clear that Jacob, like his Biblical namesake, is a fallible man. His attempt to convert Wanda is neither wholly successful nor wholly wise. Yet Jacob is a man of good faith, and his trials serve to teach him basic truths about man and God. With his wife's death, his own education reaches a kind of completion, too:

But now he at least understood his religion: its essence was the relation between man and his fellows. Man's obligations toward God were easy to perform. . . . Men like Gershon cheated, but they ate matzohs prepared according to the strictest requirements. They slandered their fellow men, but demanded meat doubly kosher. . . . Rather than troubling him to induce a Jew to eat pork or kindle a fire on the Sabbath, Satan did easier and more important work, advocating those sins deeply rooted in human nature.[93]

In the course of his education Jacob transgresses the formal rules of Judaism. Wanda-Sarah is never legally converted, they are not legally married, and they cohabit before marriage. The child born to them is not, in Jewish law, truly a Jew. Again, Singer emphasizes that law and ritual cannot always be obeyed. Jacob is compared in the novel to the patriarchs Abraham, Jacob, Joseph, and Moses. Nevertheless, there is another model never cited explicitly—Jacob is also somewhat like Jesus, the Jew. Nor is this an unlikely reference. Singer seems to be saying that in times of uncertain faith a Jew may have to question the Law in order to remind his own people of their task.

The Slave contains a number of themes central to Singer's work. First of all, it is a hopeful book. All things are possible, good as well as evil. Even in the darkest times human nature is capable of regeneration. The novel begins with an allusion to the covenant of Noah and the symbolic rainbow in the sky. God has promised to save a remnant, despite massacres and communal degeneration. History is made by the evil and Jews are pawns of that history.[94] However, Jews must retain their own history, which involves the recognition that chronological time and history are, in a sense, illusions:

Everything remained the same: the ancient love, the ancient grief. Perhaps four thousand years again would pass: somewhere, at another river, another Jacob would walk mourning another Rachel. Or who knew, perhaps it was always the same Jacob and the same Rachel.[95]

In spite of history, the essentials of human nature do not change. Every Jew comes to God in his own way, through his own free will. Every Jew relives the journeys of the patriarchs, who also must be comprehended as fallible human beings. One is not born into Judaism: those who are raised to be Jews may at heart reject the teachings; there will always be Ruths or Wandas who will accept it. A Jew, Singer infers, is a surrogate and a slave of God.

Singer creates a social situation in the novel which, in its reference to marginality, is also comparable to modern times. Having married a Gentile, Jacob walks a tightrope between the Jewish and Christian worlds. If the Christian authorities learn of Wanda's conversion surely they will punish the Jews. Therefore, Jacob and Wanda decide to hide her past from both communities by alleging that she is a mute, so as not to explain her lack of Yiddish. Of greater relevance, both communities are corrupt, headed by either demonic or exploitative men. Jacob, through his devotion, has unwittingly taken responsibility for the whole community. By teaching the Torah to a willing convert, Jacob has become one of the few real Jews in an unwilling community.

The novel deals with the problem of personal righteousness in times of upheaval. It underlines the importance of the communal order, but suggests that a Jew lives in more than one community at a time. The Jews of Pilitz ape the Gentiles in their greed and envy of power. Pogroms do not necessarily make Jews better than others. Instead, they have aggravated the tendencies toward decay within the community. Jacob, however, is never fully in either community. He is of the world but not slave to it. In seeking God, Jacob follows the Scriptural percept, "Ye shall not fear the face of man." Moreover, Singer concludes that a Jew is also supported by other, more distant communities—the Jewish people, living and dead. Eventually, when the community of Pilitz turns against him, Jacob can rescue his son and go to Palestine. In the end, Jacob's path is the match to Yasha's. Jacob becomes the Wandering Jew, choosing alienation *outside* the small community, whereas Yasha had opted for alienation *within*.

Although separated by more than a decade, *The Slave* and *Enemies, A Love Story* should be read as companion novels. Their situations are complementary, probably with intention. *Enemies* focuses on Jewish refugees from Hitler, primarily one Herman Broder, who hid in a hayloft to escape the Nazis. Like Jacob, he was cared for and saved by a Polish peasant girl, whom he later marries. They go to America where they live among Jews but keep their past a secret. Like Jacob, too, Herman's family was erased in the Holocaust, although his wife reappears in America a number of years after the war.

Herman also questions God—at times His existence and at times

His mercy and justice. "Wasn't it possible," he asks, "that a Hitler presided on high and inflicted suffering on imprisoned souls?" While he views the departure from Orthodoxy as leading to all possible worldly sins ("If we don't want to become like the Nazis, we must be Jews"), he is incapable of following the Law and resisting the world. Unlike Jacob, he does not respond to his Polish wife's desire to convert, since he himself is not observant. He feels little kinship with American Jews, assimilators who desire to evade the past by plunging into materialism. For Jacob, marriage is a sacred act which must be subject to God, even if it is not the result of a lawful wedding. Herman, on the other hand, is married to three women, each of whom serves a different need (mother, father, and lover). In having a trio of wives Herman also copies the patriarchs, but in a less significant way. In addition, he does not want children, and unlike Jacob who rescues his child, Herman flees before his child's birth.[96]

Herman, in short, is a modern man, although still beset by eternal questions. Passive in the face of a world dominated by power, Herman, like many of Singer's "modern" Jews, entwines himself in destructive personal relationships. Singer makes it clear that Herman's malaise, as well as those of the other characters, predates the Second World War:

> . . . in Herman there existed a sorrow that could not be assuaged. He was not a victim of Hitler. He had been a victim long before Hitler's day.[97]

Herman is an older Asa Heschel, a wanderer who is not sure that he wants to be a Jew. Like other American characters, he represents the full realization of the despair and confusion of modern man:

> Religions lied. Philosophy was bankrupt from the beginning. The idle promises of progress were not more than a spit in the face of the martyrs of all generations. . . . Those without courage to make an end to their existence have only one other way out: to deaden their consciousness, choke their memory, extinguish the last vestige of hope.[98]

In Singer's view, the Holocaust magnified and distorted guilts that had been festering long before. Those who suffer the most from the camp experiences are the prewar enlightened. Shifrah Puah, for example, who like her daughter Masha sprinkles references to Nazis into every conversation, becomes more pious in the United States. A freethinker before the war, the New World for her becomes a place of penance. "Guilt stared out of her dark eyes. Could she permit herself to enjoy God's bounty when so many God-fearing Jews had died of starvation?"[99] The only refugees for whom guilt is not an obsession are two Orthodox Jews, the Nissens.

The unresolved conflict between the generations that arose before the war continues, although for some the Nazis become the new elders. Masha, who has strayed further than most, is in fact something of a Nazi herself:

> The Nazis forced me to do things for so long that I can't do anything of my own free will anymore. . . . Here in America, I've come to realize that slavery isn't such a tragedy after all—for getting things done, there's nothing better than a whip.[100]

The Nazis, then, serve many purposes in this novel. On the one hand, they are used by the characters as a punishment for rebelling against parents, people, and God. The Nazis replace parents as figures of authority, hence preventing some individuals from ever separating from their elders. In the end, Masha will not leave her dead mother, and opts to join her by killing herself. In life she had likened Shifrah Puah to the Nazis, calling her "dictator" and "tormentor."

Singer intimates that some modern Jews need the Nazis as much as their forebears needed God. Lost in a world bereft of higher authority, some Jews have deified their enemy, using the Nazis to remind them of their Jewishness. In this sense, Nazi persecution is a further reminder of "chosenness" and exclusive importance. Thus the title of the novel refers to more than Herman's stormy affairs. Singer suggests as much in the ambiguous comment that prefaces the novel: "Although I did not have the privilege of going through the Hitler holocaust, I have lived for years in New York with refugees from this ordeal."[101]

Without God, modern Jews have subjected themselves to false idols—to hedonism, politics, and humanity. In another story, Singer asserts that "modern Jews are suicidal," beset by unresolved contradictions. A character explains:

> The modern Jew cannot live without anti-semitism. If it is not there, he's driven to create it. He has to bleed for humanity. . . . He preaches revolution and at the same time wants all the privileges of capitalism

for himself. He tries to destroy nationalism in others but prides himself on belonging to the Chosen People. How can a tribe like this exist among strangers?[102]

American freedom, although far superior to the oppressions of the Old World, is hardly a panacea. "Democracy seems to me to be one of the better systems," Singer once declared. [103] Democracy is more prone to encourage free choice and discourage dogma. Yet it is only a better system in a world of dark possibilities. Thus American freedom is by no means an unmixed blessing. In *Enemies*, the characters live in a mobile, unregulated state, where the law is impersonal and distant. Moreover, freedom is less meaningful in a civilization fascinated with death, where individuals are psychologically enslaved to a guilty past.

Thus behind the storyteller stands Singer, the observer of modern life, who can be strongly critical of Jews in this new world. Without a spiritual aim external to themselves, American Jews are described as materialistic and pleasure-seeking. Their rabbis are often men of the world, entrepreneurs of religion, adept at jokes and favors but with little appreciation of Torah. Notably, in Singer's works, characters who emigrate to the United States are often escapists who seek to avoid confronting life and death. [104]

In *Enemies*, Herman's elaborate deceptions actually organize his life, but keep him apart from his fellows. In *The Slave*, Jacob's ruse leads to unplanned communal responsibility. Jacob, the teacher, seeks justice within the community through example and leadership, until the community turns against him. Herman, on the contrary, neither walks with God nor with his people. Instead he deals with the people abstractly, telling them what they want to hear as a "ghost writer" for a modern rabbi. Spurned by his own community, Jacob saves his son and journeys to Palestine, where he continues a holy, if iconoclastic life. Jacob refuses to follow either the majority or the leaders of his corrupt generation, interpreting the Torah in his own manner, seeing his obligations to fellow men as paramount. Herman, unhappy with or without God, wanders away from all worldly responsibility.

Brandeis argued that modernity could be modified by idealism and reform, seeing Zionism as an antidote for despirited American Jews. Nevertheless, his optimism rested on darker images of the human prospect, and was undercut by a commitment to the very institutions which were fashioning the modern dilemma: technology, the corporation, and the nation-state.

To the multitude of Russian Jews who emigrated to America around and after the turn of the century, this strange new world represented modernity in full blossom. It was a world which fascinated or repelled, but could not be altered through mere reform. Moreover, for many of these immigrants religion was not merely personal, and in their ties to religion and community lingered intimations of an alternative world. To some, only a large-scale movement could dislodge the moorings of the system. For others, like Heschel, who viewed Torah as a demand for holy justice, political activity might bear witness to God's presence in the world. More accurately, it might remind modern man of His presence.

Singer, neither reformer nor prophet, stands closest to the traditional Jewish position. America, while perhaps a "crazy" place, is but the epitome of modernity, a further extension of developments occurring in Europe. "The people are the same"—the problems of human nature are eternal and universal. [105] A Jew must remember the eternal questions in the face of the obstacles of history. He ought avoid but understand the ways of the nations, their worship of power and denial of mystery. Like Jacob, he may have to wrestle with God in order to face his brother. In truth, for Singer, all men of God become patriarchs, recreating divine justice through simple acts of affirmation and denial, as they "continue to journey on the stormy seas." [106]

CHAPTER
4
THE IMMIGRANT EXPERIENCE: ASSIMILATING INTO AMERICA

Citizenship, as Isaac Bashevis Singer exemplifies, need not mean full assimilation and loss of traditional identity. Yet blending, fitting in, and feeling comfortable and not apart were goals as appealing to immigrants as they are to contemporary Americans. Not all immigrants were moved by such needs, and even those most avowedly "American" might retain more of the Old World than they cared to admit. For most, assimilation was an *issue*, inherent to the process of settling the new land. Cast into a world where physical and informational mobility were constantly being refined, modern immigrants could not enjoy the sense of communal separation that their predecessors had known. "It was a time for speed," Harry Roskolenko recalls, "not for permanent values."[1] The larger society was a constant reality looming in the background of consciousness.

The decision to emigrate usually predestined the crisis. The immigrant placed himself in the midst of a society which would be parental, although not in the obvious colonial sense. As noted earlier, immigrants often viewed their experience as a rebirth, with the ocean voyage symbolizing the trauma of birth, the crossing over into a new life. Abraham Cahan's "David Levinsky" is quite explicit:

> The immigrant's arrival in his new home is like a second birth to him. Imagine a new-born babe in possession of a fully-developed intellect. Would it ever forget its entry into the world?[2]

Symbols of separation and rebirth lingered stubbornly in the new land, usually accompanying a crisis of identity. Samuel Ornitz writes, in *Haunch, Paunch, and Jowl*, that "an ocean separated us" from Old World parents, to whom, he could have added, the metaphor was reality.[3] For Harry Roskolenko, born in the New World, the sea remained the vital symbol which both separated him from and kept him loyal to his parents' experience. The sea symbolized openness, and freedom from the restrictions his parents had accepted in America. Yet it also represented an option similar to the one his parents had chosen when they emigrated.

> One night I rushed off to sea, and the world of the Educational Alliance and the Lower East Side dissolved in the crow's nest. . . .I was reversing my father's route of 1895—when East Broadway, like Cherry Street, was the Jewish immigrant's ghetto. I had other boundaries, none of them self-imposed, for the next seven years, when every port in Europe became part of my natural schooling. "The time that was then" was between my father's and mine.[4]

Similarly, in Cahan's works, guilt rides the waves, recalling former beliefs now submerged within the "new self": "My former self was addressing me across the sea in this strange, uninviting, big town. . . ."[5]

As Cahan realized, being born or reborn in America would never be simple. The new environment might seem to demand and lure, overpowering the individual with a material reality which could mold his ways. Still, the mind would remember, and images of the past would haunt and govern the present. To experience conversion or rebirth, one must acknowledge rootedness in the past, and for many immigrants this proved difficult. Immigration often involved an attempt to escape from the past, as well as a personal separation from kinfolk, the finality of which (and consequent guilt) might be very painful to admit. Those who came may have desired rebirth, and the mobility and romance of America may have encouraged the belief in its realization. But for many the past was neither easy to escape nor confront.

The contrast between Old World and New, between the ghetto and mysterious America, led to confusion and guilt, a legacy often bequeathed to the future. For many it involved a search for new parental figures, Americans or "allrightniks" who seemed to be comfortable in the new environment. Some openly rejected their parents' ways, striking out on their own like Roskolenko, not realizing that they were acting on their parents' example. In many cases, American values might be the focus of familial tension, as children attempted to convert parents to the dominant norms. Values which pervaded the political realm, such as freedom and equality, would be tested in the immigrant family, with paternal authority facing the greatest challenge. Anzia Yezierska's stories and novels, for example, center around the conflict between an authoritarian father, supported by religious tradition, and his individualistic, ambitious children, who cannot appreciate his eschewal of work in America.[6]

The impulse to assimilate challenged traditional modes while it placed immigrant groups into a "subject" attitude regarding the host culture. Most of the writers dealt with here had dropped their religious orthodoxy, but were still part of the culture which religion had produced. Often they describe relatives, usually fathers, whose religion had been an obstacle to success in America. Similarly, Judaism is often seen as a badge of masculine passivity—a passivity which, in America, is associated with femininity (see also Chapter 5). If in the Old World the religious Jew was content to accept the powers-that-be, in a freer America his resignation to fate might be criticized by a more restless son (especially since the son was probably learning that activism was valued in America). The pianist Samuel Chotzinoff could not understand the "dogmatic conservatism" of his father, a Hebrew school teacher, who genuinely appreciated the poetry of the sacred books.

> What puzzled me was that this appreciation had no influence on his character, opinions, and behavior. They brought him no closer to a consideration of the misfortunes and problems of the poor.[7]

Chotzinoff described his father as a "born conformist" and while he was not a profoundly religious man, he may have been a valid exemplar of the political attitudes of the Orthodox immigrant: Man is small, immigrants are particularly weak; it is foolish to meddle with the forces of the world. Political life *within* the Jewish community was less of a danger, since the weakness of the community reminded men of their own lack of power. To the younger generation, however, religion conveyed a humanitarian spirit, which could not stop at the borders of political action. To their elders, political action meant a betrayal of God and a threat to the traditional community:

> Politically and ideologically they were at odds with their parents who leaned through habit and tradition toward conservatism and paternalism. In the minds of the older people, unionism or criticism of constituted authority and resistance to it invariably led to atheism, or at least to a slackness in the observance of the laws, and traditions of religious orthodoxy. Yet, though their expressed opinions were iconoclastic, the actual behavior of the young people was strictly, though unconsciously, in the tradition of their elders.[8]

Under the circumstances, the political orientation of the young constituted a dual rebellion. Not only were their avowed beliefs potentially harmful to an apolitical tradition, but their challenge to established American authority reflected a challenge to established Jewish authority in the religion and in the home. Political activity, even though it was aimed at changing the American scene, may have seemed too threatening to a tradition of separatism. The Orthodox were caught in the dilemma of American freedom. The freedom to practice traditional religion had to coexist with the freedom to stray from observance. Orthodoxy, to be meaningful, had to come to terms with the larger American scene. It had to concern itself with modernity without adjusting to it. That it could not, in a practical sense, is hardly a condemnation.

It might have been simpler psychologically if the "parent culture" *was* a colonial one. Certainly there were many elements of the colonial relationship: Immigrants were unschooled and powerless politically; they worked for enterprises controlled by outsiders, older Americans and assimilated German Jews; their culture was generally insular, often denigrated by Americans, even those with obvious sympathies; they looked different (Jews were often referred to as "orientals" in the late nineteenth century), and had a distinctive religion and way of life.

In theory, this quasi-colonial dependence was supposed to be a temporary condition, and most immigrants accepted this as their plight, wearing their hope as a badge of forbearance and self-respect. Initial suffering, they learned, was a necessary trial, preparing one, usually in an economic sense, for citizenship and equality. Yet this dogma could not allay an immigrant's fear and doubts; it would only give them direction. A chasm might develop between the image of America and the reality of sacrifice and toil; between immigrants reborn as free citizens and immigrants being remade into good Americans. Moreover, the Darwinian mood of the period emphasized the qualified basis of American citizenship. If people and races could be judged by their success and achievements, surely immigrants might be evaluated by their contributions to American life.[9]

Thus while Israel Zangwill was assuring contemporaries that "God is making the new American" in a country that was "the great Melting Pot where all the races of Europe are melting and re-forming," he was sure to point out that Jews were exceptional spiritual and artistic qualities to contribute to this secular age.[10] Others, such as Morris R. Cohen, Isaac Berkson, and Horace Kallen, also seemed compelled to justify Jewish virtues while arguing for cultural pluralism. The frenzy of progressive "Americanization" programs, for all their good intentions, taught that America had to be earned and immigrants had to produce.

The emphasis on contributions was at one with the tendency to postpone essential questions for future resolution. Immigrants, reborn or remade, individuals forever in the process of becoming—in this atmosphere personal identity might be lost in what Marcus Eli Ravage called "the race for American dollars."[11] Suddenly, also, the past became devalued, and a new calculus of time and ambition measured the meager present and the hopeful future. Chotzinoff, for example, remembered how his father was encouraged by a friend to change his name after his arrival in America:

> He now demanded to be told what possible good the last two syllables of our name could be to us in a country so dynamic and impatient of nonessentials as America.[12]

Here then was the dilemma clearly defined: America may have been impatient of nonessentials, yet it seemed to judge one's essence by the accident of a name. The ideal of equality contended with a system of superficial inequality that seemed to govern at least the commercial realm of public life. The liberal creed seemed to treasure individuality, yet in practice it induced a narrow conformity, which neglected or insulted cultural differences. The immigrant attracted to assimilation learned that success might demand more than the sacrifice of two syllables.

Assimilation was a natural temptation, intrinsic to the perception of citizenship, yet shrouded in ambiguity. In its primary meaning, assimilation involves likening, or conforming to a given model, standard, or ideal. It is an act of choice and may involve, for example, conforming to certain values deemed American without embracing other values or patterns of behavior. The critical factor here might be the rigidity or flexibility of the model and its own self-definition.

In twentieth-century America assimilation has frequently been viewed as a problem of the parent culture.[13] During the first three decades of the century, the pages of popular magazines and liberal journals were replete with articles on "absorbing the alien," "the minorities problem," and "life in the foreign quarter."[14] Assimilation was seen in terms of the digestion or incorporation of foreign bodies that might have to be changed in order to conform with dominant patterns of American life. Imposing this conception, itself narrow, on immigrants would equate assimilation with accepting current American values, adapting to prevalent customs and fashions, and remaking one's personal life to conform to the beliefs and preferences of America's white Protestant majority.

Even presuming this conception, the reality of assimilation was highly complex. The analogy to colonialism might again be instructive. In the colonial situation distinctions of power and status were normally related to definite national and cultural differences. The subordinate culture was overtly such, and its weaker position was rationalized in terms of paternal responsibility along with its alleged inferiority. In most instances, complete assimilation was a rare option, due to racial and political differences. The extreme options included a self-hating acceptance of both colonial rule and the colonial model, or a rebellious rejection of subordinate status with various political and psychological possibilities clustered around these poles.[15]

In America, the immigrants' situation was more complicated if less painful. Semi-colonial in their initial status, many immigrants came to realize that behind the democratic ideal there was a dominant culture and a dominant creed—the one which might or might not offer entry; the other a system of values which might or might not be worthy of assumption. To make matters more complex, older Americans liked to deny that a dominant pattern existed, or they were often genuinely confused about their own traditional values. In addition, the culture seemed to imply that becoming like other Americans involved greater individualism—in one sense, at least, the opposite of assimilation.

Thus, paradoxically, one way of fitting into American patterns was by becoming an *individual*, freeing oneself from ties to the past. This might manifest itself in the quest for personal achievement, perhaps ascending to a position of status and influence. It might involve a loosening, and even a sacrifice of family ties, which Anzia Yezierska described poignantly in her autobiography.[16] It might result, too, in a lonely quest, a romantic search for lost values in larger America, which is the theme of some of the socialist novels of this period, which will be discussed in Chapter 5.

THE HAPPINESS OF THE SINGLE LIFE

Marcus Ravage, like many of his generation, viewed his settlement in America in terms of personal transformation. "As I look back over my transition from the alien to the American state," he wrote in his autobiography, "I cannot help wondering at the incredible changes of it."[17]

That the cost was high and the changes indefinite is suggested by another passage:

Vowing allegiance to the state is one thing. But renouncing your priceless inherited identity and blending your individual soul with the soul of an alien people is quite another affair. And it is the staggering experience of the spirit—this slipping of the ancient ground from under the immigrant's feet, this commingling of souls towards a new birth, that I have in mind when I speak of becoming an American.[18]

Ravage's words raise questions as to the validity of this "new birth." An inherited identity is both involuntary and inviolable. Nor can one truly blend with an alien people. One can try, and Ravage's early autobiography recounts his attempt to assimilate, just as his later journalism is a reaction to his failure to do so. As the previous quotation suggests, his efforts may have masked a divided self.

Ravage came to America as a teenager and discovered a land that was far from his preconceived image. He found a world centered around money ("the race for dollars"), at whose altar immigrants led a dreary and sordid existence. Slum conditions seemed worse than those in Europe, and certainly less tolerable. He was disturbed, too, by the "degeneration" he perceived in Jewish immigrant life. The demands of commerce sanctioned aggressive behavior, morals had declined, and authority and age attracted less respect. Beyond this, natives were insensitive to the immigrant's culture, to his "Old World soul," and tried to Americanize him as if he were a "blank slate." [19]

Still, Ravage chose to remain, for reasons never specified, heartened by the intimation that there was an America other than that of the ghetto. It was this feeling that was to drive him out of the ghetto to the University of Missouri, and his major test of assimilation. He had, moreover, a "royal ambition," a desire for success that made him see dissatisfaction with one's condition as a kind of Darwinian law and "the rule of progress." At the same time, he could feel that the Jewish ghetto was more culturally advanced than the rest of America. The sweatshop was a nursery for intellectual freedom. Looking back on those days he would remember their intensity, along with the sense of being part of an enlightened and rejected minority. Ironically, he was reminded not of Jewish life, but of that early period "when Christianity was still the faith of the despised and lowly." [20]

Thus Ravage touches a vein that runs through the works of Jewish-Americans during this period. American Jews are like the early Christians, or like Christ himself. Young Jews understand Christ better than nominal Christians (given the racial thinking of this era, this conclusion was hardly avoidable). Suffering and sacrifice raised them above their forebears as well as the rest of complacent America. Ravage compares the ghetto intelligentsia to medieval monks, and describes his initial suffering as "my American baptism," a purification and "cleansing of the spirit." [21]

A Jew who assimilates into America becomes a kind of Christian—an essential one, a sacrifice perhaps, but one who transcends American Christians through his greater knowledge and tempered soul. America is a powerful attraction, but Ravage does not want his readers to forget that ghetto culture is somewhat superior to American culture. Nor could he forget that the intellectual and emotional qualities of Jewish life were potentially part of the sacrifice of assimilation. Ravage, like other Jewish immigrants, viewed the parent culture as a teacher. When the teacher's values seemed shabby and inferior, Ravage was quick to reverse the analogy. Given the quality of popular culture in the United States, an immigrant easily concludes that, "Whatever might be said for Americans, of the fullness of life and of the things of the spirit they know as little as children." [22]

For Ravage, whose ties to Judaism were minimal, the temptations of Christianity seem almost irresistable. Even though Christian theology often seemed unreasonable, and Jesus was worshipped in ignorance of his "fierce humanity," sometimes he wished that he, too, could be a Christian.

> When one came right down to it, it was really immense for a religion— this Christianity, with its couples and Easter bonnets, its socials, and its watches. . . . If I had been born into any one of the many indistinguishable varieites of this faith, I often ask myself would I have turned against it? [23]

Christianity pervades the culture and folkways of the new land. To Ravage, it is attractive because it is the dominant religion, and a rather secularized one at that. By his own account, it provides something of an escape from traditional worship, a religion which concerns itself with practical matters—success, achievement, and "the virtue of thrift, sobriety, and manliness." [24] Christian in name only, American religion is the religion of democratic man, catering to individual needs and worldly values. Hardly a threat to individualism itself, Christianity is appealing because it seems to stand at the heart of American social and cultural life, from which Ravage felt estranged in Missouri. [25]

His initial reaction to the University of Missouri is similar to his experience on the East Side of New York City. He is disappointed by the coldness of the campus and the sense of distance which invisibly separates people. Fellow students appear aloof, insensitive, and excessively polite. He is critical of the values of individualism—self-reliance, success, and the cult of manliness—yet seems driven toward them. In truth he is attracted to this culture, and these values are partially submerged in his own personality. Furthermore, he is confused by the nuances of this alien environment, particularly the emotional discipline which characterizes Americans. On the one hand, they seem removed and unfeeling; on the other, he is struck by their moments of warmth and personal decency. Ravage concludes that the fault most likely is his own, and even comes to see their individualism as a virtue; "an emphasis on the happiness of the single life." [26]

Ravage's desire to adjust is not complete, however. In later years, as a journalist, he seemed to swing back and forth between identifying himself with immigrants and natives. It was a harsh era for new Americans and Ravage's dualism is understandable. Yet the consequences were both pathetic and comic, with Ravage personally identifying himself in one essay with "the stalwart, adventurous elder sons of the European family who braved the wilderness and blazed the trail." [27]

In fairness, his duplicity in this essay may have been a necessary ruse, allowing him to make some points which a foreigner could not have made. The newcomer to America, he argues, shares the dependence of childhood. He needs help and guidance, emotional support, and models of citizenship. Instead, Americanization was more akin to a war, causing immigrants to react defensively in the form of "foreign colonies" within our cities.

> Americanization which ought to mean a reintegration of mankind in this hemisphere with an open mind towards the future, became through our impatience and ineptitude a thing to frighten children with. [28]

America must win the *hearts* of the immigrants. To do this, both religion and democracy must be revitalized. Falling back on the logic of progressivism, Ravage argues that American democracy has suffered from desuetude, becoming an abstract ideal, while Europe has made impressive advances. Immigrants (and here he is clearly alluding to idealistic East Siders) must be shown that democratic reforms can work in America, too. We must be true to our character, especially in the (civil) religion we preach:

> It is of no earthly use to distribute the Gospel among the heathen, unless our lives are sufficiently Christian to tally with Gospel principles. . . . It is by the tradition of the Fathers that we attempt to gain converts to our polity. . . . [29]

Immigrants, Ravage insists, want to be assimilated, although his own experiences indicates not only the pains of adaptation, but also the value of intellectual distance. His definition of assimilation remains vague, although it seems to rest on social acceptance and cooperation. While it involves a mutual acceptance, in reality the crucial factor is the practice of Christian values on the part of natives. Perhaps, also, it involves the shared recognition that Jews and Christians are not very different, especially in a secular age. Essential is a future goal, which the integrated society defines and cooperates in realizing. The polity, which is the focal point of allegiance and national character, must be a model to the immigrant, but can only be reached by taking the path of secularized Christianity.

Ravage's identification with native America in these essays is counterpoised by a different theme in a series of essays he wrote for *Century* magazine during the same period. In these pieces, Ravage writes from the perspective of a Jewish immigrant and shows great insight into the culture with which he supposedly identified. Recalling his years in Missouri, Ravage describes his initial disappointment with the materialism and narrowness of American students. They had little interest in socialism or public issues; practical concerns governed their lives. They conformed, in other words, to the ghetto intellectuals' stereotype of Americans.

He came to understand, however, that Americans approached success with an aspect of worship, spiritualizing the commonplace, driving themselves to attain an abstraction. They worshiped the big businessman, scorning professors as men who opted for irrelevance because they could not succeed in the "real" world. American students could not appreciate that being an intellectual required more talent and perhaps more courage than being a "man of affairs." This insight demanded "somewhat extraordinary penetration," which most American students lacked. [30]

Ravage echoes a note here which resonates throughout Jewish immigrant literature: the Jew *sees* better than the native, has an older wisdom, and a deeper insight. The Jew transcends intellectually, fending off the new culture through observation and analysis. "In my quality of a dispassionate observer," he writes, "I could not but be impressed with the excellent side of this unique creed, but . . . neither could I help see the mischief it was causing." [31]

The ethic of success, Ravage argues, promotes personal rivalry and the achievement of private power. To raise philosophical questions, to value culture and art, and to enjoy ease were to Americans "effeminate" ways which detracted from man's "battle for success." Worse, a sense of distrust undercut social and political life. It had become common to assume the worst motives of our best men, driving them out of public life, and encouraging instead those whose motives fulfilled our expectations.

In spite of these insights, Ravage draws conclusions that are inaccurate, at best. He will not go back to the ghetto, since he has shed socialism and now has broader concerns. In any case, "the Ghetto is dead," killed by the immigrants' desire to succeed and the natives' desire to Americanize. "America, the great leveler" has defused the passions and enthusiasm which characterized political and social life in the Jewish quarter. The "movement" had represented the spirit of the ghetto, and now that spirit, less enflamed and less noticeable, was being redirected toward other ends. Believing himself that religion was essentially an archaic remnant condemned by the logic of history, Ravage criticizes the Jewish radicals for too often seeking liberation from religion without establishing an alternative idealism.[32]

East Side radicals in his estimation could not endure the competitive demands of American life and hence have channeled their energies toward the "race for success." Ravage describes this as part of "this inevitable annihilation of imported civilizations," a "degeneration [which] comes with the poignancy of tragic death." It includes the descent into political life, as practiced in American cities:

> The revolutionary socialist has shrunk into the politician, and clamors for votes from the tail-end of a motor-car as he once angled for souls from the top of a soap-box.[33]

Local politics, like local culture, does not correspond to the polity, a distant, national ideal.

Assimilating into America may involve moral degeneration, but the "melting pot" functions well even if it is dirty. Ravage somehow manages a hopeful vision: The tragedy "is lightened by a vast, rollicking farce and a broad beam of hope."[34] The vitality of the East Side cannot die—it has been given to America. While the ghetto has been "inoculated" with Americanism, in some mysterious way it has contributed its own spirit into American life. The Jew has been the sacrifice once again, and humanity is reaping the reward.

Ravage's fragile vision could not survive the rise of anti-Semitism in the 1920s. Although his tone changed from lighthearted optimism to bitter irony, the essentials of his thought show little alteration. The Jew is still Christ, now crucified by worldly power which does not perceive its own foolishness.

For Ravage, the assimilating Jew is basically passive ("inoculated," "imported") and is used by Gentiles as a scapegoat for their own shortcomings. Analyzing anti-Semitism, he sees its roots as dual. First, Jews are a vital, passionate people who often represent extreme types—Jews stand out. "The first thing I had to do in order to become like other Americans," he recalls, "was to tone down the dramatic quality in my make-up, to become more drab and less vital." More important, Jews have created Christianity and are responsible for giving an essentially pagan civilization a conscience it would prefer to forget. "And it subconsciously hates the race from whose loins Christianity has come."[35]

Jews have to suppress their vitality and aggressiveness if they want to "pass" into America. Obviously, from his account there are some who do not want to assimilate (contrary to his earlier assertion of the death of the ghetto), and there are many who cannot shed their distinctiveness in trying to assimilate. They are perceived as Jews in spite of their own wishes, presumably because they are outstanding human types. Also, there is an important psychological polarity in this argument. Jews, and other immigrants, are vital as such, but in becoming Americans they come to feel passive, if not feminine.[36] Jews who try to conform to American standards feel overwhelmed by the new culture which they do not know and can never master. They feel weak and passive, suppressing an anger of dual purport: they are angry at both the new land and themselves.

On the other hand, Ravage believes Jews have tremendous influence, both subtle and enduring. Jews may lack power in the short run, but in reality Jews have conquered the West through "the irresistible might of our spirit, with ideas, with propaganda."[37] It is a transcending power once again, a power over and through history, a power which requires intellectual insight to recognize. Given the course of Ravage's earlier thought, it is a power which appears to compensate for feelings of passivity and rejection. Out of weakness comes ineradicable influence. Merely by being of a people who are closer to human realities and truths, the Jew has achieved this conquest. Ravage sees the Jew as the "conscience" of the Western world, the measure of its progress, and the symbol of its humanity or evil.[38]

While hardly a major thinker, Ravage is important because he articulated the dilemma and confusion of the ambitious Jewish immigrant. Moored between two worlds, neither of which felt like home, Ravage struggled to find some kind of definition of America which could conform to the spirit of his past. Since he believed this spirit to be basically parochial, it could not survive either his ambition or his desire to win a place for himself amongst Americans. Wilsonian liberalism and a mellifluous Judaeo-Christian nationalism were stops along the way, preceding a retreat to sullen marginality. In the process, Ravage remained a man divided, neither remade nor reborn.

THE PROMISED LAND

Few accounts of the immigrant experience are as eulogistic as Mary Antin's. Hers is a tale of personal success with no apparent regrets or reservations. In turgid prose and romantic metaphor she details the march of an immigrant girl into an expectant America.

Born in Russia, Mary Antin was the daughter of Orthodox parents who rapidly shed their Orthodoxy in America, believing that loyalty to the external aspects of traditional Judaism would hamper them in the "race for Americanization."[39] Her autobiography, *The Promised Land* (1914), was one of the most popular immigrant accounts of its time, and continues to be reprinted today. It is most notable for its unrestrained praise of American democracy and for the author's magnificent egotism. In a larger context, it is also an important reflection of the personal struggle involved in assimilation.

Mary Antin regarded herself as an individualist. Her independence, even as a child, is a constant theme: "aloof," "separate," "by myself," are terms she uses frequently to describe herself. Yet the loneliness which one might anticipate is not there, or at least is never avowed. Instead she tells of a prophetic vision which she always held, of rising out of the slums to live a busy, active life in the "garden of America." A child of nature, she credits her success to special endowments, along with the personal sacrifice of family and friends. In her romantic self-image, she was born with a "patent of nobility" and a longing for the richness of life. As soon as she could "toddle unaided," she began to take in the abundance of the world, which, like a magnet, she was bound to attract. Given her character and destiny, the aid of her family seemed almost inevitable, perhaps minimizing any guilt she may have felt for rising above them.[40]

Similarly, her description of the personal devotion which abetted her success freely mixed self-importance with gratitude:

> Not only the members of my family, but mere acquaintances put their little all at my disposal. Merely that a dreamer among them might come to the fulfillment of her dream, they fed and sheltered and nursed me and cheered me on, again and again facing the wolves of want for my sake. . . .[41]

Everyone approved of her success, which she would eventually redeem by becoming a spokeswoman for immigrant America. As such she remained her childhood image, a "heroine of two worlds."[42]

Still, the tone of Antin's epic does not ring true. Her importance and success are so overstated as to raise doubts, doubts which she rarely expresses about herself. Her relentless emphasis on the positive has an almost defensive quality to it, as if she could not tolerate the possibility that her vision was not real. More specifically, contradictions of fact and mood slip out which belie her one-sided enthusiasm.

Antin usually describes her Americanization in terms of inevitable triumph. She was destined to succeed in America and her rise is accomplished with little pain and no apparent sacrifice. "Being set down in the garden of America," she writes, "where opportunity waits on ambition, I was bound to make my days a triumphal march toward my goal."[43] Apart from its implied irresponsibility, there is an automaticity in this statement which hints at evolutionary logic. Talent and industry are destined to make their way in the world. Along the way, she never admits to significant conflict or personal unease. "I have never had a dull hour in my life," she relates, even in the slums, because she could always envision her eventual triumph.[44] The slums could not depress her, by her account, because as an individual she had the power to attract "uncommon things."[45]

Most of the things she recalls, however, came from outside her neighborhood, particularly her brushes with the leaders of "higher culture" in Boston. In another passage, too, she recalls "dragging through the slums." Most suggestive, she describes the experience of first and second generation immigrants in terms of "chaos" and the "disintegration" of traditional norms. Like Ravage, she sees this breakdown in Christian perspective: disintegration "is the cross that the first and second generation must bear." [46] Surely, it is impossible that a sense of disorder and confusion could have passed her by. Her exaggerated prose suggests in fact a fear of disorder.

Even the egotism which is lavished unashamedly throughout her tale is countered by nuances in her narration. Not only does the extent of her self-importance hint at self-doubt, but her pose is usually that of an observer, rarely a part of the things which she describes. Her frequent references to noble friends are undercut by her failure to recount any intimate relationships, and by the number of friends she appears to have (too many for intense friendship). Tellingly, her friendships are remembered in a distinctly utilitarian way as "materials" from which she made her "after-life" in free and open America. [47]

For one who naturally ascended on a motor of destiny, "after-life" is a curious expression. Antin fluctuates between viewing her life as the inexorable development of qualities she always possessed, and seeing it, on the other hand, as a "new birth" which involved the death of an earlier existence. Thus, in the "Introduction" to her autobiography, she appears almost schizophrenic in her account of the assimilation process. In describing her early experience she writes, "I am just as much out of the way as if I were dead. . . ." [48] She also admits that writing her autobiography was an attempt to be finished with her past.

In her writings, Antin's foremost identification is with America. Judaism has become a thing of the spirit alone, an "inner" call, important but private. As such, she reduces it to an ethical standard which is indistinguishable from Christianity. Loving thy neighbor, she declares, is "not far from being the whole of Judaism." [49] American democracy, in truth, takes its place, and she explicitly merges the two in thought and language. Thus, for Americans the Declaration of Independence becomes "the law of the Fathers," a creed of liberty and equality. "What the Mosaic Law is to the Jews, the Declaration is to the American people." [50]

> I have chosen to read the story of '76 as a chapter in sacred history; to set Thomas Jefferson in a class with Moses, and Washington with Joshua; to regard the American nation as the custodian of a sacred trust, and American citizenship as a holy order. . . .[51]

One effect of this, as we shall see, is to use Jewish history as a model for Americans, and to underline the point that Jews have much to teach. Of greater importance, however, is the fact that this interpretation allows her to see American history in meaningful personal terms, seemingly consistent with her background. Furthermore, her attempt to establish a "basic law" which must be rigidly followed suggests the desire for order alluded to previously, a child's desire for the world to be "nice." The alternative to such a glorious rendering of the American past, she notes, is to read history in terms of plunder and conquest, a possibility which seems to linger in the back of her mind. [52]

Antin strains to see Jewish qualities in America while she dismisses much of traditional Judaism. Basically this represents an effort to assimilate while retaining a Jewish identity. Hence, she seeks to stress certain moral qualities which Jews have and, hopefully, Americans share. Both nations, she notes, are heirs of a fundamental law to which they owe allegiance and fidelity. Both nations are voluntary in character, and value learning and achievement. Both nations are based on a conception of human dignity. Yet it seems clear that for Antin, Judaism represents a virtue of the past rather than a value of the present. [53] Certainly, rigorous loyalty to a fundamental law, for which she uses Jews as an example, is not something she desires for Jews today. In fact, she sees Jewish law as extremely inhibiting—a "wall," "fortress," and "stronghold" erected against the ravages of persecution. [54] In her view, freedom for Jews means educational and intellectual opportunity, which engenders a "widening of the Jewish spirit . . . dropping nothing by the way but what their spirit has outgrown." [55]

For Antin, America is a special place, the inheritor and transformer of the Judaeo-Christian tradition. It was the Jews who overthrew paganism, introduced monotheism, and dignified humanity. It was Christ, "a son of the venturesome race," who offered the brotherhood of man. Democracy, the American creed, is a refinement of Christian teaching, and now is a model for the world. All evolves from the Jews, she implies, but today America is the governing reality, whose mission it is to elevate mankind through being a model democracy. The Jews, being an older and intrepid people, have much to teach, even though in respect to the new land they are its eager students.[56]

Education is a vital aspect of her love for America, and she sees intellectual freedom as a large part of American freedom.[57] To Antin, the most impressive product of American democracy is its free public services, notably public education and libraries. American education expands opportunities for men *and* women, liberating a Jewish woman from the restrictions of her culture which, in her opinion, values women mainly because they can produce male children.[58] The school is a microcosm of America, the place where good Americans are made and where the teacher becomes a loco-parental figure. The school acts to free people from the unnatural restrictions of the family.

For Antin, the school is closely joined with the neighborhood church as virtuous socializers of the slums. The church, she writes, brought culture as well as "soap and water" to the neighborhood. In addition, the true teacher has a distinctly Christian quality:

> Apostles all of an ideal, they go to their work in a spirit of love and inquiry, seeking not comfort, not position, not old-age pensions, but Truth that is the soul of wisdom, the joy of big-eyed children, the food of hungry youth.[59]

Similarly, she describes her mentor Edward Everett Hale as a saint, who picked her out and made her feel important.[60]

In spite of her inclination to Christianize her experience, Antin's view of the teacher is close to that of traditional Judaism. Teachers are profoundly important people whose aspiration for truth signifies a transcendant power.[61] God made the world, she asserts, and created teachers to show people how to live in it. Significantly, her definition of a true teacher excludes those who become involved in politics. In a sense, teachers are the highest statesmen.

Writing in 1914, a time of international tension and domestic strife over "foreigners," Antin strongly opposed limitations on immigration. Her argument was predictable, but bold—America must live up to its creed of brotherhood, even if it demands material sacrifice. More important, her analysis of American life—including the hopes of the immigrant and the fears of the nativist—gives us some insight into the complexity of her own Americanization.

Clearly, most Americans fail to meet her expectations. Among these are the rich and the poor who, products of extremely different conditions, seem to oppose immigration without much consideration. The man in the street is easily influenced by "catchwords" rather than logic. Most Americans, she believes, have a biased view, because the newspapers report lurid and uncommon immigrant events, and because they are poorly led. Americans, it would seem, are basically a good folk whose essential virtue is encumbered by social and political restraints. Many Americans are increasingly involved in the curse of materialism, as "the canker of selfishness is gnawing at the heart of the nation." 62 This bane has always been with us, but in the past it had been balanced by a God-given remedy—the vision of brotherhood and equality. "The love of self, absorption in the immediate moment, are vices of the flesh which fastened on us during the centuries of our agonized struggle for brute survival." 63 These vices are more prevalent today among native Americans than among immigrants and account for much of the indifference which newcomers find in America.

Antin saves her strongest censure for politicians. As most Americans fall short of national ideals, so do most politicians pale before the majesty of our institutions. America's real enemies are not the immigrants. Instead, they are the "venal politicians" and businessmen, who try to blame the immigrant for all the faults of an unregulated capitalism. 64 Where the immigrant goes wrong, one can find sordid American conditions which have tempted him. Like Ravage, she argues for domestic reform and a reinvigorated civil religion.

There are gaps in this argument which hint at the ambiguity of her own experience. America, it would appear, was hardly a "garden" for earlier immigrants, the ancestors of contemporary natives, whose struggle for survival hardened their hearts. Why the new immigrants are free of this curse is not explained, although she intimates it is because of the productive capacity of modern capitalism. As previously noted, the style of her autobiography reflects a rampant individualism and the same "love of self" she sees in native Americans. In fact, most of her references to the achievements of new immigrants are characteristically aggressive:

> What is the galvanizing force that impels these stranger children to overmaster circumstances and bestride the top of the world? Is there a special virtue in their blood that enables them to sweep over our country and take what they want? [65]

Immigrant ambition, of course, is not the result of racial factors. Like Brandeis, she stressed the importance of ideals and visions which can produce sacrifice and achievement. Yet the obvious influence here is Emerson, critic of bourgeois materialism, yet admirer of the "captains of industry." This is consistent with Antin's deification of nature and her Boston upbringing. Like Emerson, too, her ultimate resort was a blind faith in progress, the hope that human development "will culminate in a spiritual constitution capable of absolute justice." [66]

Becoming an American, as desirable as that might be, was not an end in itself. To Antin, America was a missionary to the world, a forerunner of universal democracy. Being true to the American creed meant restating and teaching it to Americans, both old and new. It might mean, as Antin was willing to chance (and as this world view was bound to promote), standing apart from Americans who might resent the stream of criticism attached to her river of praise. In the process, too, she was willing to obscure Judaism in the rhetoric of Christianity and liberal democracy, while on the personal level she fled from the darker side of the self.

PLURAL AMERICA

The most important response to the Americanization offensive was the idea of cultural pluralism. Surfacing shortly before World War I, this school of thought has endured, with various modifications, until the present. Its followers have included native Americans, such as Randolph Bourne, who, anxious over the growing uniformity and impersonality of modern America, saw in ethnic diversity the potential for renewed communal life. [67] In the main, however, its adherents have been ethnics themselves, searching for a way to define America, and thus fit into it. [68]

The term itself arose with Horace Kallen, who spent nearly half a century proselytizing this view. Like Brandeis, Kallen was a German Jew of Harvard training and Zionist commitment, who shared many of the justice's attitudes, although he articulated them more precisely. A modernist and a progressive, he argued on intellectual grounds which were generally standard during that era. Ethnic loyalty, for example, was viewed as "emotional and involuntary," the result of hereditary racial factors.[69] The Jews, Kallen argued, had been restricted by primitive religion and external prejudice from expressing their inherent nationality. Now, under the sway of secular rationalism, Jewish nationality could find self-expression in Zionism.[70]

Cultural pluralism would do for American Jews what Zionism would do for world Jewry. True to pluralist theory, Kallen invested the group with a wholistic identity which earlier liberalism had retained for the individual. Real democracy in America, he argued, must primarily be a democracy of groups. Moreover, national cultures within America have much to contribute, as ethnic heterogeneity has always been an important element in our progress. America, Kallen concluded, should be "a federation or commonwealth of national cultures, a cooperative version of Europe, an example to all mankind."[71]

In respect to politics, Kallen was fairly typical of his age. Although political autonomy was a necessary aspect of the Zionist program, there was little place for politics among the many nationalities which composed America. In truth, Kallen distrusted politics, and even dropped out of the Zionist movement in time, due to disagreement over the role of the Zionist organization. Genuine cultural pluralism would demand political changes as well—a renaissance of localism, for example—to which Kallen's thinking was directly opposed. His conception of federalism, in fact, envisioned ethnic groups as dependents of a powerful and distant nation-state. In his image of a plural America, its political and economic life would be a "single unit," which would serve as a foundation for both group distinctiveness and cooperation.[72]

At the core of Kallen's thinking lay a rigid division between emotions and rationality. A man of the secular age, he came to see the value of traditional groups in the emotional life of the individual, but looked upon these attachments as essentially nonrational. Economic and political life demanded planning and coordination, and had to be divorced from the passions which religion and nationality could engender. The effect of this, among other things, was both to orient these attachments towards the private realm as well as to undercut the basis of the ethnic community. As admirable as Kallen's defense of the immigrants was, it could not repel the modern goliath. Cultural pluralism, to use his own words, would offer "isles of security, reservoirs of life"—an escape from modern life, rather than a challenge to it. [73]

A few years after Kallen introduced this idea, another work was published which tried to confront the same problem. Isaac Berkson's *Theories of Americanization* (1920) is a rare piece, a consciously theoretical work by an Eastern European Jew concerned with the problem of assimilation and Jewish identity. Like Abraham Cahan, Berkson was worried about the impact of modern life and economic advancement on Jewish identity. Ironically, Berkson, the director of the Central Jewish Institute, was more pessimistic than Cahan, whose David Levinsky is essentially unchanged by economic gain, To this educator, the disappearance of Jewish culture in America was a definite, if distant possibility.

As a theorist, Berkson left much to be desired. A disciple of John Dewey, he suffered from the era's overriding concern with adjusting traditional liberalism to modern conditions. But Berkson's major interest was to reconcile ethnicity, not religion, with majoritarian liberal democracy. In so attempting, he converted Judaism into a national culture and democracy into a "new religion." More so than Cahan, he reflected the ambivalence and self-distrust to which the man who straddles two cultures is prone.

The faults of Berkson's argument are unfortunate because his critique of prevailing theories of Americanization is full of insight. He chides Americanizers for trying to suppress individuality, for always assuming that immigrant traditions are alien. Allegiance and loyalty result from feeling "as kin with other citizens," but this does not mean that family loyalties ought to be eroded. [74] "The assumption was that breaking down a loyalty of seemingly smaller range leads of itself to a wider loyalty. It does not, necessarily." [75] He indicates, too, that other theories, seemingly friendly to the immigrants, are based on untenable assumptions, usually racial. For example, he points out that Kallen's "Federation of Nationalities" theory is racist, since it argues that ancestry is destiny.

Berkson's approach is founded on an assumption often unshared by other progressive intellectuals: the ethnic group has the right to exist and endure. As the individual has a right to life, so too does the nationality or ethnic group. Its existence is a complete right, which others cannot evaluate, since they cannot appreciate "the validity of an experience" particular to one group. Although Berkson states that there are commonalities of experience which transcend a single group (and allow emotions born in family and community to extend to institutions beyond their limits), it is crucial for him to fit the ethnic experience into a liberal framework of rights and unique group identity. Also, while an ethnic group in theory need not justify itself, it is significant that he disregards this assumption in practice. Hence he provides an extended discussion of how the Jewish group will contribute to the larger culture. In other words, implicitly recognizing the uncertainty of the rights argument, he feels obligated to show that ethnic groups also have "utility." [76]

Berkson's emphasis on the value and utility of nationality groups may be related to his evolutionary bent. Most evolutionary theorists had seen Americanization and the melting pot as stages of inevitable growth, assigning ethnic groups to a traditional past destined for extinction. [77] Berkson employs the same theme to counter the Americanizers: why should modern America be ruled by its traditional Anglo-Saxon past? However, the use of evolutionary theory locks him into a utilitarian argument. What can a nationality give the larger culture? How can it further progress? Therefore, even when he describes the virtues of ethnic loyalty with great persuasiveness, he subverts his argument by assuring that these virtues are causes of higher or future goals. Ethnic loyalty, for example, "promotes spiritualization of the individual's aims and purposes." Through close family ties, intimacy is fostered as well, "which seems basic to a real human touch and understanding." [78] In the long run, he believes, ethnic loyalty, particularly in the Jewish situation, can foster both national loyalty and international understanding.

Evolutionary theory, he notes also teaches us of the universality of force, an elemental aspect of our existence. Religion and philosophy then do not deal with reality, but reflect our aspirations, "describing universes better than the one we live in. . . ." Nor does democracy really exist; instead, it is a religious ideal, "a Messianic hope," which "comes not to destroy all other religious faiths but to fulfill." [79] Although older ideals are important to it, democracy is a possibility of modern life alone, since science and technology have provided the world untold opportunities.

The governing message is fuzziness. Berkson never defines democracy with anything near precision, nor does he take on the assumption of conflict so central to evolutionary thought. He blithely suggests that the emotional conflict which multiple loyalties might produce is not a problem, since "conflict tends to be resolved into harmony."[80] Instead of leading to possible antagonism or frustration, the experience of conflicting loyalties will encourage us to seek common denominators in both cultures, in the end, fostering a liberal, international outlook.

In reality, Berkson does not envision multiple loyalties as a problem because he does not want to think about them. His assurance that conflict will be "rationalized" is an apt description of his own intellectual processes. Political and cultural allegiances, he asserts, are really separate. A Jew can give "spiritual allegiance" to Palestine, but "he must by virtue of the duty that his oath of citizenship implies, give a complete allegiance to America."[81] Significantly, Berkson accepts the narrow conception of political allegiance of the Americanizers, equating it with loyalty to state policy. He sees ethnic political organization as a "menace" and politics as an impersonal "duty." The educational process, he concludes, is the only legitimate way of maintaining cultural plurality in the United States.[82]

Predictably, then, a note of defensiveness characterizes his justification of minority rights. Berkson accepts, even in denying it, the prevalent view that minorities need to explain themselves. Furthermore, he has no complaint with majority rule, even though he assumes that we are all unique and generally incapable of understanding one another's experience. The test which he proposes for minority rights—that minorities should be assumed good until proven evil—he does not consider applying to the majority as well.

Berkson avoids the question of what exactly constitutes "evil," although he suggests certain criteria of evaluation. Scientific demonstration and common sense show that some divergencies are harmful and evil (such as unhealthful sanitation). In addition, there is a "whole range of activities universally acknowledged to be evil."[83] This vague reliance on science and public opinion suggests again that Berkson is wary of the power of the majority.

Berkson also persists in the trend, so common to the writers dealt with here, of converting Jews into model Christians. Democracy, the "new religion" that will join Jews and other nationalities to America, is a Christ-like faith, the fulfillment of all faiths. Democracy assumes individualism along with an intricate social interdependence. It does not abide selfishness. It seeks harmony, altruism, and resolution of conflict. Coincidentally, the Jewish people reflect similar virtues, since they are an international people "whose interests include and are inextricably woven with the interests of many peoples. . . ." As a historic minority, Jews are dependent on the spread of liberal thought. Most important, and most Christian in the popular view, the spirit of the Jewish people is one of self-abnegation: "Its supremacy is hoped for in terms of service, not in terms of acquisition."[84]

In other words, Jews are neither an aggressive nor an angry people and can contribute meaningfully to the democratic faith. As such, Berkson manages to make Jews messianic, too, seeing them as the Christians of a future "one world."

APPROACH AND AVOIDANCE

The attribution of Christian values to Jews was intended to make them more acceptable to native readers. Better educated and social- ized than other Jewish immigrants, these writers were most sensitive to the stereotypes of Jews as aggressive and self-seeking.[85] Jews also needed assurance that they were not a grasping people. Antin and Ravage never really confront their own ambitions which were major forces in their urge to become acceptable Americans. The desire to as- similate involved a powerful ambition, if not an angry challenge to the dominant culture (particularly a culture that encouraged individual achievement).[86] Viewing yourself in Christian terms might absolve your hostility, while at the same time assuring that you were really like other Americans—except that you were a degree better because most Americans were but nominal Christians.

The appeal of Christian metaphors may have had other sources worthy of attention. Most Jews were close enough to their past to feel comfortable with, or perhaps need, religious models. Judaism and Protestant Christianity *are* similar in certain respects although these writers chose to identify with a mild and benevolent Christ, rather than with the demanding God so typical of early American Protestantism. [87] Most important, some Jews probably did feel like secular Christs: more advanced and enlightened than their own people from whom they feared scorn and rejection; and more advanced and civilized than the Gentiles, who deluded themselves with the frills of formal religion.

Thus I am not suggesting that these Jews were becoming Americans through a quiet conversion to Christianity. For one thing, they were too imbued with both secularism and Jewish loyalties to be genuine converts. If anything, their thinking reflected a further decline in Judaism—an emphasis on nationality instead of religion, a movement towards ethics and ideals and away from Torah. This would continue in ensuing years with the growth of the Conservative movement in Judaism along with the secular compromises it made regarding serious religious questions. [88] Antin, Ravage, and Berkson were attracted to Christian imagery because it allowed them to preserve some marginality and ambivalence; to portray Jewish uniqueness and commonality at one and the same time. Similarly, their emphasis on Jews as *teachers* of old and relevant truths may have served a similar function.

Their ultimate position was marked by ambivalence and confusion. In one sense, they desired to preserve a special identity as Jews, even if this self-concept was now modernized or Christianized. At the same time, they desired to assimilate into an America which reflected Jewish values and traditions. In this version, Jews could stand out as cultural priests and prophets, teaching Americans their own traditions. Another scenario, which also illustrated these same tendencies, saw Jewish assimilation as partial, because America itself was evolving towards a universal community based on seemingly Judaeo-Christian values. In this conception, too, Jews would be in the vanguard as teachers and models.

If anything was a sacrifice here it may have been a more active political role. Optimally, a healthy assimilationist program would demand assertion on the part of the minority cultures of the virtues of their way of life. It would demand debate and criticism along with the willingness, on the part of both majority and minority, to make some changes in their customary ways. Inevitably, it would involve political participation beyond the formal act of voting. Yet benevolent and service-oriented Jews, concerned with acceptance, were reluctant to approach a realm which the dominant culture associated with conflict, and their own culture had viewed with distrust.

Certainly, a distinction has to be made here between political ideals and politics, between statesmanship and electioneering, between the august polity and the bosses. These writers were generally attracted to distant political forms, while denigrating the mundane realities of American politics. [89] Their perspectives were often national and international, as distinct from the narrower ethnic group which they approached with ambivalence. Moreover, genuine involvement in American politics, practically or intellectually, might be too much of a commitment for Jews, who despite their prose may have wished to remain a step apart from American life.

Loyalty to the distant nation was consistent with the experience of the Diaspora, when most Jewish communities had come to rely on the central authority for protection. Beyond this, allegiance to the nation and its ideals could provide a personal guide without the risk of political involvement at the local level. For those who were attracted to American assimilation and were likewise ambivalent about their Jewish identification, genuine political involvement may have appeared too threatening. Political life, embracing visible commitments in action and words, may have personalized issues which a more distant allegiance left less obvious and more abstract.

CHAPTER

5

THE IMMIGRANT EXPERIENCE: THE PERILS OF AMERICA

For those Jewish immigrants who were committed to social change, the new nation presented a political reality which differed in several ways from their own experience. In the Jewish community of Eastern Europe, local political issues were entwined with questions of religion and law, although always subject to practical accommodations with external forces. A higher law and morality were integral to communal life, although the necessity for group survival, along with tendencies towards conservatism in religious life, sometimes suppressed their application. Judaism encouraged its adherents to see life, and hence politics, in distinct moral terms. But the religion, as well as the conditions of Jewish life, fostered an acceptance of political reality.

Many of the more radical Jewish immigrants, to be sure, considered themselves to be political emigres from Russia, not from the shtetl. Yet czarist Russia was also a remote political climate for those who wanted to understand American political life. The autocratic nature of government in Russia and Eastern Europe, founded on a rigid class structure, often promoted in secularized Jews a desire to transform society through revolutionary action. Politics was frequently viewed in terms of moral extremes and subversive activity.[1]

The American environment, on the other hand, was characterized by different political expectations. While Americans also liked to measure political life by high moral standards, usually derived from a religious tradition, this inclination was significantly modified by other aspects of American life. Neither American traditions nor conditions seemed to foster the demand for revolution. Moral urgency was more likely to produce reform rather than revolution, and many reformers had little taste for politics. Reform movements were often sporadic and lacked a foundation in ideology. Within American politics, compromise was encouraged by a complicated structure of government, a variety of interests, and the assumption that political activity was secondary to the rewards of economic achievement.

Most Jewish immigrants arrived here during a period in which local politics seemed dominated by bargaining and practicality.[2] Urban political culture swayed between "machine" and reform modes. The machine seemed to cherish practicality and compromise as ends in themselves, supports for its own power and survival. Reformers, in contrast, were more moral but less adept, uncompromising and often ineffective. Moreover, reformers were often quite narrow in their social and economic goals, and their morality, while akin to the Jewish experience, might seem ultimately irrelevant to Jewish radicals.

Some Jewish immigrants, in the least an articulate minority, came to see America as a politically corrupt nation, whose decay was more obvious because of the virtue it had seemed to promise. To a disappointed immigrant this virtue was usually associated with an earlier cherished image, which itself may have been utopian in its demands. Their early experience in America caused many immigrants to feel as if they had fallen into a society with lower moral standards and a shameful public morality. As we have seen, this theme was not unusual—Aleichem, Singer, Cournos, and even Ravage expressed various degrees of disillusionment. Yet Aleichem accepted this demoralization, viewing it with an aging humorist's sense of sad resignation. Singer, devoted to his new land while rejecting its follies, sees all modern states as corrupt. Cournos and Ravage, while ostensibly rejecting America, were driven by American standards of success.

For others of the immigrant generation, dissent and criticism became banners behind which one marched on a journey into America. If America never seemed good enough it might be because the new country promised so much, or because one could not admit to new affections without breaking loyalties to a distant past. This is not to deny the sincerity of the critics or the validity of their judgments. The failings of America were painful lessons, especially in the light of expectations which had been aroused. What should be noted, however, were the ways in which bitter criticism often reflected an attraction to America. If those who were most concerned with fitting in seemed to maintain an unrecognized distance, those who seemed most alienated were often extremely sensitive to the lures of the new land.

For the most part, those who chastened America did so from the corner of modernism rather than tradition. The socialists accused America of backwardness. Europe, it seemed, particularly Germany, took socialism more seriously in doctrine and law. Labor organization in America was stultified by a narrow individualism which Morris Hillquit, along with other Jewish socialist leaders, saw as a relic of an earlier stage of economic development.[3] To many Jews socialism became a symbol of modernity and beyond, a means to universal enlightenment. America, along with one's fellow Jews, would have to be raised to a higher plane of civilization.

"THE SOCIALIST OF THE POOR DEVIL"

To socialists like Morris Hillquit and Meyer London the question of Jewish identity was apparently a minor issue. Hillquit hardly concerned himself with it, distancing himself from any conscious identification. Hillquit saw his own cultural influence as German and Russian, and tended to condescend toward early Jewish life in the United States. Thus in recalling the initial problems in organizing Jewish workers, he describes them as "dull, apathetic, and unintelligent," "pitiful"—utterly devoid of assertiveness and the ability to defend themselves.[4] A half-century of labor organization had transformed them, however, "from a race of timid, submissive, cheerless and hopeless drudges" into a group of men and women who were self-reliant and possessed self-respect.[5]

In a similar vein, the socialist theoretician Hayim Zhitlowsky saw the task as one of enlightening the entire Jewish people:

> We, the carriers of ideals of universal human progress, had to appeal to the people with our message about quite a new world, the world of modern, progressive West European culture. Vis-a-vis this world the whole Jewish people were like the ignorant masses.[6]

When Meyer London came to Congress he also sought to separate himself from the commonly held image of the Jew. Yet unlike Hillquit, he was forced to acknowledge Jewishness as part of his identity:

> . . . I shall accomplish one thing that is not in the platform of the Socialist Party. I hope that my person will represent an entirely different type of Jew from that type Congress had been accustomed to see.[7]

In the midst of an overwhelmingly Gentile Congress, London could hardly avoid being conscious of his distinctive background. Among New York socialists Hillquit might be less so.[8] With its strength firmly rooted in the Jewish neighborhoods of the Lower East Side, New York socialism, under Hillquit's captaincy, maintained both an evolutionary and intellectual approach which sometimes alienated its political brethren. New York socialism reflected, in rough terms, elements of traditional Jewish life: an emphasis on learning and argument (London, true to form, posed himself as a teacher to his fellow congressmen); a zeal for social betterment, along with a resignation to the impossibility of rapid, utopian change; and finally, an almost religious approach to socialism.

References to the religious nature of socialism were common among Jewish socialists of this era. Hillquit referred to socialism as "my ideal and religion and one of the principal interests in my life."[9] Harry Roskolenko remembers the socialist leader as a "tzaddik" (a wise and holy man), and the Socialist Party as "our political Messiah. . . ."[10] Abraham Bisno, the leader of the Chicago cloakworkers, liked to express his social and industrial morality in terms of "Thou shalt" commandments. His description of early socialist activities in Chicago recalls more of the spirit than the substance: "We were all inspired with the missionary spirit to convert everyone to whatever our doctrines might be."[11] Meyer London's 1904 campaign letter combined the old rhetoric and the new, urging his brethren to reject "the soul-crushing traditions of the past," and to accept "a new political faith if convinced of its soundness. . . ."[12]

The older faith, of course, was never based on soundness and the likening of socialism to religion did an injustice to both. True, socialism encapsulated roles which religion earlier had fostered—the teacher, the prophet, and the scholar, for example. Socialism also captured passions and faith that the culture previously had encouraged toward ends sanctioned by religion. But the socialists' goals were allegedly of this world, and their approach to worldly affairs was supposedly scientific, practical, and materialistic. If guided by ideals of a perfect society, they were far from worshipping a supernatural deity.

Against the boredom and drudgery of everyday life, socialism offered a hope and an escape. America seemed to stimulate an asocial individualism, propelling settled immigrants into private enterprises which absorbed their talent and industry. "The more energetic and intelligent of our people," the labor leader Abraham Bisno admitted, "left their work benches and went into business. . . ."[13] Disliking socialist politics for being unworldly and impractical, Bisno concentrated on union activities instead, finding in it "human attachments" almost familial in their depth. Socialist labor activity, if nothing else, brought people together in a higher moral brotherhood. Bisno saw American politics as essentially corrupt and irresponsible, with the labor union as a fragile but virtuous alternative. Although frequently undercut by the competitive quality of America economic life, the labor movement seemed to have more of a sense of solidarity and morality than there existed in the political realm.[14]

Similarly, Hillquit saw the socialists of this era as politically inept. However, the virtues of intimacy and solidarity which Bisno discovered in the labor union, Hillquit found in the socialist movement. Hillquit saw the socialists of this period as members of an intimate and elevated communion, which he analogized to the early followers of Christ. He, too, noted that these early socialists were not "practical politicians." They constituted a small, intense fraternity, bound together by common belief, although they were unappreciated and often derided by the masses. Thus, in Hillquit's eyes, they shared more than "a *mere* political kinship."[15]

The sense of being members of an exclusive moral fraternity grew out of and reinforced the intellectual distance between leaders and followers. The socialists, as modernizers, had a perhaps unwonted affinity with that liberal American world which they challenged. London's comment in Congress that "the Republicans are the Socialists of the rich. . . . I am the Socialist for the poor devil," takes on deeper meaning in this light. On some level, these antagonistic socialists had certain assumptions in common: a belief in progress; a faith in science

and intellect; and a tendency towards universalism and political cen-
tralization. In this respect, London assured Congress that suppressing immigrants' native languages was not a good idea, since a common language could not be achieved through "mere edicts." The government should aim, he went on, at "bringing up" the people to cherish American institutions and culture.[16]

Jewish socialists, who considered themselves to be pioneers on the
frontier of enlightenment, almost inevitably gravitated to an emphasis on intellect and knowledge. London's role in Congress—the wise
and didactic philosopher with an air of patient prevision—was indica-
tive of this tendency. Taking a distinctly non-Marxist approach, London argued that the only difference between the present and the past
lay in the greater diffusion of knowledge in the modern world. Ultimately, if the facts could be diffused to all the people, then wars could
be eliminated, as their causes would now be understood. Democracy,
honesty, and above all, knowledge, were necessary to facilitate progress.[17] In words and action, he implied that America required teachers in political life who could persevere in the long and difficult task of
mass education.

As a socialist, London believed that human salvation depended on
"love guided by intelligence" and an "enlightened will."[18] Human
hearts, weak but inherently good, were easily misdirected by poor education and a distorted vision of the world. Government ought to be
entrusted to men with ideas, to men who reason and think in a "modern" way. Like Brandeis and the progressives, London placed great
faith in education and educated men, hallmarks of the era which was
to follow.

"WOMEN ARE THE JEWS OF THE SEXES"

It is reasonable to assume that the type of Jew that London did not
want to be fit the traditional stereotype of unworldly passivity. Socialism, although it attracted attributes and roles typical of Jewish culture, also reflected an *active* attempt at changing the world. "I hate to
be condemned to inaction," London once remarked. "I must participate in the work of the world, although some of it may be work of mischief."[19] Likewise, Hillquit viewed the socialist task as an arduous

commitment to "education, organization, and struggle," which aimed at transforming the minds of "the passive millions of workers" throughout the modern world.[20]

In later years communism would attract the radicals' desire for action and worldly power. Socialism, communism, and a missionary Christianity provided models of participation and commitment, and also traced a path of sexual role adjustment to American life. Some of the virtues of socialism—its concern with human welfare, the health and working conditions of the common man, and social justice— might seem overly maternal without a corresponding emphasis on power, solidarity, and action. Characteristically, in many of the socialist novels of the period it is frequently a strong woman who inspires activity. It is also noteworthy that women played an important role in the Jewish labor movement during this era.[21]

The character of the Jewish man is a pervasive theme in the literature of the period. The traditional standards of Jewish masculinity were radically different from those which prevailed for men in America. The stress on scholarship and piety had fostered a necessary sense of alienation and unworldliness. The Jewish male, at his best, would persevere in the intellectual and spiritual realms, arguing, questioning, rebelling, and surrendering to God. It was the Jewish woman who, in many cases, governed the practical life, raising the family and sometimes administering a business enterprise. Obviously, many Jewish males succeeded in business and other practical endeavors. However, the religious scholar was an esteemed cultural role, a role which successful businessmen might pressure their sons to fulfill.[22]

In America much of this had to change or become adapted to the new environment. The turn-of-the-century United States, in a surge of modernization, emphasized action and practice, the values of a business civilization. In intellectual life, too, as Morris Cohen would encounter, the Jamesian stress on "tough-minded" pragmatism would challenge the speculative and contemplative style. In the short run, of course, most Jewish immigrants had little real choice anyway: once or would-be scholars had to pursue more practical careers to survive. But for some, men, in particular, adaptation to America might involve a painful attempt to discover one's true self.

The crisis of Jewish identity then often involved a crisis of male identity. Socialism, and later communism, offered an appealing resolution: a spiritual life dedicated to making real changes in the world. Raised in households characterized by strong maternal affection, Jewish males had to find their way in a new land where the traditional model of their father was often spurned. That the act of immigration often symbolized a rejection of this model only intensified the difficulty; it did not relieve it. Some, like the main character of Elias Tobenkin's *Witte Arrives*, attempt to assume the more traditional role. His uncle explains that boys like Emil Witte are often misunderstood, because most people conceive of power only in aggressive terms:

> Most people can only see power when it is manifested in a strong arm, athletic physique, or daring feats. But there is another sort of power in the world, a more fruitful power frequently—the power which resists passively and endures patiently. Emil has that power.[23]

Emil's father had chosen to remain Orthodox, which to his son meant dropping out of the "race for prosperity." Emil, more worldly and ambitious, wants to make something of himself, and chases success in the newspaper profession. Typically, Emil is an ambivalent soul, who in spite of his alleged strength of character, desires a degree of worldly influence through his ability to observe and communicate. As a journalist, he is essentially a loner, a romantic who sees himself as a socialist and personally identifies with the poor. In a municipal lodging house in Chicago he feels this identification in the broadest of terms. In this place, where "manhood commanded no respect," Witte is reminded of himself and his father, and of the fortuitous circumstances which have kept them from this condition. He sees the passivity of the poor as part of a universal trend, symbolic of "the helplessness of the individual in modern society."[24]

Witte's identification with the poor and alienated, along with his search for a modern American and Jewish "manhood," involves mainly a personal quest. Seeing modern life as a condition of fear and insecurity imposed on isolated individuals, Witte fails to discern that this reality was his own rather than his father's. His father, although religiously isolated in a small midwestern town, has both the security of the old faith along with the respect of his Gentile fellow townsmen. The younger Witte, more adrift in America, has no such bonds and his anxieties are aggravated by his chosen profession, which is notoriously unstable and competitive. In truth, Witte is much the individualist, and the novel is primarily a romantic study of personal achievement within the trappings of socialism. Witte's outlook in many respects fits well with Spencer or the anarchist, Max Stirner. His marriage is described in terms of a contract; his wife promises to support herself and do nothing to obstruct his career (significantly, she has a background of revolutionary activism in Russia). Witte feels "in debt" to his wife for her sacrifices, yet when he learns of her pregnancy he does not feel it in joint terms and agrees that their decision to have an abortion is truly imposed by "society." [25] Although Witte considers himself to be a disciple of his socialist uncle, who is an acceptable personal and political model, he ends up embracing the New England tradition (almost literally, since he marries a New England Protestant after his first wife dies)—and the wrong one for a socialist, that of Emerson.

Witte's marriage to an old-stock New Englander seems to represent a further movement away from his father, although it may have actually been an indirect profession of loyalty. For one thing, New England symbolizes the oldest and most Hebraic of American traditions —it is potentially comparable to Witte's own background. Secondly, the events and mood of the novel imply an unresolved oedipal situation which is deepened by social and political factors. Witte's first marriage to a Jewish women is structured to avoid excessive personal dependence. More important, it concludes with her death, which psychologically may symbolize the danger of marrying a woman like one's mother. The novel ends with his second marriage, which promises happiness, but resolves nothing. Certainly it leaves Witte's quest for "manhood" unresolved, implying that it could be solved by discovering the right woman and ignoring Witte's relations with men and the community.

In a curious way some Jewish socialist writers such as Elias Tobenkin often accepted basic tenets of the individualist ethos which seemed to alienate them. Socialist characters like Witte are too often presented as heroes and romantic loners, who challenge or suffer the crassness of the new society. Witte's "manhood," for example, is that of the quixotic victim. He is an outsider within, having no strong ties to any community or group. As lonely individuals, usually disappointed in love and extremely oriented toward personal achievement, these characters supposedly represent the better half of the "David Levinskys" who went astray in America. They have chosen a higher path, but their souls are troubled by concerns similar to those of their seemingly assimilationist brothers.

Samuel Ornitz's two novels of immigrant adaptation also highlight many of these issues. In *Haunch, Paunch, and Jowl,* published in 1923, Ornitz excoriates the type of Jewish man which the American experience has produced. Meyer Hirsch, a successful lawyer and politician, is a man dominated by his material success (symbolized by his large paunch), childless, and living without real love. In the end, surrounded by material comfort and the results of American success, Hirsch is still sensitive enough to admit his doubts—"Tell me, life, tell me, what's it all about. . . ."[26]

Yet true to the naturalism and socialism of the period, Ornitz places his character in the broader environmental perspective. Hirch is pictured as an almost inevitable product of early Jewish slum existence and is as much the victim as the victimizer. There is a constant reminder in this novel that Hirsch could have been something better. While he chose the wrong path, it is nevertheless clear that ghetto conditions and American values strictly limited the alternatives, and that some young men were bound to choose the immoral way.

America, in Ornitz's view, is a corrupt place which perverts the values of the young men of this generation. "It was a sordid generation," he writes, "a generation creeping out of the mud into the murk." Whatever sensitivity survived the years of youth was submerged under a callous exterior that society necessitated.

> There was nothing in the conspicuous examples of American life to inspire anything else. Politics stank of corruption and chicanery. Big business set even a worse example. Daily the people were treated to scandal after scandal in commerce, industry and government. . . .[27]

In this decadent world, a man must inhibit his feelings, his kindness and compassion, in particular, if he is to confront the hard grind of American life. Witte's mother, too, had heard even before arriving in the new land that "America often transforms men. The struggle for existence makes them hardhearted, destroys their finer sensibilities."[28] Success in America means "playing the game" and in doing so limiting one's manhood in a serious, even perverse way. Manhood becomes difficult to realize, since some of its genuine qualities of feeling have been automatically relegated to the "feminine" sphere.

Politics is also portrayed as a game, perhaps the most corrupt of all.

One says what the people want to hear, catering to base needs, manipulating the courts, using influence to get ahead. To Ornitz there is little compensation for all this chicanery. A party organization is merely an extension of individual ambition, a primary example of the system of push, pull, and favoritism which degrades American life. The organization uses the people; the politician manipulates the organization. The public good is left to the reformers, who are usually hypocrites, or the socialists, who are on the right path, but are sometimes misguided.

Ornitz's characterization of Meyer Hirsch as a political man parallels this scenario. In addition, it is consistent with a traditional stereotype of the *Jewish* political man. Hirsch is a political schemer—a shrewd operator and "wheeler-dealer," a court politician who uses his intellect to get ahead. Even as a youth, his political role in the neighborhood gang was that of the counselor who took few real risks:

> I take my place next to Boolkie, as self-appointed adviser, strategist—anything—except fighter. In time, I have made this position for myself, always playing the part that involves no personal danger and by sheer push, assertion and brass have become ex-officio everything. . . . I am a sort of prime minister of our gang state, and Boolkie kneads pliantly under my flattery. . . .29

It is clear that for Ornitz this is neither an admirable masculine role nor an admirable political role. In fact, even its aggressive aspects are quite mixed—push, assertion, and brass are traits more frequently found in Ornitz's Jewish women characters, as of course, flattery might be, too. Furthermore, Hirsch is seen as a coward, who takes little direct responsibility or risk. At best, he is a divided, incomplete man, who uses power for petty and base ends.30 His political life, as described by Ornitz, symbolizes the descent of the Jewish man in America.

In a later work—published in 1951, but a novel of the immigrant generation—Ornitz places these themes in a more intricate context. In *Bride of the Sabbath* there is a strong association between a passive, downtrodden Judaism and the male figures who are ordained to represent it. Although strongly denied within the text of the novel, sexual themes are very important in this book. The "decline of the patriarchal Jew," described by Hutchins Hapgood,31 is reflected in Ornitz's writing by the absence or early death of fathers, the turning

away from religious traditions which are essentially masculine, and by
the characterization of Jewish men as passive and possibly feminine.
While Ornitz relentlessly singles out the male chauvinism of Jewish
religious observance, he also likens the male treatment of women to
the Christian treatment of Jews. To most people, "women are the Jews
of the sexes," similarly ostracized and maltreated, and perceived too
as the source of all evil. People also believe, he asserts, that Jews have
the same psychology as women. 32

More accurately, these observations give Ornitz the impression that
Jews have the psychology of women. He also suggests that Christians
are perhaps unavoidably attracted to Jews, as men are drawn to wom-
en. Christianity has created a "compulsion" to associate Jewishness
with evil which is "as powerful as the sexual compulsion." 33 Finally,
the entire novel makes it evident that Ornitz himself has ambivalent
feelings about women, and possibly sees them as the origin of evil.

Saul, the main character of this book, grows up in a household
dominated by women—his mother and grandmother—who have endured better than their men the transformations of the New World.
His father, a student of Talmud in Russia, is forced into the sweatshops and dies early, a broken man. His grandfather, although not an
ineffectual man, has similarly fallen from social grace. He had been a
rather prosperous storekeeper in Russia, and something of a scholar
as well. A good man, but a poor provider because he will not exploit
those who work for him, his "failure" is viewed in sexual terms, particularly by his wife. "Pick yourself up!" she exhorts. "Be a man
again!" 34 The most positive male figure predictably is an uncle, a
socialist writer, who is continually referred to as a man of intellectual
power and authority. Nevertheless, Ornitz's general impression of
Jewish men is that they are not complete people. History has produced
a Jewish man, "conditioned by centuries of survival by means of non-
resistance"—a passive creature who will not fight back. Significantly,
it is Jewish women who are depicted as the rebels, the fighters, who
must push their men into combat. 35

The passivity of Jewish men is the other side of the power and aggressiveness of Gentile males. The submissiveness of the Jewish man
is contrasted to the aggressive sexuality of Christian men. At an early
age Saul is sexually attacked by an Irish street gang. When a member
of the gang started to touch him, "Saul fought and screamed like a

girl." 36 Irish street gangs would punish a Jewish boy by "flogging his dummy." Anti-Semitism is compared to the gonorrhea germ: it thrives on darkness and ignorance along with the acquiescence of fearful Jews who allow the virus to penetrate them. 37

For Ornitz, it is the Jewish socialist who is closest to the strength of his male traditions. Uncle Mendel, the socialist editor, is a strong figure who exhibits no confusion in his sexual role. He even has a girlfriend, a non-Jew, with whom he has a "liberated" sexual relationship. More significant, socialism is presented as being strictly in accord with Jewish traditions of protest and concern for human welfare. Liberalism, on the other hand, is seen as an attempt to evade the problem of personal identity and social commitment:

> Naturally, many of the elders turned Socialist as a reaction against the sweatshops. Who wouldn't? As a rule, the children did not altogether sell out, rather becoming liberals identified with no party or ideology. And this was what they wanted: not to be identified.38

To become a liberal might mean greater acceptance in American society, but it promises the greater loss of one's Jewish and socialist self. Socialism corresponds to the universal and ethical traditions of Judaism and allows Jews, especially Jewish men, to adopt roles which are agreeable to both historical and religious experience. Uncle Mendel is offered as a teacher and prophet, warning America and its Jews about the evils of social injustice. Socialism allows Jews to combine intellect and spirit with the promise of social change. At the same time it allows them to pursue adaptation in a more comfortable, predominantly Jewish environment. 39

Socialism also provides a key to eventual assimilation in its relationship with Christianity. Saul, raised as an Orthodox Jew, moves away from Judaism in his late adolescence. The influence of Christian missions in the neighborhood and Christian teachers at school, in addition to the egalitarian teachings of his uncle are important here. He chooses medicine as a career (under the influence of a strong woman), but gives that up after he begins to work for a Protestant welfare agency. Saul becomes everything but an avowed Protestant, describing himself as a Christian socialist in politics. His job brings him into daily contact with society's downtrodden, whom he approaches with a mixture of august intellectual detachment (he is writing a book) and

Christian benevolence. Saul works with the insane, people who were so forgotten "that it seemed he cured several of them merely by giving them a kind look or word, their gratitude heartrending."[40]

Saul's attraction to Christianity, eventually symbolized by his marriage to a Catholic woman, is only temporary. Ornitz implies that their relationship is almost necessary if he is to understand himself as a Jew. Saul is fascinated with Christ and realizes that he, as a Jew, can understand him better than most alleged Christians. His primary model, Uncle Mendel, in fact symbolizes the convergence of Judaism, socialism, and Christ.

Even as a boy, Saul had begun to understand that his uncle was "more Jewish in his feelings" than his grandmother, who was seemingly more pious in her ritual observance. Being a Jew, Ornitz suggests, means embracing certain universal emotions, perhaps to a greater degree than other people. These feelings, moreover, ought be applied to political as well as personal life, and should not be limited or replaced by an emphasis on ritual. While this lesson is more Christian than Jewish, Ornitz attempts to merge the two religions in the socialist character of Mendel. His uncle, Saul came to appreciate, loved and admired Jesus "as a Jewish teacher and revolutionary. . . ."[41]

Ravage's assertion that Christians do not really know Christ is matched in Ornitz's novel by the intimation that Jews understand Jesus better than alleged Christians. Ornitz implies that America's salvation does lie in Christ, but only when both Christians and Jews join to acknowledge Christ as a Jew. In describing the religious education of Jewish boys in America, Ornitz comments:

> But Christians and Jews seemed to have occultly agreed not to teach either of their young that Jesus had had a totally Jewish childhood and upbringing, Heaven forbid, lest it make the former sympathetic to Judaism and the latter to Christianity.[42]

A *true* understanding of Christ could unite most Americans, not only by lowering obstacles to assimilation, but by providing a political agenda derived from a Judaeo-Christian tradition of social justice. Presently, Ornitz asserts, it is the Jew who is closer to this tradition and hence the temptation, or perhaps necessity, to bring this message to both Jews and Christians who are blind to it—the temptation to *be* Christ. Thus, in *Bride of the Sabbath*, Saul returns to a Jewish identification only after his teachings have spurred his Christian wife to enter a nunnery. In *Haunch, Paunch, and Jowl*, one Christ-like character becomes a wandering missionary, traveling and working through the land, attempting to convert workers to the idea of "one big union." Another, a romantic figure of great beauty and poetry (his name is David), dies young after marrying and "saving" a Gentile prostitute.

It is significant that in each of these cases the reformer or savior figure is either apolitical or extremely detached from American politics. Typically, the most political of Ornitz's admirable characters is Mendel, but even he is less concerned with political activity than he is with trying to understand and transform those values that pervade American life and politics. He is a Marxist and a socialist, but he has little to do with Marxist organizations in America. His activities, apart from journalism mainly involve internecine intellectual disputes with other East Side socialists.

Ornitz seems to suggest that a true political Jew must rise above practical politics in America, which is sordid and corrupt. In doing so, he may find the genuine model of Jewish manhood, which is a Jewish Jesus Christ. As prophet and teacher, he must penetrate the mind and spirit which govern the actions of men. While American life offered male models that were crudely aggressive, the Jewish tradition, as Ornitz saw it, could teach men how to relate to politics and transcend it at the same time.

SEX AND SENTIMENT

As noted earlier, Ornitz also intimates that adapting to the American public sphere may have been easier in many instances for Jewish women than it was for Jewish men. Jewish women are portrayed as willful and aggressive, less bound by traditional status than their male counterparts. Since, for Ornitz, public life is essentially decadent, this portrait, although it reflects some admiration, is highly unflattering. Nor is it entirely surprising. Judaism had consistently portrayed women as corruptors and temptresses who led men away from moral righteousness. Closer to the earth, women were seen as more easily prey to its godless norms. Furthermore, Jewish women had partaken extensively in commercial life in a public setting. Their adjustment to America was probably less demanding than that of the Jewish man whose religious code had required a greater sense of distance from the world of affairs. The religious Jew had to feel discomfort in the Gentile public domain.

For many socialist writers, fascinated with the Enlightenment and the hope of progress, America was also a great temptation. The public realm may have represented "feminine" power in certain respects because it promised so much and because in truth it was so appealing, its power a lure as well as a danger. Unused to political power and half-convinced that Jews were too passive and hence feminine, socialist writers often endowed the political realm with tremendous potential. In addition, we must remember that the position of ethnic groups in early twentieth-century America was at least semi-colonial. American or Americanized women may have symbolized status and power, forbidden fruits of great allure.

Beyond these possibilities, the prevailing image of America was of a place of great opportunity and looser standards. Coming from a background in which a moral and communal order were given great value, an immigrant Jew might see America as a place where the old supports to personal order were threatened, too. American liberty could easily be interpreted as libertinism, and life in American cities provided numerous examples of sexual freedom which could stimulate this interpretation. Hence, to male writers the association of America with female temptation was by no means bizarre.

These themes appear in sharpest relief in the works of Abraham Cahan, perhaps the best of the early Jewish socialist writers in America. A revolutionary activist in Russia, Cahan came to the United States as a young man and went on to become a "lord" of the Yiddish press, to paraphrase George Seldes.[43] Once in America, Cahan quickly learned English, and by the turn of the century was a frequent contributor to American newspapers. He soon turned to writing fiction, his achievements culminating in *The Rise of David Levinsky* (1916), one of the classic works of immigrant literature. All the while —in fact, for more than forty years—Cahan edited the *Jewish Daily Forward*, and served as both teacher and spokesman for Jews who were struggling to become Americans.[44]

Significantly, too, Cahan showed great sensitivity to the problems of assimilation and adaptation. He wrote in both English and Yiddish, and his English works deal primarily with the apparent transformations which Jews experienced in the United States. Although he often took the predictable socialist line on religion—that it would fade away with social and economic changes—Cahan was usually alert to Jewish issues. [45] An early and somewhat lonely advocate of Yiddish journalism, Cahan argued that Jewish workers must be reached through the traditional culture. This emphasis on a Jewish means to a socialist end, however, masked an essential fact which stands out in most of Cahan's English works, at least: Socialist concerns are usually assigned second place to Jewish issues or general immigrant problems. In addition, Cahan's strong attachment to Old World life included an identification with Orthodox Judaism which is unmistakably present in his writings.

Cahan's life almost epitomized the course of the Russian Jewish socialists who came to America. Raised in Vilna to be a religious scholar, Cahan in his early adolescence chose to follow other paths. His discovery of science freed him from his belief in and fear of God. He saw his own father as a failure, a "sad" man, who "fumbled in meeting the vicissitudes of life." He describes his father as a weak person, overly sensitive, and easily mistreated:

> Years later, while reading Dostoevski's *The Brothers Karamozov*, I recognized my own suffering in his description of a young lad's reaction at seeing his father insulted and belittled. [46]

The younger Cahan was attracted to secular pursuits, first seeking to learn a trade, and then becoming an ardent student of Western knowledge. Cahan became deeply involved in the revolutionary ferment that was sweeping through Russia, which he described as a kind of religious passion. [47] What these activities meant in broader terms may be inferred from his novel, *The White Terror and the Red* (1905), which is an account of a band of underground radicals in czarist Russia. The two main characters are Pavel, a disillusioned and fatherless youth of the Russian nobility, and Clara, a poor Jewish girl of high idealism and a sacrificial nature. Clara's father is practically inert. A pious, unworldly man, he is treated like a baby by his tough-minded wife. Similarly, Pavel refers to the present Russian nobility as "a lot of idlers . . . a lot of good-for-nothings." [48] For both Pavel and Clara the older male generation apparently can provide no models for the future.

Typically, it is the example of Clara, who makes a forthright public

speech, which draws Pavel into the clandestine revolutionary movement. Equally important here, however, is Pavel's relationship with
his mother, with whom he identifies the goals of the revolution. When
he finally tells her of his activities ("uncovers his soul to her"), she experiences "an unwonted state of mental excitement," and feels "ini-
tiated into a strange ecstacy of thought and feeling. . . . His world
lured her heart also," Cahan writes:

> Her heart was deeper in his movement than he supposed. It was as if
> every barrier standing between her and her son had been removed.[49]

Symbolically, then, revolutionary activity has familial and sexual
implications. The revolutionary movement, inspired by women,
pushes a man towards heroism and sacrifice. Being a member of the
Russian underground means, paradoxically, that one can totally transcend all father figures (real father, czar, and God), and through a
corresponding fantasy, can win one's mother. Perhaps this is why the
revolution cannot be successful, and why, in the course of the novel,
Pavel and Clara cannot consummate their love.

Cahan himself remains somewhat distant from his characters, although there is little doubt as to his political sympathies. Although
The White Terror and the Red was a novel of his youth, it reflected
magnetic yearnings which are present throughout the course of his
works. In writing, at least, Cahan was able to resolve some of the difficulties which appear so consistently in his fiction. His pragmatic
socialism suggests likewise that he was able to temper the romance of
revolution with the realities of American life. In another story, about a
former socialist who becomes a wealthy doctor, Cahan took aim at
dogmatic socialists who were unwilling to face human political realities. The doctor, in spite of his success, is a man of good "heart," who
performs small, but sincere charities for other people. His spirit,
Cahan writes, is not that of an "eagle," who flies among the stars, and
looks down at mankind. The doctor's spirit, instead, is that of an
"ordinary hen,"—unlike that of many socialist intellectual "eagles,"
who, in their detachment, did nothing to help people.[50]

That the doctor is compared to a hen implies that Cahan's "resolution" was hardly complete. In America, the heroic revolutionary had
to give way to the pragmatic socialist, a less appealing male model,
and he gave way with great reluctance. The Old World and old prob-

lems were strong magnets, perpetually drawing one back. Despite his advocacy of pragmatism and moderation, Cahan was always attracted to the romance and warmth of his youth, which he associated with his hometown in Russia. "If all is permissible and danger is absent," he wrote, "socialism becomes diluted and revolutionary heroism becomes impossible" [51] Later in life, recalling what the "sacred idea" of socialism had meant to his own development, Cahan wrote, as if of an old and enduring love:

> You are as young to me as I myself was twenty years ago; you give me light in my darkest moments, you give me a shred of self-respect when, in the humdrum course of things, I sometimes lose faith for a moment in my own decency. [52]

It is important to stress these sexual and romantic themes because they reappear so frequently throughout Cahan's writings that they often seem to be the paramount issues. Clearly, other themes are at work here, too. Revolutionary activity is appealing because it joins Jew and Gentile in a higher, "sacred" activity. After joining the movement, for example, Pavel feels that his life has taken on "the infatuation of a moral awakening, of a political religion, of the battlefield." [53] The goal of the movement is the toppling of unjust authority, which is more important than creative political aims, which are rather unformed. In addition, it is significant to note that Cahan here, as in other works, is fascinated with the Russian nobility, and most certainly identifies with them. There is a line of association which connects Orthodox Judaism and the old Russian nobility, both traditional aristocracies, with the revolutionary activists, who represent the true nobility of the present and future. [54]

In a like manner, when Cahan came to the United States, after being forced out of Russia for political reasons, he saw himself as a member of a chosen minority among Jews and immigrants. Once again, this was a courageous, active minority, willing to confront a dangerous world. Being a socialist set him apart from "ordinary immigrants" who were "just running away" from the old country. [55] Again, the theme of heroic masculinity is important in this context. Most immigrants, Cahan felt at the time, were acting out of cowardice and sought America as a mere escape. His escape, on the contrary, was ennobled by danger and provoked by a political quest, in Russia, and in the New World, too.

Revolutionary Russia looms as a constant backdrop in Cahan's works, a past alternately sentimentalized and forgotten, and at times appreciated as a stepping-stone into a new life in America. More often than not, sentiment stifles adaptation to America. A typical theme in Cahan's fiction involves the Eastern European aristocrat (Russian nobleman, Jewish socialist, or Orthodox Jew) who despairs at the loss of spiritual values in America. The story of "Tzinchadzi of the Cat-skills" is illustrative in this respect. Tzinchadzi is a Russian noble-man, now living in America, who constantly mourns his memories of lost love. In the end, he changes his name to Jones, becomes a wealthy merchant, but remains forlorn. He no longer yearns for his old love, but he misses his yearnings. The pain which memory can revive is in itself a form of pleasure as well as an offering of loyalty. "I have thought it all out," Jones says, "and I have come to the conclusion that a man's heart cannot be happy unless it has somebody or something to yearn for."[56]

The heart always draws one back. In *Yekl* the main character, alone in America and liberated from marital responsibilities, is liter-ally haunted by visions of his father. America offers mobility, and with it, delusions of personal freedom. Here physical distance—between America and Europe and within America itself—allows Jake (Yekl) the illusion that he can evade old obligations. Nor is there a strong moral or communal order to provide some sense of direction. Instead, the laws of the state seem distant and impersonal. Their impact on Jake is indirect, though profound, and they help to liberate him from Old World ties. The end of the tale is probably symbolic, with inten-tion: Jake gets a religious divorce from his traditional wife and then goes to the neutral and secular City Hall to marry his Americanized and promiscuous sweetheart. The concluding scenes convey a mes-sage that may or may not have been intentional—that in America sta-bility and order lie in marriage and family, in finding the "right part-ner"[57]

"FANTASTIC EXPERIENCES . . . MARVELOUS TRANSFORMATIONS"

Cahan is fascinated with the transformations which seem to occur in the New World, along with the Jews' ambivalence regarding them. For most immigrants, he suggests, transplantation and mobility promote the *illusion* of change. The heart does not change, nor does the character that was formed in childhood.[58] In the "topsy-turvy world we have here," the formerly poor may become rich, and hypocrisy may be rewarded with wealth and status.[59] Nevertheless the psychological nature of the Jewish immigrant seems to be static.

In Cahan's writings, America is pictured as a land of danger and temptation, usually symbolized by libertine women. In addition, America's decadence is sometimes the reflection of an immigrant's self-image, engendered by guilt at leaving parents, brethren, and tradition behind. The spirit of venture arose in Russia and drove the immigrant toward America, to avoid and correct his father's plight, and possibly—this lingered in fantasy—to replace him. The guilt felt at leaving parents behind only reinforced psychological ties which had never been truly loosened in the Old World, particularly ties to the mother. Parental memories haunt Cahan's characters, inhibiting them from creating healthy relationships in America. Unrequited love, frustrated passions, impotence, and the unsuccessful search for the right woman are their common inheritance. Unresolved personal histories combine with changes in the political and social environment to foster ambivalence and marginality.

Cahan's most powerful work, *The Rise of David Levinsky*, well reflects his concern with estrangement and frustration. Isaac Rosenfeld was close to the truth in describing it as a traditionally Jewish novel.[60] The novel focuses entirely on Levinsky and his apparent success in America through the rise of his garment "house." (The "rise of the house of David" is probably intentional irony.) Levinsky, however, is hardly convinced of his own success. He is a lonely, unhappy man, a wanderer without any essential meaning to his life. In reality, wealth has not transformed him; instead it has taken him further away from his true self, which he associates with childhood. Furthermore, he views his anxiety and sadness as basic Jewish qualities.

> There is a streak of sadness in the blood of my race. . . . I cannot sing myself, but some tunes give me thrills of pleasure, keen and terrible as the edge of a sword. Some haunt me like ghosts. But then this is a common trait among our people.[61]

Levinsky's father had died when he was an infant, and he was reared by a doting mother who wanted him to become a rabbi. The mother is murdered by a gang of toughs whom she had confronted after they had attacked the passive David. After his mother's death Levinsky loses interest in religion; in fact, he loses interest in almost everything. He thirsts "for some violent change, for piquant sensations. . . . Then it was that the word America first caught my fancy." [62]

Like Aleichem, Cahan implies that America appealed to the less serious side of man, to youthful spirits, to the desire for novelty. He also suggests that America appealed to those who were seeking a new identity. Thus Levinsky admits that he was lured to America for reasons other than its great abundance. The United States impressed him as a land "of mystery, of fantastic experiences, of marvelous transformations." [63]

Most likely, Cahan was building, in part, on his own memories of arriving in America. In his autobiography, he relates how American freedom both delighted and baffled him. After a few days in the United States he abandoned his plan to join an experimental socialist community because he began to feel much more attracted to the "seething life" of New York City. The appearance of freedom, in the sense of liberation from prior restrictions, was a constant source of excitement to him. He also recalled, however, that America's freedom confused him, as it warred with his prior image of this country as a "capitalist prison." In addition, the experience of freedom, and its importance, contradicted the conditions of his first jobs, in which he worked "like a slave." [64]

Cahan, like his Levinsky, was attracted to the openness of America. From the start, however, Cahan was sensitive to the perils that Levinsky would not recognize. Levinsky saw the immorality of urban America, and was often repelled. Still, he fell victim to the commercial ethos that dominated American life. In America his aggressiveness is channeled into economic pursuits. Even politics has a basically economic goal—to take over cities and control their wealth.

David Levinsky comes to see American politics as a form of commerce, contractual and unsavory. Significantly, he learns about political parties from a prostitute who describes the party as "a lot of people who stick together." Unconcerned with ideals or justice, American politics seems to rest on personal transactions:

> Favors, favors, favors! I heard the word so often in connection with politics, that the two words became inseparable in my mind.[65]

Politics here lacked seriousness and intellect, rather appearing as a game, a sport, or a way of acquiring personal wealth and power. [66]

The amoral nature of American politics seems related to the real tragedy of men such as Levinsky. Men living without apparent limits are easily deluded into fantasies of individual power, especially through economic pursuits. Moreover, since the political realm subordinates itself to business values, there may be great and dangerous power in economic life. Cahan suggests that such power brings isolation and loneliness, and alienation from the true self.

While Cahan may have intended this as a Marxist analysis, his portrait of Levinsky undercuts its effects. Levinsky is ambivalent in the Old World, before he has even heard of America. A good son and scholar, on the one hand, he is also strongly competitive and extremely envious of his wealthy classmates. Once freed from the restraints of religion and community, he is susceptible to the seductions of American enterprise. [67] Capitalism does not transform Levinsky. It allows him to evade the quest for inner meaning and truth, a quest to which he had never been committed before coming to America. Levinsky's tragedy is that he is mostly aware of his evasions; intimations of a better, more profound life are always close to his consciousness. His attraction to socialists, for example, is based not on their political aims, but derives from the kind of life they seem to lead and that he senses he is lacking. They are more communal, more intense, more Jewish, and more European than his Americanized friends.

For Levinsky, and perhaps for Cahan as well, salvation is symbolized by a woman. [68] The persistent reminder of Levinsky's failure in love also derails the socialist theme. Levinsky's problems in this regard have little to do with socialism or capitalism. He came to America as a young man with a powerful maternal attachment, and with ideas about sex that associated women with Satan. Levinsky is attracted to women who are inaccessible—either because they are married or because they are not interested in him. In addition, the women who attract Levinsky are usually associated with men who have character traits he admires. Dora, with whom he has an affair, is married to a sharp businessman who has helped him. His great unrequited love, Clara Tevkin, is the daughter of an esteemed poet Levinsky remembers from his youth. In another story, an unsteady marriage is held together by the partners' mutual respect for the wife's father, a rabbi recently deceased. Cahan's stress on messianic women may have veiled some confusion over sexual identity, but it also may have screened a lifelong search for an ideal father.

Women are either messianic or satanic, comparable perhaps to the possibilities and dangers which stand behind the mystery of America. At their best, women are the source of the highest ideals as well as the object of the highest sacrifice. At their worst, they are dangerous sinners, best kept at a distance. Cahan often portrays women as heroic revolutionaries and labor leaders, but with like frequency he poses them as superficial, manipulative, and cunning. This is particularly true of Americanized Jewish women. The main character in the story, "A Providential Match" is typically distrustful:

> They look more Christian than Jewish, and are only great hands at squandering their husbands money on candy, dresses, and theatres. A woman like that would domineer over him, treat him haughtily, and generally make life a burden to him. 69

Women are dangerous because they remind man of his passion, his anger, and his fear of dependence. Cahan's characters are moved by great passions, political and sexual, which they are never able to consummate. Levinsky, never happy in love, could reconcile himself with the thought that his rise had helped make American women the "best dressed" in the world. He covered up women and thus seemed to control the passions he feared in himself. Levinsky's plight was linked to dual impulses regarding women: the desire to sacrifice and achieve for a beloved mother, along with the desire to keep women at a safe distance.

In the end, Levinsky remains the same, materially successful by American standards, but inwardly estranged from an America in which he could not commit himself to anything enduring. Moreover, Levinsky has few meaningful ties to his old culture, since he has spurned religion, and also lacks a family life which might connect him to a Jewish community. The socialists, on the other hand, present a more appealing alternative. The socialists have real bonds with the past, a past of heroic models and maternal ideals. They reflect at least a semblance of community—a serious, intense, and committed fellowship. Most important, perhaps, the socialist life provides both political values and emotional support, allowing its adherents to adapt better than the "successful" Levinsky.

For those immigrants who could not accept a religion they viewed as outmoded and reactionary, socialism provided more than a political agenda which could help shape a new world. Socialist theory offered the hope of a future society in which the values of justice and charity could be generalized to all people. This society would be a comfortable place, although at present Jewish socialists were part of an unpopular minority. For this minority, socialism provided a kind of home, and it sometimes provided the models and examples for which the old home seemed no longer relevant.

Clearly, too, the place of the socialist minority replicated the eternal social posture of the Jews, with one major difference. The socialist movement was open to all people and actively sought converts to its creed. Thus the comparison with Christianity which, as we have seen, came easily to a number of Jewish socialist writers. Socialism, like Christianity, was viewed as aggressive and political, whereas Judaism was seen as unworldly and passive. Also, as discussed in the preceding chapter, the tendency to Christianize one's identity was typical of Jews who straddled the worlds of tradition and American modernity.

To men like Cahan, Hillquit, or Abraham Bisno, socialist activism also provided an avenue of assimilation unavailable to most immigrants. It allowed them to learn more about America and to meet older Americans on theoretically equal grounds. It joined men in a movement which seemed to minimize religious or ethnic differences. While bringing them closer to America and an American creed, socialism offered rigorous standards by which to measure and judge America's achievements and failures. It also furnished, as Cahan intimated, a moral orthodoxy, as well as a source of resistance against the seduction of American life. Moreover, its European roots were important in maintaining, often unconsciously, older ethnic ties. Socialism might help a man seek the best in America while warning him of its perils, both personal and political.

Most of these Jewish socialists were apt to acknowledge that the struggle to transform America was frustrating, and possibly futile. The struggle, as I have suggested, was really dual: trying to build socialism in America and concomitantly, fending off the appeal of an amoral freedom to susceptible human natures. In the end, despite the maintenance of personal integrity, there may have been no clear political and social achievements outside the trade union movement.

Cahan lived to see the decline of the Socialist Party during the New Deal, along with the mass defection of Jewish voters which symptomized its fall. Hillquit liked to think that the New Deal proved that socialist agitation had had some effect, although he admitted that the ultimate goal required years of struggle and work. [70] Perhaps Abraham Bisno, twenty-five years before Franklin Delano Roosevelt, was the most realistic:

> There was activity; there was life, active and vigorous life. In the end, it all made for development, for some indefinable end, but there was no coherence in a social way. [71]

While socialism provided a vision of a new world, the veritable new world for all immigrants was America. Without intention, perhaps, those who embraced this creed found a way of enduring their transition to America. For many, in their eventual adaptation to American life, socialism became the sacrifice, and, as Samuel Ornitz inferred, liberalism became its ambiguous replacement. Irving Howe is correct in reminding us that the evaluation of socialism as part of an "inexorable process" of adaptation is overly deterministic and treats too lightly the intentions of the earlier generations. [72] The decline of socialism was not inevitable, nor can we prove that the immigrant's state of mind led directly towards an accommodation with dominant norms in American life. However, we can appreciate the nuances in the thought of new Americans at a particular point in time, and thus hope to comprehend how an eventual accommodation was made possible.

CHAPTER

6

MORRIS R. COHEN: THE JEW AS A LIBERAL

Morris R. Cohen once complained that Louis Brandeis, a man he deeply admired, was limited by the basic themes of the old liberalism, notably a belief in free competition and "a general fear of bigness."

> Having been brought up on the Continental Liberalism of 1848, which was also the liberalism of Jeffersonian democracy, Justice Brandeis naturally speaks in its individualistic terms.[1]

The milieu that nurtured Morris Cohen in his formative years was markedly different from that of Louis Brandeis. Cohen was not a native American. He spent the first twelve years of his life in Russia, which he left in 1892. Unlike Brandeis, whose parents were enlightened German Jews of a middle-class professional background, Cohen was raised in the Orthodox tradition by parents who knew economic poverty for most of their lives.[2]

Like most Eastern European Jews who voyaged to America, Morris Cohen came from a premodern culture in which religion and community were of primary importance. As Isaac Bashevis Singer has indicated, this milieu had begun to feel the impact of modernism even before the start of massive immigration, but its cultural supports were still strongly rooted in tradition. To German Jews such as Brandeis, religion and community were less important than reason and family. They were, as Cohen suggests, somewhat Americanized before coming to America. To those raised in the world view of Russian or Polish Jewry, America was more foreign and demanded a greater adjustment. In addition, as Cohen noted, this adjustment was complicated by the fact that the Jews of Eastern Europe had felt themselves superior to the non-Jewish culture that surrounded them.[3] Ultimately, in his approach to American life, Cohen, like many of his brethren, came to dwell on reason and family. But this apparent similarity obscured significant differences between the old and new immigrants.

Brandeis and Cohen were both "liberals" in their own estimation, yet their approaches to political and social issues differed in significant ways. A socialist in his early years, Cohen was never strongly attached to capitalist institutions or values, of which Brandeis viewed himself as a protector. Cohen chided Brandeis for his individualism, particularly for his emphasis on the "right to privacy," which Cohen viewed as an evasion of human needs and social necessities. While he admired Brandeis's challenge to judicial formalism, Cohen went much further than the justice, criticizing the political role of the Supreme Court as both inappropriate and undemocratic. Cohen, in fact, had a tempered faith in politics which distinguished him from other liberals of that or succeeding generations.[4]

Of equal importance, for our concerns, the two men approached Judaism from very different directions. Brandeis identified himself with Jewish causes late in life, perhaps as a reaction to the emergence of anti-Semitism in Boston in the early part of the twentieth century. He approached Jewish issues from the standpoint of an American progressive, seeing Zionism as an extension of liberal thinking to group and nationality questions. Zionism apparently never led him to any serious thinking concerning Jews in American life. For Brandeis, as it was for many others, Zionism constituted a way of normalizing the Jewish situation.

Cohen's ties to Judaism were established in his early years, becoming somewhat less taut as he grew older. At an age when Brandeis had earned honors in a German "realschule," Cohen was a student of the Talmud in Russia. Coming to New York, he entered into the life of a city with an exceptionally high percentage of Jews in its population. While he came to see Jewish identity as familial and cultural, his background enabled him to map out a personal journey which was both consciously and unconsciously Judaic.

Unlike Brandeis, Cohen was more concerned about Jews in America, perceiving Zionism as basically an evasion of this issue.[5] Zionists, Cohen believed, avoided the basic question of how Jews could live in a secular society. Moreover, he believed that the Enlightenment, to the extent it had truly existed, had helped the Jews. A return to a "glorious past" of poverty and exclusion was ludicrous. Zionism, in his estimation, was fundamentally incompatible with the American tradition. It was illiberal, tribal, and exclusive, susceptible to the "dangers which inhere in all forms of nationalism. . . ."[6]

Cohen's early experiences influenced him in other important respects. His father chose to follow the path of German Jewry in America, starting out as an itinerant peddler in upstate New York. His failure in this line of work led him to sweatshop and factory labor in which he toiled for the rest of his life. His father's experience impressed upon the younger Cohen the cruelty of economic individualism and "the reality of class oppression and the consequent class struggle."[7]

Cohen departed from the Orthodox faith in his teens, reason providing him no evidence of a personal God who could be influenced by human prayers or deeds. Nor could he believe that "the Jewish religion had any more evidence in favor of its truth than other religions."[8] Nevertheless, his Talmudic training and religious upbringing remained as a solid foundation for what he described as "my own journey from the medieval to the modern age. . . ."[9] Like many other emancipated Jews in America, Cohen seemed to refashion an originally religious zeal into a spirited intellectual drive. Talmudic study proved to be of practical value as a whetstone of certain intellectual skills, notably logic and memorization. Eventually logic and scientific method seemed to replace religious orthodoxy as means of organizing the world in a coherent vision.

Cohen professed to love truth and intellectuality as ends in themselves, apart from their practical implications. This affection for impartial truth, Cohen believed, was a trait more apt to be found among Jews than in other groups. It was also a reflection of Cohen's distance from American philosophy and society, both of which he considered to be too enamored with practicality and materialism. Of major contention in his disputes with John Dewey was his insistence that philosophy need not, and often cannot, be useful.[10] Thus, in the first chapter of *American Thought, A Critical Study*, there is an almost bitter tone to Cohen's discussion of American attitudes toward the intellectual life, attitudes which he associated, somewhat inaccurately, with our Puritan past.[11]

This sense of distance from prevailing norms, however, had deeper roots, for Morris Cohen was consciously not entirely of this world. Seeing the use of reason as "the crown of life," he disdained both dogma and experience, warning that excessive worldliness can blind us to our ignorance and the mysteries of existence.[12] Perhaps because of this generalized alienation, Cohen could cling ardently to other American values, especially political liberalism and pluralism. As we shall see, these attachments were not uncritical—Cohen was not orthodox in his liberalism. As an immigrant and a Jew, Cohen saw liberalism as a value to be treasured in a land that was strange from the beginning.

THE NATURAL FAMILY

Cohen's ease with his Jewish background was qualified by a hint of discomfort over his identity as a Jew. His uncharacteristic imprecision in this area could be connected also to some critical assumptions within his general outlook. Jewish identity, he argued, "is not altogether a voluntary affair" determined by one's beliefs. Instead, "we are Jews by descent": "No change of ideology—no matter how radical—can make a man cease to be the son of his parents."[13]

While he assumed that Jewishness is imposed, like it or not, by the accident of birth, he also viewed it as the result of external realities. Group loyalty, he concluded, is a "natural" thing, people being more comfortable with "their own kind." Hence, the exclusion of Jews from various realms of American life must be viewed in terms of the normal inwardness of other groups. We are born into groups, and are perhaps destined by this fact:

> One is born a Jew without being consulted about it, and continues to be regarded as one no matter what moral or religious views he professes.[14]

Since Jews are creatures of birth, background, and "social existence," it is "neither safe nor dignified to ignore our peculiar inheritance."[15] Jews will feel better and contribute more to civilization if they are conscious of their past, understanding its virtues along with its faults. Nor did Cohen mean this in a superficial sense. He advocated, for example, the study of Talmudic Judaism as a part of a larger effort to adapt the traditional religion to some modern conditions. In his writings he frequently cited the influence of a Judaic rearing on his own philosophic views. His was a Judaism without the clear voluntary commitment to God and people which marked the epitome of the old faith. It was an automatic Jewish identity, which others, less familiar with the qualities in Jewish culture which Cohen embraced, might accept as a greater burden than blessing.[16]

It is important to emphasize the somewhat grudging undertone here not to denigrate Cohen's thought, but to point out some regions to which his thinking would not extend. Certainly, there was much practical truth in Cohen's perspective, and it appeared particularly relevant to an age that was rapidly reifying the group (a reification he criticized in *Reason and Nature*[17]). Moreover, he was a man who cherished his citizenship and identified strongly with individual Americans. Consequently, in this area, he may have displayed an unusual sensitivity to prevailing conceptions. Even so, his serious defense of the virtues of cultural diversity and pluralism contrasts sharply with the superficial attention paid to these issues by others dealt with here. Despite the admirable clarity of his intellect, Cohen was a fairly new citizen during a period in which enormous pressures environed the question of assimilation. On a personal level, these pressures combined with changes in Jewish culture to produce ambivalence and inconsistency.

Cohen's unwillingness to identify the Jew with belief tended to reduce Jewish identity to a congeries of traits that history and culture have bequeathed to its current heirs. Jews are characterized, he suggests, by "tenacity," a love of learning, a desire for social betterment, and greater verbal directness than other groups.[18] His emphasis on family and background would make genuine conversion improbable, yet any classification of Jewish qualities surely may include many individuals of Gentile background. Cohen criticized modern Judaism for placing too much reliance on history, for believing that "a knowledge of the past will breed loyalty to it."[19] Seemingly, his own position was not far from this, although he would most likely argue that knowledge would *awaken* loyalties already established.

In respect to the "Jewish question," Cohen leaned towards cultural, if not racial determinism, perhaps because it established personal identity as being beyond argument and apparently beyond tension. For himself, however, the past was inseparable from the actualities of the self, and his own world view derived from a conscious and discriminating study of history. A skeptic toward religion, he nevertheless arrived at a piety in many ways consistent with that of Judaism.[20] Yet his lack of clarity on this issue provided an uncertain standard for others of less learning and profundity.

Cohen liked to calculate the possible longevity of the Jewish people, countering those who feared that Jews were rapidly succumbing to the lure of assimilation. His projections rested on probable rates of intermarriage, assuming again that the family itself had become the key institution of Jewish culture. By making Jewish identity an a priori matter of family, Cohen could discount the spectre of complete assimilation, since the level of Jewish marriages appeared likely to remain high enough to preserve the group. This approach ignored potential distortions or dilutions of Jewish culture, and seemed strangely superficial in contrast to his obvious concern with spiritual values and personal belief.[21]

Of greatest importance, Cohen's stress on familial and cultural influences in regard to Jews seemed to contradict his philosophic emphasis on reason and logic. Might not logical analysis lead some men to reject their family and ethnic group? Are all families virtuous? Logic, too, assumes the ability to make an independent judgment, to use one's "free mind," even concerning the influence of one's background. Even though group interaction appears to be natural (which, for Cohen, seemed to mean unconscious, or fixed by early training), there are often those within a cultural group who are quite detached from its social life. In addition, it is plausible that Jewish parents might consciously raise their children to reject their background— and for these children volition might be a critical issue.

The position which Cohen took on these matters thus bore a certain resemblance to that of others we discussed earlier, especially Brandeis, Kallen, and Antin. Family comes to represent traditional, sometimes archaic attachments, usually separate from the more secular society and public life. Family becomes the repository of emotion, if not irrationality. While Cohen struggled to go beyond the rigid distinctions between tradition and modernity, and private feelings and public beliefs, so typical of older liberals, he was still in part captured by them. Accordingly, Cohen implied a division between reason and nature in his relations with his family:

> I have a right and indeed a duty to profess any ideas which seem to me true and change those views if I am given reasons for doing so. But my having been born in my particular family and my natural association with my kindred are not a matter for argument.22

There is an intimation here that the intellectual realm is separate from the familial, that intellectual freedom may indeed have to be unexpressed within kindred ties. Family and culture teach us a way of life, good or ill, and invariably contribute to the irrational bases of our personality. Moral judgments, Cohen asserted, derive from attitudes and feelings that are "habitual." This bedrock of personality, "the roots of our accustomed faith," is difficult to overcome, and leads us to "almost instinctively abhor" certain attitudes in other people. 23 Thus the strength of logic, in part, derives from its ability to liberate us intellectually from the restrictions of our background and personality. So, too, the appeal of liberalism derives from the fact that it enables us to exceed the bounds of our "hereditary class prejudices." 24 In sum, philosophy permits the individual to transcend the limitations of birth and upbringing, and serves, in a sense, as a way of adapting to the larger world.

> Every one of us in born into a certain class of beliefs which are considered absolute truths. Philosophy enables us to analyze and compare these "absolute" truths and find their relative values.25

For Cohen, the "absolute truths" and "hereditary class prejudices" of his background and personality were associated with the paternal traditions of Judaism. His own father was a distant figure, a man who worked alone in America for a few years before he could bring his family across. Reared during his formative years by an often tyrannical Orthodox grandfather, Cohen came to see "oriental" tradition as authoritarian and narrow-minded. 26 His emphasis on matrilineal Judaism—being a Jew by descent through the mother—must be seen then as the other side of his rejection of the paternal tradition.

Cohen's reconciliation with Judaism required a Christian mediator, the philosopher-educator Thomas Davidson, who reminded him of the biblical prophecy: "In thy seed shall all the nations of the earth be blessed!"[27] Davidson urged him to pursue and "live truth," to disdain worldly goods, and to appeal to the heroic in one's self and in fellow men. Cohen described his relationship with Davidson as being "like that of an affectionate father and son."[28] His identification with Davidson was a fortuitous path of adjustment to the New World—learning from an American who taught him to seek universal truth as a Jew.

Davidson's teachings built upon earlier lessons which Cohen had absorbed from his grandfather, particularly the value of being distant from excessive worldliness. In truth, despite his hereditary and cultural approach to Judaism, and his oft-stated skepticism, Cohen was attracted to religious thought and rhetoric.[29] His approach to liberalism, as we shall see, was colored by a view of human nature which the old religion had taught. Outwardly skeptical about monotheism, Cohen nevertheless avowed a belief that "there was a God of morality, but even beyond this there was a God of nature."[30] His Judaic training fostered a sense of alienation from this world, at the same time instilling a faith in the possibilities of human action and improvement.

Within Judaism, Cohen identified with the prophetic tradition against the patriarchal formalism of Orthodoxy. Witnesses of God, criers against injustice, the prophets were the symbols of the search for eternal truth, symbols that joined Jew and Christian. As rebels against dogma, they stood on the perimeter of worldly affairs, judging, castigating, and reminding men of their errors. Similarly, Cohen viewed logic and scientific method as universal measures of truth, liberating us from the bonds of traditionalism, yet preventing our falling prey to the anarchy of modern life. The philosopher's role, moreover, combined prophet *and* priest, preserving eternal truths, as well as the *search* for eternal truths:

> ... philosophers, I take it, are ordained as priests to keep alive the sacred fires on the altar of impartial truth, and I have but faithfully endeavored to keep my oath of office as well as the circumstances would permit.[31]

Cohen's peculiar liberalism swung between a concern with eternal truths (for example, truths of human nature) and a constant reminder of eternal tests for truth. His approach was usually negative—to arrive at wisdom by comprehending fallacies, resolving contending forces, and showing that truth was a precious complexity somewhere beyond the thoughtless certainties which most of us cherish. More often than not, Cohen seemed fascinated with destroying false idols of intellectual authority, using logic as a "weapon" to decipher "the dizzy whirl of change." [32] The effect of this was to establish Cohen's reputation as a narrowly critical philosopher, rather than as a creative thinker. [33] While there is some truth in this charge, it overlooks the consistent premises which were at the foundation of his analytic style, and it denigrates the creative potential in the critical role.

THE PHILOSOPHER'S CALLING

Cohen was a philosopher for whom liberalism was primarily an intellectual phenomenon. As an intellectual, he was admittedly detached from the world of affairs which he knew was, more often than not, an illiberal world. Most men, he confessed, under the normal conditions of stress in modern life, could not be expected to be tolerant or open-minded. Human nature itself was a basic limitation. Self-interest moved most people toward a natural concern with the results rather than "the rules of the game." [34]

Liberalism, then, as an intellectual phenomeon, was mainly confined to the life of the university and academic societies. Yet even in these realms it remained more an ideal than a reality. Men of science, Cohen allowed, are probably not any more tolerant or politically liberal than those in different careers. Since "tolerance is a virtue that seems to thrive only in a certain leisure, in a certain cultivation," then it would seem that philosophers are most likely to approach the genuinely liberal temper. [35] Given their detachment, Cohen believed that they should assume the special responsibility of protecting the standards of liberal civilization. Accordingly, in respect to intellectual life, a serious philosopher should claim a form of magistracy by employing the rules of logic to ensure order, censure fallacy, and critically judge all apparent truths. [36]

Philosophers ought to protect the rules of intellectual discourse—the validity of reason, the need for evidence, and the value of experimentation—in the face of a world which is often pressured to abuse them. Thus philosophers are not and ought not be political men. Politics is an art with standards only occasionally complying with those of science and philosophy. The example of Cicero, Cohen believed, indicates the wisdom of philosophic men refraining from affairs of state. A political man should be able to employ the intellectual rules of philosophy, knowing full well their limitations in the affairs of men. (They might teach him, for example, that he should be illiberal in many cases.) Cohen, as well, hardly purported to be a philosopher of politics. He was, on his own terms, a gadfly of politics, a critic whose standards were the ideals of liberal civilization. For Cohen, a philosopher might be king, but in his own realm separate from, though possibly above, political life.

There is an almost medieval note to Cohen's thoughts on this subject. Philosophy, he argued, is vital to a culture because it embodies aspects of our essential nature. The love of play, the desire to think, as well as curiosity and wonder are traits common to humanity, but which may be suppressed or encouraged given the quality of the culture in which we live. Just so, a philosopher whose work may have no practical "utility" has a vital calling, peculiar to his talents and inclinations. He is a thinker, distinguished by his fealty to the standards of reason and investigation. This calling naturally involves a responsibility—to these standards and to society at large. Indirectly, then, philosophy has a relationship to politics, if not *over* politics. As Cohen described it, the philosopher has an "office" with obligations to assess and judge the community to whom he is responsible.[37]

Since the pleasures of the mind are generally discouraged in America, the philosopher who accepts his calling is something of a rebel. Here, the natural fascination with motion as equivalent to "the blessed life" crowns pragmatism as our national philosophy, sacrificing philosophic distance to "our thinly optimistic faith in the mechanical law of progress. . . ."

> Against this view, the wisest and best of mankind—those, at any rate, whom mankind most reveres: the prophets, the great religious leaders, the artists, the great scientists—are a continuous protest.[38]

There is a clear parallel here with Singer's position, as well as with that of traditional Judaism. For Singer, a Jew must be witness to eternal questions and mysteries, a nay-sayer to the myths of modernism.

Similarly, for an Orthodox Jew, the keeping of the covenant through Torah represented both loyalty to the Almighty and "a continuous protest" against the transgressions of most men. For Cohen, the true philosopher may have to alienate himself from the ways of the world, and in America, from the ways of other philosophers, too. Singer, of course, argues deeper that a Jew may also have to alienate himself from the ways of other Jews.

American philosophy, Cohen advised his colleagues, has an excessive fear of "other-worldliness."[39] Chance, uncertainty, and mystery are realities which scientific progress obscures but cannot deny. Fearful of social alienation, American intellectuals either feel compelled to prove their social usefulness or are overly concerned with changing a world from which they feel distant. The best course is that of personal discipline, intellectual rigor, and a "wise resignation" to human limitations and the world man has made. Thus Cohen, often prizing his alienation, stood on the outside of the philosophical mainstream—a "stray dog" in his own description—constantly returning to "eternal truths [which] demand eternal repetition."[40]

BETWEEN TWO WORLDS

Cohen tended to interpret the American reality from the perspective of an immigrant. Writing in an era when domestic attitudes towards immigration were increasingly negative, Cohen continually emphasized the importance of immigration in American history. The immigrant, he argued, has made the dominant contribution to the special virtues of the American experience: the idea of America as a land of promise and hope; the enduring belief in popular sovereignty; and the image of America as a non-imperialist nation. The vitality of American liberalism in the nineteenth century was based on "the absence of besetting fear."[41] The immigrant brought optimism and energy to the American scene, continually infusing it with the spirit of adventure and opportunity. Twentieth-century America, more closed and sensitive, is beset by fear of foreign ideas now symbolized by the newly arrived immigrant. Cohen believed that immigration and the frontier spirit were the key elements in American liberalism, as well as "the dominant forces that have produced whatever is distinctive in American thought. . . ."[42]

It would be a mistake, however, to place Cohen among those who glorified the immigrants' background. In his autobiography he related how East Side Jews sometimes embellished their experiences for the sake of the willing ears of American journalists. The ghetto he knew had more than spirit—it had poverty, hard work, crime, and unhappy men in taxing, tedious jobs. Many Jewish homes, he recalled, were rent by "explosive tension" between the generations. Moreover, most immigrants came from cultures which, despite their virtues, were often narrow and repressive. It was the *process* of immigration (the "heroic epic" of his parents) and assimilation which contributed that valuable dynamic to American life. Immigrants were mobile, open to change, and resilient.[43]

If Cohen avoided romanticizing the ghetto, he still saw profound differences between urban and rural life in this country—to the favor of the former. He viewed the cities as seedbeds of liberalism, where toleration and mutual understanding are forced upon people by the very conditions of survival. In cities the intellect is broadened by the variety of cultural types; ethnic self-consciousness fosters both the unique and the universal. Small towns and rural areas, on the other hand, promote either narrow conformity or an old-fashioned individualism discordant to the needs of modern society. In the city a person is freer to choose his friends, while at the same time he can preserve a necessary anonymity. Reversing the Jeffersonian image, Cohen saw danger to the best American traditions emerging from the hinterlands, from small farmers who compose the most conservative group in society.[44] In other words, he viewed traditional American culture as he viewed all traditional cultures, as often narrow and conservative.

This culture, he conceded, has had its virtues. Developing out of Calvinist roots, rural life in America has been characterized by its emphasis on self-government and political decentralization. Calvinism also encouraged the growth of democratic representation as well as a "democratic temper," derived from the belief in our general equality before God.[45] At the same time, Cohen argued, our strong religious heritage has been responsible for many of the flaws of American life. Our often exceessive individualism, our fear of government, the social pressures which urge conformity—these, among other things, are also the bequests of our Puritan past. In this regard, Cohen saw no difference between early and late Puritans, thus tracing our lust for business back to the original Puritans. [46] While "traditional Americans" were once immigrants also, seemingly their conservatism derived from their religious background, the fact that they have become settled in America, and the rural nature of their cultures. [47]

Pressures to conform clashed with the cultural pluralism which immigrants had brought to American life. Cohen placed great value in pluralism in both philosophy and politics. The use of reason teaches us the fallacy of monistic explanation. More important, it indicates the limits of human knowledge and hence the need for intellectual humility in a world of unknown possibilities. There are many paths to truth and the good polity is one which encourages the journey by keeping the roads open. America had been particularly blessed by the concordance of demography with philosophical process: The continuing stream of immigrants has induced tolerance while concurrently depositing new values and ideas on the American earth. Still, Cohen's pluralism stopped short of dogma. While cultural pluralism and political decentralization were important values, they ought not be generalized. Extreme pluralism could indeed be dangerous, threatening human individuality with the pressures of the small group, while denying the state its rightful sovereignty. "The evils of an absolute state," he wrote, "are not cured by the multiplication of absolutes." [48] Furthermore, in modern society centralized economic and social policies are often a necessity.

Although Cohen valued America as a "blessed" country, there were aspects of American life which consistently dissatisfied him. His critique reflected the ways in which America fell short of immigrant (and human) needs, and the extent to which pluralism often went unrealized. Along with other immigrants, he lamented the dilution of European values in this country. The acceptance and creative use of leisure, respect for the intellect, a stronger sense of community, and a deeper emotional life—these echoes of de Tocqueville resound throughout Cohen's works. Like Ravage, Cohen often found native Americans cool and reserved, apparently lacking in intensity and self-understanding. Jewish students at City College, he recalled, were not afraid to carry an analysis of ideas "beyond the points where polite conversation generally stops." On the other hand, "the more placid Western students . . . were less interested in bringing to light their own first principles. . . ." [49] Cohen's pluralist ideal—and he was frank to admit that it was an ideal—involved the coupling of European and American virtues: Americans need to be taught the wiser use of freedom.[50]

However much Cohen cherished America's liberal environment, he was also sensitive to its limitations. Liberalism frees us intellectually from the bonds of tradition and from our ingrained prejudices. Liberalism also provides tolerance as well as an atmosphere of political freedom. Yet, for Cohen, this negative freedom was not in itself the key issue. All legal systems "protect certain kinds of freedom and suppress other kinds."[51] Individual freedom, too, could not be separated from social responsibility and communal goals; our individual actions inevitably redound in the social sphere. In a sense, all men are born guilty, with responsibilities to society and their fellow citizens.[52] Freedom, he urged, is a social and political issue, requiring serious debate and analysis. A liberal environment needs limits as well as direction, forms of guidance to which all men can contribute. Most important, as we shall discuss later, Cohen implied that it requires a political focus.

Ultimately, however, Cohen's assessment of American liberalism was touched by inconsistency, influenced perhaps by his ambivalence as an immigrant. The European virtues lacking in America, especially personal intensity and emotional depth, unavoidably chanced those vices which Cohen associated with traditional cultures—prejudice, irrationality, and repressiveness, for example. The connection seems inevitable, moreover, because Cohen often intimated that emotions are bound to habits and instincts that are almost natural to our character. The basic strength of a liberal philosophy, according to Cohen, is its ability to transcend these possibly inherent traits of character: it frees us *intellectually* from the "limitations of our hereditary class prejudices."[53] To refer to prejudice as "hereditary," however, is to evade the issue. Physical factors which signal prejudice in the anti-Semite are inherited, but not the prejudice itself. The implication of this comment is that prejudice is natural, and ineradicable, and that liberalism allows us on one level—the intellectual—to escape it. Thus Cohen's view of liberalism suggests an irreconcilable division between intellect and emotion, and possibly between thought and action. In addition, this makes liberalism but an uncertain guide to action, since the "real" world does not offer a solid foundation for liberal values.

Cohen was attuned to these difficulties, and struggled with them, generally reconciling himself to liberalism as an intellectual process. Yet liberalism still left its adherents between two worlds—the world of family, tradition, and the realities of human nature, and the world in which truth is pursued for its own sake. This general division does not discount other possibilities which Cohen essayed, such as liberalizing one's religion, or attempting to implant one's tradition into American intellectual life. Yet one man is small, and tradition and culture are monuments difficult to dislodge. Always suspicious that the desire for solutions was a human conceit and weakness, Cohen opted to endure the difficulties but remain true to them. [54]

LIBERALS AND JEWS

Cohen's liberalism rested on unlikely supports. He rejected, for one thing, many of the hallmarks of the older American liberalism—individualism, the glorification of freedom, the belief in inevitable progress, and the judicial a priori rationalism which likened the Constitution to holy writ. At the same time, he was reticent to embrace the prescriptions of twentieth-century reformers who were unwilling to attempt necessary intellectual and institutional changes. Thus his consistent call for the dimunition of the Supreme Court to a purely judicial role separated him from other critics who wanted to change the philosophy of the Court.

His deviation from traditional liberalism began with his conception of human nature. Older liberals, such as Brandeis, were usually less concerned with this matter, stressing instead natural rights or individual potential. Cohen saw human nature as essentially divided by contrary tendencies. People had a basic desire to know and learn, but were also characterized by a "will to illusion" which subverted their efforts. Man desires to express individuality and free choice, but may also seek to evade decisions, preferring to lose himself in a higher cause or in another's personality. Our ability to think and reason is often outweighed by an unfathomable irrationality. To a great extent our personal development depends on how and what we are taught, and the good teacher tries to liberate our minds by exposing the fallacies which frequently govern them:

... though I am liberally skeptical I have a firm faith that if you remove
certain obstructions the free mind will thrive by its own energy on the
natural food it can gather from its own experience.[55]

This positive faith in human intellect which has been tutored to
"know the false" is one of the bases of Cohen's liberal spirit. Our souls
are moved by freedom and fear, the one impelling us toward expansion and growth, the other restricting and organizing our efforts. Both
are necessary, or inevitable aspects of life, and the best we can strive
toward is an intelligent balance between these forces. Ages, along with
individuals, are often characterized by the dominance of one or another of these emotions. In fact, Cohen tended to conceive of all human activity in polar terms, similar to his analysis of human nature.[56]

Faith in human potential therefore had to be a tempered faith because human history is characterized by permanent evil and great
tragedy. Liberal historians had erred in their "jaunty and atrociously
optimistic belief in the inevitability of progress. . . ."[57] Even in the
best of times, human nature is fairly constant, and our faith must coexist with a fatalistic presumption of human travail.

Cohen's emphasis on the need for wise teaching also characterized
his political vision, particularly his critical evaluation of the Supreme
Court. Cohen's critique of the American political structure derived in
the main from his concern with law, a concern which he perceived as
an outgrowth of his early Talmudic studies. The Hebraic conception
of the law, like the Greek, differs from the liberal view which sees the
law as a brake on human freedom and individuality. Ever since his
childhood, Cohen recalled, he had viewed the law as an assertion of
the right *way*, "a pattern of life," instead of a system of rules which
were necessarily alien to the individual.[58] Men are by nature "full of
deadly tendencies" along with the potential for kindness and love.
Law, like Torah, indicates the way to the good life which must involve
restrictions on human freedom. Like the Puritans of whom he was so
critical, Cohen believed that the law of a good society is "wisdom organized to combat natural evil."[59]

In the United States, however, the law was often enmired in unfair-
ness and confusion. Not only was the law wrongfully administered in
many cases (especially in regard to labor), but it was the product of
both philosophical and political illegitimacy. American legal thought
had been anchored in an old-fashioned natural rights theory which

viewed the Constitution as scripture and the judge as mere interpreter. Beneath the language of natural rights was embedded an individualistic social philosophy unrealistic in its premises about human nature.

Cohen assailed the problem from various perspectives. A primary danger was the illogic of permitting an eighteenth-century document to govern the contemporary scene. While a Constitution is desirable as a guide to positive action, it ought not be held sacrosanct. Furthermore, as Beard had shown, the Constitution was written by men of a philosophical bent opposed to democratic government. Historical precedent, while worthy of respect, may be wrong or irrelevant to current ethical problems. Rational analysis, experimentation where possible, human experience, and a respect but not obeisance to traditional rules must all be brought to bear on contemporary problems.

In Cohen's view, this was only part of the morass into which law was sunk. Of equal danger was the way in which contemporary law was made. The mythology of jurisprudence in the United States would have us believe that judges hand down decisions already immanent in the Constitution. This "phonography-theory" of the law, as he called it, belied the fact that judges had social and political philosophies, the more influential because they were unarticulated. The effect of this has been to confound the legal and moral, and to endow judges with undue political power. Political and moral responsibility was deflected from the people and the legislature to the courts, where judges were often not of high quality. The legitimacy of law, instead of resting upon rational, ethical, or political foundations, derived instead from the perpetuation of myth.[60]

Ultimately, Cohen believed, the problem could only be alleviated by a change in political structure. The dogma of the separation of powers, borrowed from Montesquieu, had obscured the practical sovereignty of the judicial branch. Judges have traditionally been private lawyers, usually aligned with conservative business interests. Their judicial role and often narrow social background have separated them from contemporary reality, which is certainly much more accessible to a more numerous legislative body. Even our greatest judges, Cohen added, have been ignorant of social and economic matters crucial to proper decision making.[61]

The obvious conclusion is that the American legislature, like the

British Parliament, should make the law. If it is unwise to permit a multimembered bicameral body to make the law because human nature cannot be trusted, then how much more unwise is it to grant this power to nine insulated men? Cohen claimed no illusions regarding political action. Nevertheless, he believed that it was clearly demonstrable that men are capable of legislating intelligently. Progress, by no means inevitable, is possible. American government, founded on fear and the frustration of political action, must be permitted to act and to plan, if necessary.

> It is argued that government is influenced by popular passion, while business is dictated by deliberate judgment. But the passion may be generous, and the deliberate judgment of business men directed to pecuniary profit may have evil consequences.[62]

Cohen's faith in the potential of political action was based more on the particular virtues of the legislative branch—its large membership, its greater intimacy with public issues, and its style of debate and compromise—rather than on a wholesale belief in democracy itself. Cohen found some of the social manifestations of democracy to be quite repellant. Courting "King Demos" often meant a lowering of cultural standards as well as a vulgarization of complicated truths. His perception of individual "callings" taught him that all were not equal; not all men could be highly educated, for example. Cohen's appreciation of the contemplative life attracted him to elements of aristocratic society, or to the genuine bourgeois culture of nineteenth-century liberalism. Still, democracy reflected the basic truth of our *general* equality before the infinitude of our ignorance, or perhaps before the majesty of God. Democracy also symbolized the best of the American experience—"the promise of freedom for the development of human energy, liberated by free education and the abolition of hereditary class distinctions."[63]

This qualified confidence in legislative politics, distinctive as it was in relation to the anti-politics of many reformers, fit snugly into Cohen's broader liberal approach. To Cohen the legislature seemed a superior forum because it provided a better law-making *process*. While his anger at the Supreme Court was instigated by the conservatism of its decisions, his criticism tended to focus on the ways in which structure and process had sabotaged wisdom. Although his political affiliation was that of a moderate socialist, he came to it by means of a liberal methodology, which itself remained his primary loyalty. Liberalism, however much he might attempt to confine it to means rather than an end, was really much more. It was an ennobled faith, "a faith in a process rather than in a set of doctrines...."[64] Moreover, it was a faith which allowed its devotee a detachment from worldly battles and hazardous doctrines.

Just as socialism served as a higher moral and intellectual focus for some Jews, so too did Cohen's approach place him above what he perceived as the narrow limits and fallacies of most political disputes.[65] This approach, he advised, allows us to evaluate alternatives and devise new solutions. It separates us from the passions of partisan conflict, although sometimes it provokes the hostility of all those involved. Liberalism, then, elevates the individual above his own passions and prejudices along with those of others, but still provides a relevant direction to political life.

As a Jew, Cohen deemed liberalism to be an absolute necessity. America's liberal spirit had offered the Jew a new homeland, while protecting his right to be himself. Thus Jews had the greatest stake in liberalism and should preserve its virtues with a watchful eye. Anti-Semitism is often but a forewarning of a broader attack on democracy. Since Jews had been most susceptible to the evils of reaction, they had a special sensitivity and responsibility in this domain. They held "the teacher's supreme obligation, that of sharing knowledge."[66] Jews, like philosophers, must be the guardians of liberal civilization.

In terms of practical politics, the same lesson pertains. Jews are almost *bound* to side with the liberals:

> It is true . . . that the only friends we have in America today *are* the liberals, and if we should do anything to antagonize them by adopting an anti-liberal philosophy, we should certainly cut ourselves off from any possibility of having the cooperation of any part of the American public when we are in trouble.[67]

Given the nature of Cohen's liberalism, these strictures would require that all Jews become detached scholars or that Jews withdraw from social and political action. Cohen advocated neither, but he did know that men are usually not liberal.[68] Hence, while Jews may not adopt an "anti-liberal philosophy," given his assumptions about human nature, they will probably not *act* liberally, and if they do, their actions might be foolishly sacrificial or plainly unwise. Moreover, based on Cohen's definition of a liberal, how could liberals be partisans, and how could Jews a priori be partisan to them?

Clearly, from these perspectives, liberalism represents to the Jew more than an admirable intellectual approach. Cohen implied that Jews have both a personal and political interest in supporting all forms of liberalism. The weakness of the Jews demands their support for certain cultural values—reason, pluralism, and free discourse, for example—almost as a kind of political position. Although many human inclinations are repressive, Jews should neither act on them, nor encourage them in others, since Jews will probably suffer. Since Cohen assumed a distinct separation between a logical approach and an often illiberal reality, this creates an unavoidable dilemma for the Jew. Should a Jew support the political stance of liberals, because they are his friends, even when logical analysis may show this position to be fallacious?

Most important, Cohen's position implies that Jews ought to preserve a fair distance from political conflict. Jews can be critics, judges, and intellectual arbiters, but political action itself may imperil their always vulnerable status. It is significant that Cohen's major political effort, his creation and leadership of the Conference on Jewish Relations in the 1930s, was basically an attempt to apply a liberal intellectual approach to Jewish affairs. It was an attempt to facilitate political action by establishing the facts through abstract analysis. This scholastic approach provides the Jew with an apparently neutral sphere on the edge of political life, although relevant to it. This tenuous and difficult position might assuage the tension of being a citizen and a Jew at the same time.

On this and many levels, liberalism represented a compromise for Morris R. Cohen. Because of this, perhaps, Cohen himself, beyond the appeal of his intellect, was an attractive and mediatory figure to both energetic immigrants and older Americans disillusioned with accepted intellectual patterns. "His life," one writer has commented, "was a field on which the inheritors of two cultures met to talk and look each other over."[69] Between tradition and modernity, ethnic ties and the lure of assimilation, and political estrangement and political commitment, liberalism provided a "free city" for the anxious soul. It offered an escape from the rigidities of the past along with a rigorous critique of the fallacies of the present. It also allowed its adherents, in important but incomplete ways, to maintain a Jewish identity on American soil.

CHAPTER
7
CONCLUSION

Contemporary interpretations of Jewish political thinking in America often agree on certain critical points. First, it is usually assumed that Jews are dependable liberals, an eternal minority group inevitably concerned with human rights and social justice. Jews vote Democratic—in spite of economic prosperity—and are commonly on the left wing of the Democratic Party. Studies of student radicals as well as Peace Corps volunteers show that a disproportionate number of these young people have Jewish backgrounds. Secondly, many analysts argue that Jewish liberalism can be traced, directly or indirectly, to Judaism itself—to the prophets' call for social justice or to the Torah's emphasis on justice as charity. These sources, combined with the special sensitivity of a persecuted minority group, have made Jews incline toward the left. Daniel Elazar, for example, intimates that liberalism has become an aspect of Jewish identity: "The Jews of the 1960s vote Democratic because they are liberals in the way their fathers voted Democratic because they were Jewish."[1]

Elazar goes on to assert that "the Jews demonstrated from the first that they shared the same political culture as the old line Yankees . . . the moralistic political culture."[2] This political culture, derived essentially from Old Testament law and prophecy, reflected the "classical Jewish" approach. Jews, from this perspective, have always been liberals and progressives in this country, fighting the battles of the

French Revolution on American soil. Predictably, Elazar almost entirely discounts the Diaspora experience before America, as well as *its* relationship to classical biblical ideas. The American experience, he believes, has helped Jews revert to their genuine traditions, which are biblical and political.

> Though classical American political thought owes much to classical Jewish political ideas, the most that can be said of the great majority of the Jewish immigrants (who came to America with little political knowledge or concern) is that their Jewish heritage predisposed them to be perhaps tangentially receptive to the fundamental American political ideas.[3]

Elazar comes close to making the same argument that Antin, Ravage, and Ornitz made years before: Jews and Christians are really very similar, and being part of an American Christian culture has brought Jews closer to their own roots. By linking modern Jews with their more political roots among the ancients, Elazar ignores the political alienation and skepticism that were part of life in the Diaspora. Moreover, the similarities between the Jewish tradition and that of American Protestants, while significant, cannot erase the differences between these cultures, including those of political background and experience.[4]

Other analysts of Jewish life in America have also stressed proclivities towards liberalism and political activism. Irving Howe, for example, noting the "highly disproportionate" number of Jews in radical and protest groups, suggests that activism is important to Jewish distinctiveness in modern America because it perpetuates the sense of a unique tradition. For Howe this vigorous political tradition descends from the age of Jewish socialism.[5] Similarly, Stephen D. Isaacs, in a recent book, lauds the "Jews' hyperactivity in politics," which he regards as "the ultimate proof of their Americanization."[6] However, unlike Howe and Elazar, Isaacs derides the "myth" of Jewish liberalism, explaining Jewish political attitudes as the product of distrust and insecurity, a defense against conservatism instead of an assertion of an inherent idealism.

Undoubtedly these interpretations of Jewish political attitudes are not without truth. Nevertheless, as I have already implied, what they exclude or ignore is often as significant as what they emphasize. Many

Jews are on the left, and Jews generally are more socially and politically active than the average American. Yet *most* Jews, like most Americans, are not politically active. [7] Thus an explanation of their distance
from political life might be as useful as one which interprets the activism of a minority. In addition, we have seen how complex the inclinations of some earlier politically minded Jews really were, and how they
often maintained a sense of alienation from American life. Moreover,
many Jews who have pursued political involvement have sought the
borders of political life. Isaacs, in this regard, constantly relates current Jewish political activity to traditional modes, especially that of
the court Jew. While this involvement might be illustrative of Americanization, the forms it takes—the fund-raiser, the staffer, the
scribe—are often marginal to the essence of American politics. [8]

These explanations also fail to appreciate the full import of Judaism and the Jewish experience in political terms, picking and choosing
instead those aspects of the religion which seem to support Jewish political energy. Howe is correct in citing the influence of the Jewish
socialist tradition, but there are traditions of resignation and unworldliness which have been important as well. Elazar, as already indicated, generally discounts the Diaspora view of political life which
governed Jewish culture for almost two thousand years, a view which
emphasized distrust of politics, rather than commitment. In truth,
the Jewish religious tradition contains enough variety to inspire conservatism as well as radicalism, and apathy along with commitment.
Hence the religious interpretation of Jewish liberalism and activism is
based more on rationalization than fact, omitting elements of Judaism that have been essential to it. As Philip Roth has perceptively
noted, this neglect might be a result of the Holocaust experience: an
attempt to deny the alleged "passivity" of Jews by stressing mastery
and power. [9]

This conscious concern with the past and its meaning, and this
attempt to explain, if not legitimize, the present by wedding it to a
tradition are efforts perhaps more important than the accuracy upon
which they are based. They indicate in contemporary Jews an orientation which their forebears felt with similar intensity: the desire for a
unique and continuous identity in a world where Jews can live like
everybody else.

We have seen how some Jewish immigrants, in their American

metamorphoses, clung to old attitudes and roles, sometimes altering them, sometimes inventing new ones. We have seen how immigrant Jews preserved a sense of distance if not alienation, how they created social and political roles which compared to Diaspora experience, and how they often opted for irresolution in the face of an attractive America and a powerful, and sometimes equally attractive Jewish tradition.

In these respects, the Jewish experience has not been unique, although it has probably been more intense than that of other ethnic groups. For most immigrants, loyalty to group and tradition, as well as crises of identity, were hardly abstract issues. For Jews, however, a path separate from the nations had been a way of life, a demand which penetrated time and place. To Jewish-Americans these issues have been more intense because they derive from religious and social realities which have endured for ages, inscribed in a written tradition which has been an unavoidable reminder of the past. Moreover, unlike other groups which have an "old country" that might invigorate the past through ties of kinship and sentiment, Jews have been bereft of this connection, most obviously since the Holocaust, but to some degree even before. Israel has aspired to this role, although its qualifications are ambiguous. The Jewish settlement in America is larger and, in a sense, older than that in Israel. Besides, Israel's secularism, as well as its efforts to modernize and dispel an Old World image, make it an uncertain source of tradition.[10] The concern of Jewish-Americans with the past, of which this work itself is an example, thus might reflect an attempt to find an "old country," and a continuous identity, even within the American experience.

As we have seen, the issues which emanated from the transplantation of Jews to America had a more profound effect on Eastern European Jews than on their German predecessors. German Jews came generally from an enlightened background which prepared them well for the liberalism they would seek out in America. Furthermore, the faith which many retained in religion was often a private faith, which could adjust easily to an America in which personal belief seemed protected and was ostensibly separate from the public sphere. While many German Jews regarded the United States, and Judaism, as illustrative of universalist ideals, later Eastern European immigrants, particularly the socialists, would use a universalist ideal to critique

America, and often their fellow Jews. If, for the Germans, the cosmo-
politan ideal was fixed firmly in American liberal democracy, some of
the later immigrants would find it in socialism, or in a "judaized"
modern liberalism. In certain ways, the German Jews did create a
model of political adjustment—specifically, for someone like Mary
Antin, and generally in the sense of attempting to establish American citizenship on the basis of a creed. Some, like Oscar Straus and
Louis Marshall, and in subsequent years Marcus Ravage, would relate to the American polity in terms of its spirit and fundamental
beliefs.

As the example of Brandeis best indicated, some of the early generations began to feel a need to reform American life, along with Jewish-American life as well. Americans needed a new cause or inspiration, which many looked for in a renewal of private religion and
others, such as Brandeis, in the Zionist movement. Just as Schiff and
Straus aspired as Jews to epitomize American values, Brandeis would
argue that Jews, but especially Zionists, displayed the choice qualities
of the American character. Ultimately, America itself, the older
America of individual freedom and achievement, was the real model,
as Brandeis injected into Zionism the traits he cherished in America.

Brandeis saw the true end of reform as the rebuilding of character
in Americans and Jews. However, this notion of character was essentially independent of communal influence and support. Individual
character was the groundwork of "self-reliance," allowing its posses-
sor to rise above community into a more mobile society.[11] To many of
the Eastern European Jews discussed here, however, personal development depended more on the spirit and quality of the community, on
its laws both formal and informal. Their traditional origins made
them more sensitive to the distinctively modern aspects of American
culture, inducing both attraction and repulsion. Their need for spiritual substitutes to traditional Judaism led many to probe and analyze
American beliefs, cognizant as they were that society and culture are
teachers of the growing person.[12]

Even for those who embraced the substitutes, the religious tradition
lingered in the background, a point of departure and a possible point
of return. Surely the appeal of religious rhetoric to people like Cohen,
Antin, or even Ravage bespoke more than a fealty to parents or to the
immediate past. Guilt drew people back, but sometimes the guilt

paralleled and obscured a genuine emotional appeal which seemed irrational, if not embarassing, in the modern era.

In modern America, immigrants encountered a political realm which also represented a possible alternative to tradition. Too, immigrants such as Cohen, Singer, and Heschel, recognized the importance of law and politics, seeing them as sources of teaching and moral direction. Some Jews, accustomed to a religious commitment which transcended human limitations, sought political substitutes that could never suffice. The Diaspora experience had taught that political loyalties must always be partial and secondary. In freer, more accepting America where religious faith was less of a magnet, one had to wrestle with the temptations of politics as a primary, and consuming loyalty, whether it be to the nation or to a political faith. Some, like Singer and Cohen, accommodated themselves to what we might call a "loyal alienation," involving the courage of criticism as well as a necessary distance from the "ways of the nation." For Singer, this position has also involved criticism, albeit indirect, of the ways of Jews when they have strayed from the path of questioning.

Political adaptation seemed to conclude in an ambiguous liberalism which, as Samuel Ornitz suggested, preserved older concerns but permitted a relaxation of commitment. If Cohen and Ornitz are any guide, the liberalism toward which the Eastern Europeans tended supported older attitudes as much as it assimilated newer ones. As this study suggests, the political thought of Jewish immigrants often maintained older conceptions of politics, even in indirect form. Indeed, Morris R. Cohen, one of the most avowedly liberal of those studied here, was at the same time a complex thinker whose liberalism departed from the standard mold. Liberalism for Cohen was fundamentally an intellectual faith, which involved skepticism and separatism, not succumbing to the fallacies of past or present. Singer, more skeptical and traditional, has implied that all politics, however necessary, chances dangerous responsibilities, and that modern politics only magnifies the dangers as it enhances the power. Unlike American conservatives, however, Singer does not place great faith in individual or societal actions as an alternative to politics. Singer distrusts all human power, all human attempts to deny mystery.

Singer, Cohen, and Aleichem come closest to the older Jewish view of political life which the Diaspora had nurtured. Confronted with the

complexity of modern America, they clung to a preference for perennial wisdom, even if it could now focus mainly through negation—
through knowing the false. In this view, the Jewish role was one of
posing questions, critically judging the terms of political and social
debate, or avoiding politics to dwell on eternal human problems. Thus
what emerges from many of those studied here is less a philosophy of
politics than a philosophic stance towards politics. Others, Cahan or
Antin, for example, were less satisfied with their distance from the
nation, and wrestled with the dilemma in different ways, without any
clear resolution. Yet even Cahan, more politically oriented than the
rest, as a novelist was mainly concerned with individual problems in
modern society. He endeavored, with the others, to deny modern
politics, to show that the state is both beyond perennial human problems and before eternal mysteries.

   This work also indicates that for many Jewish immigrants it was the
prophetic tradition within Judaism that held the greatest appeal. The
prophet, like many of these immigrants, paced the perimeters of political and social life, chancing the ostracism of society, while seeking
to echo its true values and perhaps forgotten concerns. The prophets
lacked formal political power, yet spoke of eternal truths that could
transcend and possibly shape the environment of practical politics.
For immigrants who embraced concerns which separated them from
Jewish-American as well as from American culture, this tradition of
protest, with its relevance to politics along with its distance from it,
may have appeared most appropriate.

   Traditional Judaism always distrusted political power as a danger
to a higher loyalty. Moreover, the intimacy of power and religion was
considered a possible hazard to spiritual and intellectual growth,
since it gives to ideas the seductive protection of doctrine. Wedded to
power, thought tends to become detached from inquiry and questioning becomes a potential danger to the state. In place of this, Judaism
offered a covenant of faith and community, a "spiritual home" for the
Orthodox and unorthodox, and a tradition of law and morality. Politics was limited to the vulnerable realm of local and organizational
life, where it was secondary to higher religious concerns and the need
for group survival.

   In an age when much of the old way of life has fallen into the realm
of anthropology, it is important to recognize those remnants of the

past that may endure in our midst. Cultures often change slowly, and the "hydra-head" of tradition sometimes stands stubbornly behind a modern facade. This book points out some of the ways in which older political attitudes lingered into the immigrant experience. As suggested earlier, these attitudes may still be immanent within contemporary experience.

The past, even when its outlines have been accurately approached, need not serve as an autocratic "guide to the perplexed." Many immigrants discovered, with the title figure of Herman Melville's *Redburn*, that the old guidebooks no longer seemed to fit the patterns of the new city.[13] They carved out roles and clung to attitudes that represented compromises between separatism and participation, and between the Jewish tradition and their perception of America. For some, these compromises may also have been "holding actions"—affirmations, however unsure and incomplete, of older modes which no longer had a safe place in the logic of contemporary life.

Nevertheless, if the search for Jewish identity relies on history and tradition, one is bound to wrestle with the realities of the past, despite their conflict with present aspirations. Prior experience can neither be duplicated nor felt. Traditions are easily created or romanticized. Still, probing into history can convey to us essentials, general truths, that broadly defined the conditions of existence. Where one seeks identity through the past, these essentials become inevitable sources of guidance.

Years ago, the philosopher Ahad Ha-Am asserted that the endurance of Jews in the modern world required the "Judaization of politics" rather than the politicization of Judaism. The "Judaization of politics," in his view, had less to do with politics itself than with the assertion of values that could pervade and direct political life. Instead of changing the world, serving humanity, or pursuing the other compromises toward which they have been oriented, Jews, Ahad Ha-Am argued, should continue their true mission—"a fulfillment of their own duties . . . an end to which everything else was subordinate. . . ."[14] Jews must persist in a way of life, involving not mere loyalty to tradition, but loyalty to traditional questions as well. This persistence, he urged, was an end valuable in itself, and was not part of any service to the world.

To pursue this mission in America would involve changes so major that they can only exist as distant standards. There would have to be a renewal of religion, in its almost literal sense—a relinkage or "binding back" with an older faith, an adaptation not necessarily a reproduction of it. It would demand a genuine cultural pluralism, a "transnational America" in Randolph Bourne's terms or Michael Novak's current vision.[15] Obviously, too, there would need to be a reassertion of localism, along with the vitality of local political life.

These changes appear unlikely, if not illusory, and perhaps, in the face of the impetus of modern life, "holding actions" are all that can be expected. Nevertheless, the prototypes of pluralism, local government, and communities built around questions of belief exist within both Jewish and American history. For those who examine the past, as if in search of something lost or true, they endure as inescapable points of direction.

APPENDIX

BIOGRAPHICAL SKETCHES

MARY ANTIN

Born in Russia in 1881 of middle-class parents, her family emigrated to America in 1893. She was educated in Boston schools and later at Columbia Teacher's College in New York City. She won acclaim in 1912 for *The Promised Land*, but published only one book thereafter. She lectured extensively between 1913 and 1918, but her public career ended with a nervous breakdown at the end of the decade. She died in 1949.

ISAAC BERKSON

Born in 1891 in New York City, Berkson was an educator and a philosopher of education. He received an advanced degree at Columbia Teacher's College, where he came under the influence of John Dewey. A director of the Central Jewish Institute, he was also supervisor of the New York City Bureau of Jewish Education. He taught both philosophy and education at the City College of New York. He died in 1975.

ABRAHAM CAHAN

Born in Vilna, Russia, in 1860, Cahan came to America as a young man for political reasons. Arriving in New York at the age of 22, he worked in the sweatshops while studying law at night. However, his interests drove him toward writing and literature in which he won a reputation as a journalist and man of letters. Editor of the *Jewish Daily Forward* for fifty years, Cahan also authored many works of fiction, including the immigrant classic, *The Rise of David Levinsky*. He died in 1951.

MORRIS RAPHAEL COHEN

Born in Russia in 1880, he came to the United States at the age of 12 with his large family. He was educated in the New York public schools, the City College, Columbia University, and Harvard. He later taught for many years at City College. Cohen's major philosophical interests included logic, law, and the philosophy of history. A man of wide-ranging intellectual interests, he wrote for liberal journals and in his later years published his major philosophical works, including *Reason and Nature* (1947). He died in 1947.

JOHN COURNOS

Born in Russia in 1881, he journeyed in early adolescence with his family to America where they settled in Philadelphia. Cournos worked in various jobs, including newspaperman, before going to Europe in 1913. In 1917 he published *The Mask*, the first novel of a trilogy, centered around the autobiographical character, John Gombarov. Cournos wrote other works of fiction along with literary essays, poetry, and translations before his death in 1961.

ABRAHAM JOSHUA HESCHEL

Born in Poland of old religious family, Heschel attended religious and secular schools in Poland and Germany. He came to America in the 1930s. He taught at the Jewish Theological Seminary and many other institutions. Rabbi, author, and lecturer, Heschel published many books, including *The Prophets* (1962) and *God in Search of Man* (1955). He died in 1972.

MEYER LONDON

Born in Russia, he came to the United States as a young man. Here he studied law and began practicing around the turn of the century. He was active in the socialist politics of the Lower East Side of New York City, running for the State Assembly, and then for Congress. In the years during and after World War I, he was the only Socialist representative in Congress, where he became a constant dissenter. He died in the 1920s.

SAMUEL ORNITZ

Born in New York City in 1890 of newly arrived immigrant parents, Ornitz studied at City College and New York University and spent ten years in various forms of social work. After publishing *Haunch, Paunch, and Jowl* (1922), Ornitz went to Hollywood where he spent many years writing for films and theater. After World War II he was blacklisted as part of "the Hollywood Ten." He died in 1951.

SHALOM RABINOWITZ (*Sholom Aleichem*)

Famed Jewish writer and humorist, Aleichem was born in Russia in 1859 and died in the United States in 1916. He lived only a few years in this country toward the end of his life.

ISAAC BASHEVIS SINGER

Born in Poland in 1904, the son and grandson of rabbis, he studied to be a rabbi but forsook a religious calling to become a writer. Before coming to the United States in 1935, Singer was a journalist and translator in Warsaw. In the United States, although writing exclusively in Yiddish, Singer has become a major contemporary author.

ANZIA YEZIERSKA

Born in Russia in 1885, Yezierska came to the United States in 1901. She worked her way out of poverty, went to college, and published stories and novels which received sympathetic and sometimes enthusiastic reviews. Her *Hungry Hearts* (1920) won her a reputation along with a Hollywood contract. In later years she worked as a journalist and essayist.

NOTES

INTRODUCTION

1. Gilbert K. Chesterton, *What I Saw in America* (New York: Dodd, Mead, 1923).

2. See Louis Hartz, *The Liberal Tradition in America* (New York: Harcourt, Brace, 1955). On religious thought in America, see Sydney Ahlstrom, *A Religious History of the American People* (New Haven, Conn.: Yale University Press, 1972). On the idea of an American "civil religion," see Russell E. Richey and Donald Jones, ed., *American Civil Religion* (New York: Harper & Row, 1974).

3. A valuable, although dogmatic, treatment of the costs of becoming an American may be found in Michael Novak, *The Rise of the Unmeltable Ethnics* (New York: Macmillan, 1971). See also some of the essays in Thomas Wheeler, ed., *The Immigrant Experience* (Baltimore: Penguin, 1972).

4. Thomas Jefferson, "Notes on Virginia," in Albert Ellery Bergh, ed., *The Writings of Thomas Jefferson* (Washington, D.C.: Thomas Jefferson Memorial Association, 1907), II: 118-21.

5. W. Lloyd Warner and Leo Srole, *The Social Systems of American Ethnic Groups* (New Haven, Conn.: Yale University Press, 1945).

6. Exod. 19:6.

7. Jacob Katz, *Exclusiveness and Tolerance* (London: Oxford University Press, 1961) is a good survey of the issue of separation.

8. On the status of "covenant" thinking in modern Judaism, see Eugene

Borowitz, "Crisis Theology and the Jewish Community," *Commentary* 32 (July 1961): 36-42, and *A New Jewish Theology in the Making* (Philadelphia: Westminster, 1968). See also Abraham Joshua Heschel, *God in Search of Man* (New York: Farrar, Straus, & Cudahy, 1955).

9. Erik Erikson has similarly noted the traditional and modern impulses in Jewish life as a factor in German anti-Semitism. See his essay, "The Legend of Hitler's Childhood," in *Childhood and Society* (Middlesex, Eng.: Penguin, 1965).

10. David Singer, "Voices of Orthodoxy," *Commentary*, 58 (July 1974): 54, 60; and Mark Wischnitzer, *To Dwell in Safety* (Philadelphia: Jewish Publication Society, 1948).

11. On the Jewish "Enlightenment," consult Michael A. Meyer, *The Origins of the Modern Jew* (Detroit, Mich.: Wayne State University Press, 1967); and Jacob Katz, *Out of the Ghetto* (Cambridge, Mass.: Harvard University Press, 1973), and *Tradition and Crisis* (New York: Free Press, 1961).

12. John Winthrop, "A Model of Christian Charity," in Perry Miller, ed., *The American Puritans* (Garden City, N.Y.: Doubleday, 1956) is a relevant example. For an example of later literature, see Ole Rolvaag, *Giants in the Earth* (New York: Harper, 1928).

13. Charles Liebman treats a similar theme, "survival versus integration," in his study, *The Ambivalent American Jew* (Philadelphia: Jewish Publication Society, 1973). The issue of Jewish participation was stressed by native Americans, as in Mark Twain's "Concerning the Jews," in Charles Neider, ed., *The Complete Essays of Mark Twain* (Garden City, N.Y.: Doubleday, 1963).

14. See Leo Baeck, *The Essence of Judaism* (New York: Schocken, 1948) for a discussion of pluralism within traditional communities.

15. Stuart Rosenberg discusses these issues in *The Search for Jewish Identity in America* (Garden City, N.Y.: Doubleday, 1965).

16. Isaac Deutscher, *The Non-Jewish Jew, and Other Essays* (New York: Hill and Wang, 1968).

17. Quoted in Irving Howe, *World of Our Fathers* (New York: Simon & Schuster, 1976), p. 641.

18. John Murray Cuddihy attempts this kind of analysis in *The Ordeal of Civility* (New York: Basic Books, 1974).

CHAPTER 1

1. Much of this discussion draws on the major points of Part One of Hannah Arendt, *The Origins of Totalitarianism* (New York: Harcourt, Brace, 1966), although the emphasis here is somewhat different. See also, H. G.

Adler, *The Jews in Germany* (South Bend, Ind.: University of Notre Dame Press, 1969) and P.G.J. Pulzer, *The Rise of Political Anti-Semitism in Germany and Austria* (New York: Wiley, 1964).

2. See Pulzer, *Rise of Political Anti-Semitism*; and Arendt, *Origins of Totalitarianism*, especially pp. 21, 24. On this era, see also Fritz Stern, *The Politics of Cultural Despair* (Garden City, N.Y.: Doubleday, 1965).

3. See Michael Selzer, ed., *Zionism Reconsidered* (New York: Macmillan, 1970).

4. Philip Roth's essay, "The New Jewish Stereotypes," is an excellent statement of this concern. It is reprinted in Selzer, *Zionism Reconsidered*, from *American Judaism* (Winter 1961).

5. Michael Selzer, *The Wineskin and the Wizard* (New York: Macmillan, 1970), and *Zionism Reconsidered*, notably his introductory essay. Similar issues are raised in Georges Friedmann, *The End of the Jewish People?* trans. Eric Mosbacher (Garden City, N.Y.: Doubleday, 1967).

6. See Jacob Katz, *Exclusiveness and Tolerance* (London: Oxford University Press, 1961); and Louis Wirth, *The Ghetto* (Chicago: University of Chicago Press, 1928).

7. Arendt, *Origins of Totalitarianism*, p. 23.

8. Ibid., pp. 8, 23.

9. Charles Liebman, *The Ambivalent American Jew* (Philadelphia: Jewish Publication Society, 1973), especially chapter 7.

10. Salo W. Baron, *The Jewish Community*, Vols. I-II (Philadelphia: Jewish Publication Society, 1942), I: 208. Among other sources used in this discussion of Jewish political institutions are Louis Finkelstein, *Jewish Self-Government in the Middle Ages* (New York: Feldheim, 1964); Mark Zborowski and Elizabeth Herzog, *Life Is With People* (New York: International Universities, 1952); and Selzer, *Wineskin and the Wizard*.

11. See Deut. 14:25, 16:11, among many similar references.

12. Deut. 1:17; and Exod. 20:3.

13. Selzer, *Wineskin and the Wizard*, p. 221; also pp. 213-36.

14. Leo Baeck, *The Essence of Judaism* (New York: Schocken, 1948), pp. 51-55.

15. Quoted in Theodore Reik, *Jewish Wit* (New York: Gamut, 1962), p. 29.

16. 1 Sam. 8:7.

17. 1 Sam. 8:20.

18. 1 Sam. 12:13-15; see also 1 Sam. 15:24.

19. Baron, *Jewish Community*, II, especially chapters X, XI, XVI.

20. Selma Stern, *The Court Jew*, trans. Ralph Weiman (Philadelphia: Jewish Publication Society, 1950).

21. Exod. 18:19-20.

22. Exod. 4:12, 15.
23. Isaac Bashevis Singer, *In My Father's Court* (New York: Farrar, Straus & Giroux, 1966), p. viii.
24. Baron, *Jewish Community*, II: 86.
25. The literature on the "tzaddik" and Hasidism is large. One recent example is Elie Wiesel, *Souls on Fire: Portraits and Legends of Hasidic Masters*, trans. Marion Wiesel (New York: Random House, 1972).
26. This aspect of the pre-American experience is covered in Ezra Mendelsohn, *Class Struggle in the Pale* (Cambridge, Eng.: Cambridge University Press, 1970); and in Ronald Sanders, *The Downtown Jews* (New York: Harper & Row, 1969).

CHAPTER 2

1. See Lee M. Friedman, *Pilgrims in a New Land* (Philadelphia: Jewish Publication Society, 1948); and Stephen Birmingham, *The Grandees* (New York: Harper & Row, 1971).
2. On the German Jews in America, see Henry L. Feingold, *Zion in America* (New York: Twayne, 1974), especially chapters V and VII; Anita Libman Lebeson, *Pilgrim People* (New York: Harper, 1950); and Stephen Birmingham's popular treatment, *Our Crowd* (New York: Harper & Row, 1967).
3. Ande Manners, *Poor Cousins* (New York: Coward, McCann & Geoghegan, 1972); and Irving Howe, *World of Our Fathers* (New York: Simon & Schuster, 1976), especially chapter 2.
4. Michael A. Meyer, *The Origins of the Modern Jew* (Detroit, Mich.: Wayne State University Press, 1967); and Jacob Katz, *Out of the Ghetto* (Cambridge, Mass.: Harvard University Press, 1973).
5. Quoted in H. G. Adler, *The Jews in Germany* (South Bend, Ind.: University of Notre Dame Press, 1969), p. 51.
6. Quoted in Adler, *Jews in Germany*, p. 36.
7. Meyer, *Origins of the Modern Jew*.
8. Isaac Mayer Wise, *Reminiscences*, trans. and ed. David Phillipson (Cincinnati, Ohio: Leo Wise, 1901), p. 331.
9. On these questions, see Israel Knox's excellent biography of Isaac M. Wise, *Rabbi in America* (Boston: Little, Brown, 1957).
10. Naomi Wiener Cohen, *A Dual Heritage, The Public Career of Oscar S. Straus* (Philadelphia: Jewish Publication Society, 1969), p. 73.
11. Oscar S. Straus, *The American Spirit* (New York: Century, 1913), pp. 291-92. See also Oscar S. Straus, *The Origin of Republican Form of Government in the United States of America* (New York: Putnam, 1926).

12. Louis Marshall, "The American Jew of Today," *Harper's Weekly* 49 (December 2, 1905).

13. The charter is reprinted in Charles Reznikoff, ed. *Louis Marshall, Selected Papers and Addresses*, Vols. I-II (Philadelphia: Jewish Publication Society, 1957), I: 30.

14. Louis Marshall to Rev. Dr. Joseph Stolz (Dec. 12, 1906), in Reznikoff, *Louis Marshall*, I: 22.

15. Marshall was a member of the Board of Directors of the National Association for the Advancement of Colored People. He also gave legal aid to several minority groups. See Morton Rosenstock, *Louis Marshall, Defender of Jewish Rights* (Detroit, Mich.: Wayne State University Press, 1965), pp. 28-29.

16. See Hannah Arendt, *The Origins of Totalitarianism* (New York: Harcourt, Brace, 1966); and Selma Stern, *The Court Jew*, trans. Ralph Weiman (Philadelphia: Jewish Publication Society, 1950).

17. On the involvement of Jews in politics during this period, consult Lawrence Fuchs, *The Political Behavior of American Jews* (Glencoe, Ill.: Free Press, 1956).

18. Judah Benjamin of the Confederacy was a prominent forerunner. Oscar Straus and Henry Morgenthau had served as foreign ambassadors, and Straus had also held a Cabinet post under President Theodore Roosevelt.

19. Melvin Urofsky, *A Mind of One Piece, Louis Brandeis and American Reform* (New York: Scribners, 1971), p. 151.

20. Most of Brandeis's references to political parties were hostile.

21. One story about Brandeis quotes him as saying that a Zionist speech by Nahum Sokolow in 1913 "brought me back to my people." This story is related in Melvin Urofsky, *American Zionism from Herzl to the Holocaust* (Garden City, N.Y.: Doubleday, 1975), p. 126.

22. The conservative nature of progressivism is stressed in a number of works. See, for example, Gabriel Kolko, *The Triumph of Conservatism* (New York: Free Press, 1963); and James Weinstein, *The Corporate Ideal in the Liberal State* (Boston: Beacon, 1968).

23. Quoted in Alpheus Thomas Mason, *Brandeis: A Free Man's Life* (New York: Viking, 1946), p. 28.

24. Brandeis to Howard White (Feb. 6, 1913) in Melvin Urofsky and David W. Levy, eds., *The Letters of Louis D. Brandeis*, Vols. I-IV (Albany: State University of New York Press, 1971-75), III: 25.

25. Max Lerner, "The Social Thought of Mr. Justice Brandeis," in Felix Frankfurter, ed., *Mr. Justice Brandeis* (New Haven, Conn.: Yale University Press, 1932), p. 10.

26. Dean Acheson, *Morning and Noon* (Boston: Houghton Mifflin, 1965), p. 96.

27. Brandeis to Jacob de Haas (Aug. 7, 1917), in *Letters*, IV: 302.

28. Louis Lipsky, *A Gallery of Zionist Profiles* (New York: Farrar, Straus & Cudahy, 1956), p. 156.

29. See Mason, *A Free Man's Life*, p. 39.

30. Brandeis to Joseph R. Marble (July 21, 1913), in *Letters*, III: 45.

31. Alpheus Thomas Mason, *The Brandeis Way* (Princeton, N.J.: Princeton University Press, 1938), p. 31.

32. Interview in *Current Literature* (March 1911).

33. Norman Hapgood, *The Changing Years* (New York: Farrar and Rinehart, 1930), pp. 184-201, especially p. 199: "One of Justice Brandeis' constant objections to material excess is that it stops the conquest by the spirit of our own universe; it makes us no longer active inside but passive."

34. Brandeis to Amy B. Wehle (Jan. 20, 1877) in *Letters*, I: 14.

35. Brandeis to Alfred Brandeis (March 26, 1921), in *Letters*, IV: 546-47.

36. Brandeis to Alfred Brandeis (Oct. 16, 1914), in *Letters*, III: 330-31.

37. Brandeis Letter to the Editor, *Jewish Daily News* (Nov. 5, 1915), in *Letters*, III: 631.

38. This was an element in Chaim Weizmann's eventual clash with Brandeis. Weizmann, for example, preferred the more earthy Louis Marshall, even though Marshall's attitudes on Zionism were for many years less positive than those of Brandeis. See Chaim Weizmann, *Trial and Error* (New York: Harper, 1949).

39. Quoted in Mason, *A Free Man's Life*, p. 604.

40. Brandeis to Harold Laski, quoted in Alexander Bickel, *The Unpublished Opinions of Mr. Justice Brandeis* (Cambridge, Mass.: Harvard University Press, 1957), p. 120.

41. Brandeis to Frederika Brandeis (July 20, 1879), in *Letters*, I: 42.

42. Bickel, *Unpublished Opinions*, p. 124.

43. Brandeis to Felix Frankfurter (Jan. 16, 1921), in *Letters*, IV: 528.

44. Paul Freund, "Mr. Justice Brandeis: A Centennial Memoir," *Harvard Law Review* (March 1957): 770.

45. Bernard Flexner, *Mr. Justice Brandeis and the University of Louisville* (Louisville, Ky.: University of Louisville Press, 1938).

46. *Gilbert v. The State of Minnesota*, 254 U.S. 325.

47. Quoted in Mason, *A Free Man's Life*, p. 585.

48. Brandeis to Norman Hapgood (July 21, 1917), in *Letters*, IV: 300.

49. Ibid., p. 300.

50. Quoted in Mason, *A Free Man's Life*, p. 520.

51. Brandeis was undoubtedly aware of the political capital involved in making an issue into a question of democratic procedure. This may account in part for the fact that while he usually appeared to be a democrat in princi-

ple, he did not always appear to be a democrat at heart.

52. See, for example, Acheson, *Morning and Noon*, chapter 5.

53. Brandeis to Julian W. Mack (Nov. 17, 1920), in *Letters*, IV: 506-07.

54. Acheson, *Morning and Noon*, p. 100.

55. Brandeis to Caroline Hibbard (March 18, 1913), in *Letters*, III: 48. The influence of Frederick Louis Taylor on Brandeis's commitment to efficiency is obvious.

56. Brandeis's letters are remarkable for their concentration on facts and logistics. Even his Zionist correspondence, written during the difficult days of World War I, is almost entirely devoid of emotional response to the sorry plight of the Jews abroad. One of his strongest published letters conveys his feelings about commercial espionage, which he called "nasty" and "nauseating" See Brandeis to Felix Frankfurter (Nov. 26, 1920), in *Letters*, IV: 510.

57. "The Road to Social Efficiency," in Louis D. Brandeis, *Business A Profession* (Boston: Small, Maynard, 1914), p. 51.

58. Jacob de Haas, *Louis Dembitz Brandeis: A Biographical Sketch* (New York: Bloch, 1929), p. 152. This work includes full transcripts of many of Brandeis's Zionist speeches, along with excerpts from some others.

59. de Haas, *Louis Dembitz Brandeis*, pp. 161-62.

60. Hapgood, *The Changing Years*, p. 197.

61. de Haas, *Louis Dembitz Brandeis*, p. 176.

62. Ibid., p. 179.

63. Ibid., p. 172.

64. Ibid., p. 157.

65. Ibid., p. 199.

66. See Andy Logan, *Against the Evidence* (New York: McCall, 1970); and also Manners, *Poor Cousins*.

67. de Haas, *Louis Dembitz Brandeis*, p. 168.

68. Brandeis to Alfred Brandeis (April 23, 1921), in *Letters*, IV: 552.

69. Brandeis to David Lublin (Sept. 29, 1918), in *Letters*, IV: 356.

70. Brandeis's neglect of socialism here is significant.

71. See Urofsky, *American Zionism*, chapter 7. See also Yonathan Shapiro, *Leadership of the American Zionist Organization, 1897-1930* (Urbana, Ill.: University of Illinois Press, 1971).

72. de Haas, *Louis Dembitz Brandeis*, p. 190.

73. Brandeis to Lydia Littman (Dec. 2, 1914), in *Letters*, III: 380.

74. Brandeis to Horace Kallen (Feb. 10, 1915), in *Letters*, III: 426-27.

75. Quoted in Cohen, *Dual Heritage*, p. 144.

76. See Urofsky, *American Zionism*, p. 226.

77. On Marshall's pessimism, consult Louis Marshall to Irving H. Fisher (Aug. 14, 1922) in Reznikoff, *Louis Marshall*, II: 819.

78. Naomi Wiener Cohen, *American Jews and the Zionist Idea* (New York: Ktav, 1975); and Urofsky, *American Zionism*.

79. The economic basis of anti-Semitism in America is explored in Carey McWilliams, *A Mask for Privilege* (Boston: Little, Brown, 1948).

80. Marshall to Chaim Weizmann (Jan. 17, 1927), in Reznikoff, *Louis Marshall*, II: 762.

81. Quoted in Urofsky, *American Zionism*, p. 141.

CHAPTER 3

1. On the immigration of Eastern European Jews to America, consult Mark Wischnitzer, *To Dwell in Safety* (Philadelphia: Jewish Publication Society, 1948). Political activism in Russia is discussed in the early chapters of Ronald Sanders, *The Downtown Jews* (New York: Harper & Row, 1969).

2. See, for example, Abraham Cahan, *The Education of Abraham Cahan*, trans. Leon Stein, Abraham Conan, and Lynn Davison (Philadelphia: Jewish Publication Society, 1969).

3. Bruno Bettelheim, *Children of the Dream* (New York: Macmillan, 1969), develops this point in contemporary perspective.

4. Another alternative, important at the time but not elaborated on here, was Shimon Dubnow's nationalism, which attempted to secure a place for Jews as a distinct group within Eastern Europe. See S. M. Dubnow, *Nationalism and History: Essays on Old and New Judaism* (Philadelphia: Jewish Publication Society, 1958).

5. Marcus Eli Ravage, *An American in the Making* (New York: Harper, 1917), p. 46.

6. See Isaac Bashevis Singer, *The Estate* (New York: Farrar, Straus, & Giroux, 1969); Abraham Cahan, *The Education of Abraham Cahan*, and *The Rise of David Levinsky* (New York: Smith, 1951); Mary Antin, *The Promised Land* (Boston: Houghton Mifflin, 1912); and other works cited here for examples of these types.

7. David Singer, "Voices of Orthodoxy," *Commentary* 58 (July 1971): 54, 60.

8. On the Jewish settlement in New York, consult Moses Rischin, *The Promised City* (New York: Harper & Row, 1970). On the early experience of immigrants in general, see Oscar Handlin, *The Uprooted* (Boston: Little, Brown, 1951).

9. Samuel Gompers, *Seventy Years of Life and Labor*, Vol. I (New York: Dutton, 1925), p. 23.

10. Ravage, *An American in the Making*.

11. Morris Rosenfeld, *Songs from the Ghetto*, trans. Leo Wiener (Boston:

Copeland and Day, 1898).

12. An eloquent expression of this is Mario Puzo's essay, "Choosing a Dream," in Thomas Wheeler, ed., *The Immigrant Experience* (Baltimore: Penguin, 1972).

13. On immigrants and politics, see James Davies, *Human Nature and Politics* (New York: Wiley, 1963), pp. 194-212.

14. Emma Goldman, *Living My Life* (New York: Knopf, 1931), p. 1.

15. Singer, *The Estate*, p. 175.

16. Ahad Ha'Am (Asher Ginzberg), "Imitation and Assimilation," in Ahad Ha'Am, *Essays, Letters, Memoirs*, trans. Leon Simon (Oxford, Eng.: Phaedon, 1946); and Erik Erikson, "The Legend of Hitler's Childhood," in *Childhood and Society* (Middlesex, Eng.: Penguin, 1967).

17. Elia Tcherikower, *The Early Jewish Labor Movement in the United States*, trans. Aaron Antonovsky (New York: Yivo Institute, 1961), p. 73.

18. See Abraham Joshua Heschel, *God in Search of Man* (New York: Farrar, Straus, & Giroux, 1955).

19. The works dealt with here were all written in, or translated to, English. Thus I necessarily exclude an extensive literature of great value written in Yiddish or Hebrew. As noted earlier, this absence is mitigated by the emphasis here, which is on forms of adaptation and assimilation.

20. Cahan, *Education of Abraham Cahan*, p. 18.

21. This theme is obviously not unique to this chapter. It is also apparent in the discussion of Abraham Cahan in Chapter 5 and of Morris R. Cohen in Chapter 6.

22. Cahan, *Education of Abraham Cahan*, p. 282.

23. Sholom Aleichem (Shalom Rabinowitz), *The Adventures of Mottel, The Cantor's Son*, trans. Tamara Kahana (New York: Collier, 1953), pp. 333, 282; 254-255, 33. On Aleichem in America, consult Maurice Samuel, *The World of Sholom Aleichem* (New York: Knopf, 1962).

24. Aleichem, *Adventures of Mottel*, pp. 339, 334. See also the brilliant piece, "Otherwise, There's Nothing New," in Sholom Aleichem, *Some Laughter, Some Tears*, selected and trans. Curt Leviant (New York: Putnam, 1968), pp. 238-239.

25. See especially Aleichem, "Otherwise, There's Nothing New"; and "Progress in Kasrilevke," in Sholom Aleichem, *Stories and Satires*, ed. Curt Leviant (New York: Yoseloff, 1959).

26. See Curt Leviant's "Introduction" to Aleichem, *Some Laughter, Some Tears*.

27. Aleichem, *Adventures of Mottel*, p. 260.

28. Mary Antin goes furthest in her glorification of nature in *From Plotzk to Boston* (Boston: Clarke, 1899), but especially in *The Promised Land*, in

which she describes the earth as her "mother" and "teacher" (p. 132). The theme of a "return to nature," usually associated with sentiment for the Old World, was typical of many works. There is also the possibility, hinted at in recurrent symbolism, that "nature" was identified with immigrant origins through its association with the ocean voyage to America, which represented a new birth to many immigrants. For examples of these themes, see Harry Roskolenko, *The Time That Was Then* (New York: Dial, 1971); Samuel Ornitz, *Haunch, Paunch, and Jowl* (Garden City, N.Y.: Garden City, 1923); Gregory Weinstein, *Reminiscences of an Interesting Decade, The Ardent Eighties* (New York: International Press, 1928); and Ravage, *American in the Making*.

29. Cournos's hostility towards America and Americanization is most vividly expressed in John Cournos, *The Mask* (New York: Doran, 1920). This was the first of an autobiographical trilogy, centering on the character of "John Gombarov."

30. John Cournos, *Autobiography* (New York: Putnam, 1935), p. 218.

31. This theme is pervasive in *The Mask*. Similarly, it is important in his *Autobiography*, wherein he asserts that it was his fate in America "to face the world and struggle" (p. 245).

32. Cournos, *Autobiography*, pp. 244, 256. See also, John Cournos, *O'Flaherty the Great; A Tragi-Comedy* (New York: Knopf, 1927).

33. Cahan, *Rise of David Levinsky*; and Ornitz, *Haunch, Paunch, and Jowl*. Bernard Sherman notes the influence of Spencer in *The Invention of the Jew* (New York: Yoseloff, 1969).

34. Cournos, *Autobiography*, p. 229.

35. Ibid., p. 215. See also, on England, John Cournos, *Babel* (New York: Boni and Liveright, 1927).

36. Cournos, *Autobiography*, p. 218.

37. Ibid., p. 342. Again see *Babel* for this theme.

38. Cournos, *Autobiography*, p. 287.

39. Ibid., p. 342.

40. John Cournos, *A Modern Plutarch* (London: Thornton Butterworth, 1928).

41. Heschel, *God in Search of Man*, pp. 46, 169.

42. Ibid., p. 171. See also Abraham Joshua Heschel, *Man Is Not Alone* (New York: Harper & Row, 1966).

43. Abraham Joshua Heschel, *The Prophets* (New York: Harper & Row, 1962), p. 211; and Heschel, *God in Search of Man*, p. 46.

44. Mordecai Kaplan, *Judaism as a Civilization* (New York: Yoseloff, 1957).

45. Heschel, *God in Search of Man*, p. 117.

46. Ibid., p. 284; also, pp. 286-96.

47. See Abraham Joshua Heschel, *The Insecurity of Freedom* (New York: Farrar, Straus & Giroux, 1966).

48. A question not dealt with is whether "holy" political action can heighten our awareness of God.

49. W. H. Auden, "Introduction," to Anzia Yezierska, *Red Ribbon on a White Horse* (New York: Scribners, 1950), p. 19.

50. Joel Blocker and Richard Elman, "An Interview with Isaac Bashevis Singer," *Commentary* 36 (November 1963): 368.

51. Cited in Irving Buchen, *Isaac Bashevis Singer and the Eternal Past* (New York: New York University Press, 1968), p. 198. This is the best secondary work on Singer available.

52. Isaac Bashevis Singer, "A Phantom of Delight," *Herald Tribune Book Week* (July 4, 1965), p. 2.

53. Israel Joshua Singer, *Of a World That Is No More*, trans. Joseph Singer (New York: Vanguard, 1970).

54. Biographical information regarding Singer may be found in Buchen, *Isaac Bashevis Singer*, as well as in a number of Singer's essays and interviews. Buchen suggests some of the vagaries of fraternal influence, but does not develop them. He notes, for example, the recurrent Jacob-Esau theme in Singer's works. Singer's rejection of the Enlightenment, with which his brother identified, rarely is indicated in terms of personal conflict. One hint of their distance on this issue might be found in the story, "Something Is There," trans. Isaac Bashevis Singer and Rosanna Gerber, in *A Friend of Kafka, and Other Stories* (New York: Farrar, Straus & Giroux, 1970).

55. Isaac Bashevis Singer, *The Manor* (New York: Farrar, Straus & Giroux, 1967) and *The Estate*. See also *Satan in Goray* (New York: Noonday, 1955) wherein Singer suggests that the temptation to become distant from a degraded community, although understandable, should be opposed. It is a temptation to which the very pious and very intellectual are especially prone.

56. Most of Singer's novels deal with the problems of Jews in a transitional state. See *The Manor, The Estate, The Family Moskat*, and *The Magician of Lublin*.

57. Singer emphasizes that for many people the Enlightenment was as blindly accepted as religion had been by their ancestors. In many, free will was surrendered in a seemingly inexorable movement toward modernity. See "On A Wagon," in *A Crown of Feathers, and Other Stories* (Greenwich, Conn.: Fawcett, 1973), p. 287.

58. The power of Nazism over "lost" Enlightened Jews is a theme of Singer's recent novel, *Enemies, A Love Story* (Greenwich, Conn.: Fawcett, 1972), which is discussed here. This theme is even more explicit in his stories,

most notably "The Mentor," in which a female Israeli doctor, a rigid Darwin-ian, argues that "Nature knows no compassion. As far as Nature is concerned, we are like worms. . . . Nazis are enemies of the human race, and people must be allowed to exterminate them like bedbugs." Isaac Bashevis Singer, "The Mentor," trans. Isaac Bashevis Singer and Evelyn T. Beck, *The New Yorker* 46 (March 21, 1970): 42, 43.

59. Isaac Bashevis Singer, *The Family Moskat*, trans. A. H. Gross (New York: Bantam, 1970), p. 598.

60. Isaac Bashevis Singer, *The Magician of Lublin*, trans. Elaine Gottlieb and Joseph Singer (New York: Bantam, 1971), p. 1; and "The Gentleman from Cracow," trans. Martha Glicklich and Elaine Gottlieb, in *Gimpel the Fool, and Other Stories* (New York: Avon, 1967). In *The Magician of Lublin*, Singer suggests a kind of dialectic of temptation, noting that Yasha was fur-ther tempted by the lure of America.

61. Isaac Bashevis Singer, "The Cafeteria," trans. D. Straus, *The New Yorker* 44 (December 28, 1968): 32; and *Family Moskat*, p. 22.

62. Singer, *Magician of Lublin*, pp. 122-25.

63. Singer, *Family Moskat*, p. 142.

64. See, for example, Dan Levin's review of I. J. Singer's *A World That Is No More*, in *The Nation*, 213 (October 18, 1971): 379-80.

65. Singer, *Magician of Lublin*, pp. 181-201.

66. "An Interview with Isaac Bashevis Singer," p. 372.

67. See *Magician of Lublin*, p. 182. See also Judith Sloman, "Existential-ism in Par Lagerkvist and Isaac Bashevis Singer," *Minnesota Review* 5 (August 1965): 206-12.

68. Isaac Bashevis Singer, "The Key," trans. Isaac Bashevis Singer and Evelyn T. Beck, in *A Friend of Kafka*, p. 45; and *Family Moskat*, p. 21.

69. Isaac Bashevis Singer, "The Letter-Writer," trans. A. Shevrin and Elizabeth Shub, in *The Seance and Other Stories* (New York: Farrar, Straus, & Giroux, 1968); also, "Pigeons," trans. Isaac Bashevis Singer and Elizabeth Shub, in *A Friend of Kafka*.

70. See Jacques Ellul, *The Meaning of the City*, trans. Dennis Pardee (Grand Rapids, Mich.: Eerdmans, 1970), especially chapters 1 and 2.

71. Ibid., pp. 36-37.

72. Singer, "The Letter-Writer," in *Seance*, p. 244.

73. Singer, "The Son," in *A Friend of Kafka*, p. 250.

74. He alludes to this in an interview with Marshall Breger and Bob Barn-hart, "A Conversation with Isaac Bashevis Singer," reprinted in Irving Malin, ed., *Critical Views of Isaac Bashevis Singer* (New York: New York University Press, 1969), pp. 27-43.

75. Isaac Bashevis Singer, "The Lantuch," trans. Isaac Bashevis Singer

and Laurie Colwin, in *A Crown of Feathers*, p. 93. On demonology in Singer, see J. S. Wolkenfeld, "Isaac Bashevis Singer: The Faith of His Devils and Magicians," *Criticism* V (Fall 1963), 349-59.

76. Singer, *Magician of Lublin*, p. 79.

77. Ibid., p. 49.

78. Ibid., p. 77.

79. Singer, *The Estate*, pp. 353-56.

80. "An Interview with Isaac Bashevis Singer," p. 369.

81. This is a theme in many short stories. See, for example, "The Beard," in *A Crown of Feathers*.

82. Stanley Edgar Hyman has also suggested this parallel in "The Yiddish Hawthorne," in Richard Kostelanetz, ed., *On Contemporary Literature* (New York: Avon, 1964).

83. See Singer's story, "Grandfather and Grandson," in *A Crown of Feathers*.

84. See especially *The Estate*. Singer's aversion to this temptation is more explicit in "I Place My Reliance on No Man," in *Short Friday and Other Stories* (New York: Farrar, Straus, & Giroux, 1964).

85. This, of course, is the moral of Singer's famous story, "Gimpel the Fool," in *Gimpel the Fool*.

86. Singer, "I Place My Reliance on No Man," *Short Friday*, p. 212.

87. Breger and Barnhart, "A Conversation with Isaac Bashevis Singer," p. 41.

88. Ibid.

89. See, for example, "Jechid and Jechidah," in *Short Friday*.

90. Singer's children's stories hardly qualify him as a "liberal" educator. See, for example, "Grandmother's Tale," in *Zlateh the Goat and Other Stories* (New York: Harper & Row, 1966).

91. Singer, *Magician of Lublin*, p. 193.

92. There is a good analysis of this in Buchen, *Isaac Bashevis Singer*, pp. 149-72.

93. Isaac B. Singer, *The Slave*, trans. Isaac B. Singer and Cecil Hemley (New York: Avon, 1962), pp. 202-03.

94. See "Pigeons," in *A Friend of Kafka*, for this explicit theme.

95. Singer, *The Slave*, p. 228.

96. Singer, *Enemies, A Love Story*, pp. 54, 157.

97. Ibid., p. 114.

98. Ibid., p. 33. Later in the novel, Herman, while glancing through Plato's "Apologia," comes upon the quote, "Because I believe it is against nature that a better man should be hurt by a lesser one." His reaction is one of disbelief: "Was it against nature that the Nazis should have murdered mil-

lions of Jews?" (p. 198). But Singer himself seems to be saying much more. In full context, Socrates argues that death may be merely an illusion, and that the true hurt is suffered by those who punish and kill the virtuous. Plato, "The Apologia," in *A Plato Reader*, ed. Ronald Levinson (Boston: Houghton Mifflin, 1967).

99. Singer, *Enemies*, p. 50.
100. Ibid., p. 37.
101. Ibid., "Author's Note."
102. Singer, "The Mentor," p. 42. For the same theme, see "The Briefcase," in *A Crown of Feathers*.
103. "An Interview with Isaac Bashevis Singer," p. 369.
104. See *Magician of Lublin*, p. 194.
105. Breger and Barnhart, "A Conversation with Isaac Bashevis Singer," p. 29.
106. Singer, *The Slave*, p. 252.

CHAPTER 4

1. Harry Roskolenko, *The Time That Was Then* (New York: Dial, 1971), p. 15.
2. Abraham Cahan, *The Rise of David Levinsky* (New York: Smith, 1951), p. 86.
3. Samuel Ornitz, *Haunch, Paunch, and Jowl* (Garden City, N.Y.: Garden City, 1923), p. 54.
4. Roskolenko, *Time That Was Then*, p. 218; also p. 14. The desire to return to Europe to find truth, to right parents' errors, is quite common in the works of young Jewish writers, especially in the 1930s. It is associated, in part, with the appeal of Communism to young Jewish intellectuals. See, in this regard, Joseph Freeman, *An American Testament* (London: Gollancz, 1938); and Isidor Schneider, *From the Kingdom of Necessity* (New York: Putnam, 1935).
5. Cahan, *Rise of David Levinsky*, p. 109.
6. See, for example, Anzia Yezierska, *Children of Loneliness* (New York: Funk & Wagnalls, 1923), *Hungry Hearts* (Boston: Houghton Mifflin, 1920), and her autobiography, *Red Ribbon on a White Horse* (New York: Scribners, 1950). Elizabeth Stern's autobiography, written during the same period, pursues the same theme. See, *I Am A Woman—and A Jew* (New York: Sears, 1927).
7. Samuel Chotzinoff, *A Lost Paradise* (New York: Knopf, 1959), p. 141.
8. Chotzinoff, *A Lost Paradise*, p. 82.
9. On the experience of new immigrants, see Louis Adamic, *From Many*

Lands (New York: Harper, 1940); Oscar Handlin, *The Uprooted* (Boston: Little, Brown, 1951); and Thomas Wheeler, ed., *The Immigrant Experience* (Baltimore: Penguin, 1972).

10. Israel Zangwill, *The Melting Pot* (New York: Macmillan, 1909), p. 37.

11. Marcus Eli Ravage, *An American in the Making* (New York: Harper, 1917), p. 91.

12. Chotzinoff, *A Lost Paradise*, p. 60.

13. See Milton Gordon, *Assimilation in American Life* (New York: Oxford University Press, 1964); and John Higham, *Strangers in the Land* (New York: Atheneum, 1969).

14. Among the liberal journals, the *New Republic, Century,* and *The Nation* were concerned with this problem.

15. The classic work, of course, is Franz Fanon, *The Wretched of the Earth* (New York: Grove, 1963).

16. Yezierska, *Red Ribbon on a White Horse.*

17. Ravage, *An American in the Making,* p. 69.

18. Ibid., p. 173.

19. Ibid., pp. 78-79, 60.

20. Ibid., p. 157; also pp. 87, 102, 131. See also Marcus Eli Ravage, "The Tired College Man," *Century* 95 (January 1918): 376-84.

21. Ravage, *An American in the Making,* p. 112.

22. Ravage, "The Tired College Man," p. 377.

23. Ravage, *An American in the Making,* p. 231.

24. Marcus Eli Ravage, "The Religion of Sanity," *Century* 95 (February 1918): 522.

25. Ibid.

26. Ravage, *An American in the Making,* p. 234.

27. Marcus Eli Ravage, "The Task for Americans," *New Republic* 19 (July 16, 1919): 349.

28. Marcus Eli Ravage, "The Immigrant's Burden," *New Republic* 19 (June 14, 1919): 211. Also, Ravage's nativist pose allows him to look down on both immigrants and "Americans."

29. Ravage, "The Task for Americans," p. 350.

30. Ravage, "The Tired College Man," p. 382.

31. Ibid., p. 384.

32. Marcus Eli Ravage, "Absorbing the Alien," *Century* 95 (November 1917): 27.

33. Ibid., pp. 36, 35.

34. Ibid., p. 36.

35. Marcus Eli Ravage, "The Wondering Jew," *Century* 107 (February 1924): 564, 563.

36. Ibid., p. 564. This sexual theme is discussed further in the next chapter.

37. Marcus Eli Ravage, "A Real Case Against the Jews," *Century* 115 (January 1928): 350.

38. Ravage, "Wondering Jew," p. 563.

39. Mary Antin, *The Promised Land* (Boston: Houghton Mifflin, 1914), p. 247. Mary Antin, *From Plotzk to Boston* (Boston: Clarke, 1899).

40. It is significant that she refers to her mother infrequently in her works. As noted earlier, she saw herself as a child of "nature." Moreover, she criticizes the family as an institution, viewing it as a human convention that hinders individual development. As individuals evolve towards perfection the family will become unnecessary. Antin's mother and sister were traditional women who would not forsake religion, despite the father's desire to Americanize. At various other points, however, she indicates that her rise out of the "mire" of the slums was not solitary, that she brought her family with her, and did not reject them in spite of temptations to do so. See *The Promised Land*, pp. 355-58.

41. Mary Antin, *They Who Knock at Our Gates, A Complete Gospel of Immigration* (Boston: Houghton Mifflin, 1914), pp. 106-07.

42. Antin, *The Promised Land*, p. 361.

43. Ibid., p. 355.

44. Ibid; see, in general, pp. 337-58.

45. Ibid., p. 356. On the effects of Americanization on her family life, see also Mary Antin's essay, "The Making of a Citizen," *Atlantic* 109 (February 1912).

46. Antin, *The Promised Land*, p. 271.

47. Ibid., p. 358.

48. Ibid., p. xi. Other references to death in her autobiography are also quite suggestive, especially in respect to her ambivalence over assimilation. In describing the threat of a pogrom in Russia, she notes that "the cry of the hunted thrilled the Jewish world" with the usual fears (p. 140). That Christian aggression should "thrill" Jews seems strange. Too, she recalls as a child how fond she was of "playing Gentile," particularly playing the corpse at a Christian funeral (p. 106). These references suggest that "after-life" is aptly used: being an American is "playing Gentile" and also "playing dead." Assimilation also seems to involve fantasies of violence as well—violence against the immigrant's culture, and also the immigrant's "conquest" of America. See also the brief discussion of Antin in Allen Guttmann, *The Jewish Writer in America* (New York: Oxford University Press, 1971).

49. Antin, *The Promised Land*, p. 247.

50. Antin, *They Who Knock*, pp. 3-4.

51. Ibid., p. 27. Her attempt to merge Jewish and American backgrounds is also reflected in her short story, "The Lie," *Atlantic* 112 (August 1913): 177-90.

52. Antin, *They Who Knock*, pp. 27-28. It is interesting that Antin views the Declaration, rather than the Constitution, as the "basic law." Like others of her age, she was catholic in her inclinations, preferring universal truths to parochial norms. Also, cherishing the Declaration is consistent with her simplification of Judaism to an elemental ethic.

53. Antin, *The Promised Land*, pp. 359-64.

54. Ibid., p. 29.

55. Ibid., p. 141.

56. Antin, "The Lie," p. 178; and *They Who Knock*, pp. 128ff.

57. Antin relates that her previous experience of educational opportunity in Russia gave her a first taste of American freedom (*The Promised Land,* p. 111).

58. Antin, *The Promised Land*, p. 30. This liberation from Jewish womanhood is not accompanied by a redefinition of it. If anything, the result seems to be confusion. For example, when Antin refers to herself abstractly in the third person, she uses the pronoun "he."

59. Ibid., p. 218.

60. Ibid., p. 344.

61. This emphasis on the teacher is illustrated in "The Lie," where the teacher represents both the best of America and an ideal authority figure.

62. Antin, *They Who Knock*, p. 126.

63. Ibid., p. 127.

64. Ibid., p. 95. Antin's support of progressivism was also based on her dislike of politicians. In a pre-election article written to endorse Theodore Roosevelt in 1912, she envisioned a day when "our legislators shall be the clerks of the wise men of our times." Mary Antin, "A Woman to Her Fellow-Citizens," *The Outlook* 102 (November 2, 1912): 485.

65. Antin, *They Who Knock*, pp. 129-30.

66. Antin, *The Promised Land*, p. 100. See her references to Emerson in "A Woman to Her Fellow-Citizens."

67. Randolph Bourne, *The History of a Literary Radical*, ed. Van Wyck Brooks (New York: Russell, 1956).

68. On cultural pluralism, see Gordon, *Assimilation in American Life*, especially chapters 6-8. See also Louis Adamic, *A Nation of Nations* (New York: Harper, 1945), one among his many works on the subject.

69. Horace Kallen, *Culture and Democracy in the United States* (New York: Boni and Liveright, 1924), p. 124. As times changed, Kallen altered some of his premises, but generally maintained his conclusion: familial and

cultural influences replaced heredity as powerful molders of ethnic ties. See, in this regard, Horace Kallen et al., *Cultural Pluralism and the American Idea* (Philadelphia: University of Pennsylvania Press, 1956).

70. See, for example, "A Convert in Zion," "The Place of Judaism in the Jewish Problem," "Zionism and Liberalism," and other essays in Horace Kallen, *Judaism at Bay* (New York: Arno, 1972).

71. Kallen, *Culture and Democracy*, p. 116. Kallen believed that the world was evolving toward eventual unification, with even war as a contributor to this process.

72. Kallen, *Culture and Democracy*, p. 124.

73. Kallen, "Retrospect and Prospect, 1932," in *Judaism at Bay*, p. 255.

74. Isaac B. Berkson, *Theories of Americanization: A Critical Study with Special Reference to the Jewish Group* (New York: Teacher's College, 1920), p. 71.

75. Ibid., p. 69.

76. Ibid., pp. 123-32.

77. Edward Saveth, *American Historians and European Immigrants, 1875-1925* (New York: Columbia University Press, 1948).

78. *Theories of Americanization*, p. 132.

79. Ibid., p. 23.

80. Ibid., p. 129.

81. Ibid., p. 106.

82. Ibid., p. 111.

83. Ibid., p. 41.

84. Ibid., pp. 140-41, 20.

85. On anti-Semitism during the period, see Higham, *Strangers in the Land*; Michael Selzer, *Kike!* (New York: World, 1973); and Judd Teller, *Strangers and Natives* (New York: Delacorte, 1968).

86. Encouraging assimilation through individual achievement might result spiritually in isolation, which is the theme of some of the "protest" literature of this generation. See Chapter 5.

87. An example of this affinity may be found in Elizabeth Stern's *I Am A Woman—and a Jew*, wherein she describes her Orthodox father's grudging approval of the Presbyterians, because the latter behaved like Jews.

88. See, for example, Mordecai M. Kaplan's influential work, *Judaism as a Civilization* (New York: Yoseloff, 1957). On the secular trend in modern Jewish theology, consult Arthur A. Cohen, *The Natural and Supernatural Jew* (New York: Pantheon, 1962).

89. As others have pointed out, there was an ethnic factor at work here. Most cities in which Jews resided were controlled by machines dominated by Irish Catholics. See Lawrence Fuchs, *The Political Behavior of American Jews* (Glencoe, Ill.: Free Press, 1956).

CHAPTER 5

1. The political background of the more radical Russian-Jewish immigrants is discussed in the early chapters of Ronald Sanders, *The Downtown Jews* (New York: Harper & Row, 1969).
2. See the section on Jews in Nathan Glazer and Daniel Patrick Moynahan, *Beyond the Melting Pot* (Cambridge, Mass.: MIT Press, 1971).
3. See Morris Hillquit, *Socialism in Theory and Practice* (New York: Macmillan, 1913), especially chapters 1 and 2.
4. Morris Hillquit, *Loose Leaves from a Busy Life* (New York: Macmillan, 1934), pp. 16-17.
5. Ibid., p. 30. Irving Howe also shares this view of the importance of socialism and labor organization in Jewish life. See Irving Howe, *World of Our Fathers* (New York: Simon & Schuster, 1976), p. 323.
6. Hayim Zhitlowsky, "The Jewish Factor in My Socialism," trans. Lucy S. Dawidowicz, in Irving Howe and Eliezer Greenberg, eds., *Voices from the Yiddish* (Ann Arbor: University of Michigan Press, 1973), p. 134.
7. Harry Rogoff, *An East Side Epic, The Life and Work of Meyer London* (New York: Vanguard, 1930), p. 10. This work is as much a compilation of London's speeches as it is a biography.
8. On the parochialism of New York socialists, see David Shannon, *The Socialist Party in America, A History* (Chicago: Quadrangle, 1967), especially pp. 9-13, and chapter II. Biographical portraits of Hillquit and London can be found in Melech Epstein, *Profiles of Eleven* (Detroit, Mich.: Wayne State University Press, 1965).
9. Hillquit, *Loose Leaves*, p. 327.
10. Harry Roskolenko, *The Time That Was Then* (New York: Dial, 1971), p. 81.
11. Abraham Bisno, *Abraham Bisno, Union Pioneer*, with a foreword by Joel Seidman (Madison: University of Wisconsin Press, 1967), pp. 231, 106.
12. Rogoff, *An East Side Epic*, p. 22.
13. Bisno, *Abraham Bisno*, p. 100.
14. Ibid., p. 156.
15. Hillquit, *Loose Leaves*, pp. 3-4 (emphasis mine). See also, Hillquit, *Socialism in Theory and Practice*, p. 9.
16. Rogoff, *An East Side Epic*, pp. 126-27, 235.
17. Ibid., pp. 210-11.
18. Ibid., p. 250.
19. Ibid., p. 105.
20. Hillquit, *Loose Leaves*, p. 10.
21. On the militant role of women in the Jewish labor movement, see Howe, *World of Our Fathers*, pp. 295-300. See also, Lewis Lorwin, *The Women's*

184   NOTES

Garment Workers (New York: Huebsch, 1924).

22. On sex roles in the Old World, consult Mark Zborowski and Elizabeth Herzog, *Life Is With People* (New York: International Universities, 1952). As noted in an earlier chapter, the adaptation of the Jewish man in America, or the lack of it, is a common theme in early literature. Apart from the works discussed in this chapter, see also Anzia Yezierska's novels and stories, the writings of Cournos and Ravage, and some of the novels of Shalom Asch, especially *The Mother*, trans. Elsa Krauch (New York: Putnam, 1937).

23. Elias Tobenkin, *Witte Arrives* (Upper Saddle River, N.J.: Gregg, 1968, 1916). This novel is discussed in Walter Rideout, *The Radical Novel in the United States, 1900-1954* (Cambridge, Mass.: Harvard University Press, 1956).

24. Tobenkin, *Witte Arrives*, pp. 123-24.

25. Ibid., p. 193.

26. Samuel Ornitz, *Haunch, Paunch, and Jowl* (Garden City, N.Y.: Garden City, 1923), p. 300. Allen Guttman sees this novel as an example of the Americanization of the Jew, in *The Jewish Writer in America* (New York: Oxford University Press, 1971), p. 35.

27. Ornitz, *Haunch, Paunch, and Jowl*, pp. 226-27. The sordidness of life, in America and on the New York streets, was a common theme in many works of this era. Two somewhat later works which also center on this theme are Michael Gold, *Jews Without Money* (New York: Liveright, 1930) and Henry Roth, *Call It Sleep* (New York: Ballou, 1934). Both portray sexuality in sordid terms as well.

28. Tobenkin, *Witte Arrives*, p. 21.

29. Ornitz, *Haunch, Paunch, and Jowl*, p. 35.

30. Ornitz's concern with Jewish issues veils a further conclusion: "American" politicians must suffer from the same problems since the "system" is similar for them. However, Ornitz is impressed with their obvious power over Jews and mistakes this for a generalized and self-confident authority.

31. Hutchins Hapgood, *The Spirit of the Ghetto*, ed. Moses Rischin (Cambridge, Mass.: Harvard University Press, 1967).

32. Samuel Ornitz, *Bride of the Sabbath* (New York: Rinehart, 1951), pp. 355-56; see also pp. 16, 46.

33. Ibid., p. 119.

34. Ibid., p. 101.

35. Ibid., pp. 46-49.

36. Ibid., p. 41.

37. Ibid., pp. 58, 47.

38. Ibid., p. 198. This is part of a chapter entitled "The Right Not to Be," which describes Saul's departure from his Orthodox background.

39. Daniel Aaron makes a similar point regarding Jews and Communism in the 1930s in his essay, "Jews and Communism," in Peter Rose, ed. *The Ghetto and Beyond* (New York: Random House, 1969).

40. Ornitz, *Bride of the Sabbath*, p. 206.

41. Ibid., p. 161. See Anzia Yezierska's sympathetic review of this novel in *The New York Times* (October 21, 1951), p. 35.

42. Ornitz, *Bride of the Sabbath*, p. 27.

43. George Seldes, *Lords of the Press* (New York: Messner, 1938).

44. Major biographical works on Abraham Cahan include Sanders, *The Downtown Jews*; Theodore Bernstein, *The Solitary Clarinetist* (Ph.D. diss., Columbia University, 1959); Epstein, *Profiles of Eleven*, and Cahan's own autobiography, part of which has been translated into English by Leon Stein, *The Education of Abraham Cahan* (Philadelphia: Jewish Publication Society, 1969).

45. Sanders emphasizes this point throughout his work.

46. Cahan, *Education*, pp. 66, 34.

47. Ibid., pp. 103-05.

48. Abraham Cahan, *The White Terror and the Red* (New York: Harper, 1906), pp. 159, 149. For another account of revolutionary activity in Russia by a Jewish immigrant, see Melech Epstein's autobiography, *Pages from a Colorful Life* (Miami Beach, Fla.: Block, 1971).

49. Cahan, *White Terror and the Red*, pp. 196, 154, 158.

50. Quoted in Sanders, *Downtown Jews*, p. 249.

51. Cahan, *Education*, p. 229.

52. Quoted in Sanders, *Downtown Jews*, p. 270.

53. Cahan, *White Terror and the Red*, p. 173.

54. Note, for example, Cahan's generally sympathetic description of Orthodox Jewish life in a Russian village in the chapter entitled "On Sacred Ground." His description of the czar is also sympathetic. *White Terror and the Red*, pp. 1-10.

55. Cahan, *Education*, p. 205.

56. Abraham Cahan, "Tzinchadzi of the Catskills," *Atlantic Monthly* 88 (August 1901): 226. On the importance of the past in Cahan's works, see Sanders, *Downtown Jews*, pp. 238-45. Guttmann, in *Jewish Writer in America*, also sees Cahan as ambivalent (pp. 28-33).

57. Abraham Cahan, *Yekl, and Other Stories* (New York: Dover, 1970). See Sanford Marovitz, "Yekl: The Ghetto Realism of Abraham Cahan, *American Literary Realism* 2 (1969): 271-73.

58. Isaac Rosenfeld makes a similar point in his essay, "David Levinsky: The Jew as American Millionaire," in Isaac Rosenfeld, *An Age of Enormity*, ed. Theodore Solotaroff (Cleveland, Ohio: World, 1962), pp. 273-81. Rosen-

feld's interpretation of Levinsky's original character, however, is different
from the one presented here.

59. Sanders, *Downtown Jews*, p. 322.
60. Rosenfeld, "David Levinsky," p. 273.
61. Abraham Cahan, *The Rise of David Levinsky* (New York: Smith, 1951), p. 5.
62. Ibid., p. 59.
63. Ibid., p. 61.
64. Cahan, *Education*, pp. 227-28.
65. Cahan, *Rise of David Levinsky*, pp. 133, 127.
66. Cahan, *Education*, p. 352.
67. David Singer also argues that Levinsky's ambivalence was pre-American in his essay, "David Levinsky's Fall: A Note on the Liebman Thesis," *American Quarterly* 19 (Winter 1967): 696-706. Beyond Levinsky, Cahan also implies that both religious and socialist immigrants found their orthodoxies threatened by the lack of external restraints in America.
68. Leslie Fiedler also stresses the importance of the romantic theme in this novel. See Leslie Fiedler, "Genesis: The American-Jewish Novel through the Twenties," *Midstream* 4 (Summer 1958).
69. Abraham Cahan, *The Imported Bridegroom, and Other Stories* (New York: Garrett, 1968), p. 147.
70. Hillquit, *Loose Leaves*, pp. 324-32.
71. Bisno, *Abraham Bisno Remembers*, p. 240.
72. Howe, *World of Our Fathers*, p. 322.

CHAPTER 6

1. Morris R. Cohen, book review of *Mr. Justice Brandeis*, edited by Felix Frankfurter, in *Harvard Law Review* 47 (November 1933): 166.
2. There is a good deal of material available on Cohen's life. Most important is his own autobiography, *A Dreamer's Journey* (Glencoe, Ill.: Free Press, 1949). Much of this work was compiled by Felix Cohen after his father's death. Leonora Cohen Rosenfield, ed., *Portrait of a Philosopher: Morris R. Cohen in Life and Letters* (New York: Harcourt, Brace, 1961) also contains valuable material, including letters and excerpts from his personal diary. A recent critical study is David A. Hollinger, *Morris R. Cohen and the Scientific Ideal* (Cambridge, Mass.: MIT Press, 1975). This perceptive work came to my attention after the completion of the draft of this manuscript. It touches on some of the same points made here although from a different perspective.
3. Cohen, *A Dreamer's Journey*, p. 28.
4. Morris R. Cohen, *American Thought: A Critical Sketch*, ed. Felix S.

Cohen (Glencoe, Ill.: Free Press, 1954), pp. 142-44.

5. Morris R. Cohen, *Reflections of a Wondering Jew* (Glencoe, Ill.: Free Press, 1950). See also, Cohen, *A Dreamer's Journey*, pp. 226-27.

6. Morris R. Cohen, "Zionism: Tribalism or Liberalism?" *New Republic* 18 (March 8, 1919): 183; and see also Horace Kallen's rejoinder, "Zionism: Democracy or Prussianism?" *New Republic* 18 (April 5, 1919): 311-13.

7. Cohen, *A Dreamer's Journey*, p. 73.

8. Ibid., p. 69.

9. Ibid., p. 205.

10. Morris R. Cohen, "Vision and Technique in Philosophy," Presidential address to the Eastern division of the American Philosophical Association, December 30, 1929, published in *The Philosophical Review* 39 (March 1930): 130. See also "Some Difficulties in John Dewey's Anthropocentric Naturalism," in Morris R. Cohen, *Studies in Philosophy and Science* (New York: Holt, 1949).

11. Cohen, *American Thought*.

12. Cohen, *A Dreamer's Journey*, p. 190.

13. Cohen, *Reflections*, p. 14.

14. Ibid., pp. 14, 9, 46.

15. Ibid., pp. 18, 19.

16. Given his argument, the voluntary decision to join the covenant was probably involuntary. I am not asserting that in reality all or even most Orthodox Jews consciously grappled with the decision to join the covenant, through the bar mitzvah. Undoubtedly many did not. Yet it was a cultural standard or ideal which many Jewish families encouraged as such, and Jewish teaching worked toward.

17. See Morris R. Cohen, *Reason and Nature* (New York: Harcourt, Brace, 1931), pp. 386-92, 417-20. More significantly, in another essay Cohen specifically questioned the value of cultural explanations, describing them as "highly speculative" and "seldom based on adequate evidence. . . ." Nor do they allow us, he stressed, "to dispense with the often simpler philosophic issue as to the truth of the opinions studied." Cohen, "Vision and Technique in Philosophy," p. 134.

18. Cohen, *A Dreamer's Journey*, p. 220; and *Reflections*, p. 39.

19. Cohen did acknowledge the possibility of genuine conversion. See his book review of *Judaism and Christianity*, ed. Fr. Lev Gillet, reprinted in *Reflections*, p. 153-55.

20. See below, also *A Dreamer's Journey*, chapters 24-27.

21. Cohen criticized American Jewish communities for falling prey to "practical" values, and especially for demoting the role of the scholar in Jewish organizational life; see *A Dreamer's Journey*, pp. 215, 224-25. At another

point he acknowledged that cultures can change rapidly, thus undercutting his "longevity" argument, as well as his cultural determinism. See his review of Ludwig Lewisohn's *The Answer: The Jew and the World*, reprinted in *Reflections*, pp. 116-23, especially pp. 121-22.

22. Cohen, *Reflections*, p. 14.

23. Cohen, *Reason and Nature*, p. 427.

24. Morris R. Cohen, "The Future of American Liberalism," in *The Faith of a Liberal* (New York: Holt, 1946), p. 453.

25. Cohen, *A Dreamer's Journey*, p. 166.

26. See, for example, Morris R. Cohen, *The Meaning of Human History* (La Salle, Ill.: Open Court, 1947), p. 281. Significantly, he came to see the God of the Old Testament in the same respect.

27. Cohen, *A Dreamer's Journey*, p. 96.

28. Ibid., p. 108. For more on Davidson's influence, see Rosenfield, *Portrait of a Philosopher*, especially chapter 3.

29. In this regard, see Cohen's essays on Spinoza, "Spinoza: Prophet of Liberalism," *New Republic* 50 (March 30, 1927): 164-66; and "The Intellectual Love of God," *Menorah Journal* 11 (August 1925): 332. See also his essay on Maimonides in *Reflections*.

30. Cohen, *A Dreamer's Journey*, p. 212. At another point, Cohen implied a belief in a particular conception of God:

> The only god that a free man can worship is the God of light, the God that is distinguished from an abyss of darkness which He did not create but which serves as the starting point and background of all the acts and strivings that we may call divine. *Meaning of Human History*, p. 284.

31. Morris R. Cohen, "A Slacker's Apology," *New Republic* 21 (December 3, 1919): 19. In a diary note of June 12, 1902, Cohen wrote that since he was 12 years old he had wanted to be a "redeemer" to his people. His daughter suggests that this impulse faded as he became disillusioned with traditional religion. Rosenfield, *Portrait of a Philosopher*, p. 205.

32. Cohen, *A Dreamer's Journey*, p. 190; and *American Thought*, p. 31.

33. See Robert Bierstedt's review of *Studies in Philosophy and Science* in *The Saturday Review of Literature*, 32 (April 23, 1949): 19; and H. A. Larrabee's review of *American Thought* in *The Journal of Philosophy* 51 (July 22, 1954): 441.

34. Cohen, "The Future of American Liberalism," p. 455.

35. Ibid.

36. Cohen, *Reason and Nature*, p. IX.

37. See his address "In Defense of Contemplative Life," reprinted in *Faith*

of a Liberal, pp. 288-91.

38. Ibid., p. 290.

39. Cohen, "Vision and Technique in Philosophy," p. 152. See also Rosenfield, *Portrait of a Philosopher*, chapter 12.

40. Ibid., p. 369. See also Cohen, *Meaning of Human History*, chapter 10.

41. Cohen, *American Thought*, p. 46.

42. Ibid., p. 47.

43. Cohen, *A Dreamer's Journey*, p. 99.

44. Cohen, *American Thought*, pp. 23-24, 43-44, 117.

45. Ibid., pp. 115-18.

46. Ibid., p. 35. For a contrary view, see Perry Miller, *The New England Mind*, Vols. 1-2 (New York: Macmillan, 1939); and Wilson C. McWilliams, *The Idea of Fraternity in America* (Berkeley: University of California Press, 1973).

47. Also at work here most likely is Cohen's "Jewish" antipathy to agricultural life. At the start of his autobiography he notes, for example, that "I have never been ashamed of being born among people who . . . did not take the rooted plant as their ideal of life but deliberately chose to change their habitat in the course of time." *A Dreamer's Journey*, p. 3. See also, Theodore Reik's speculative and suggestive essay on Jews, "The Repetition Compulsion in Jewish History," in *Curiosities of the Self* (New York: Farrar, Straus, & Giroux, 1965).

48. Cohen, *Reason and Nature*, p. 398. On Cohen's pluralism, see ibid., pp. 396-98, 441-42; and *A Dreamer's Journey*, pp. 222-23.

49. Cohen, *A Dreamer's Journey*, p. 145. Cohen's comments regarding "polite conversation" support the thesis of John Murray Cuddihy in *The Ordeal of Civility* (New York: Basic Books, 1974).

50. Note, for example, Cohen's comment in *American Thought* on the American businessman: "Since his education has not taught him to find real satisfaction outside of his daily routine, he does not know how to spend his leisure nobly" (pp. 29-30).

51. Morris R. Cohen, Review of *Freedom, Its Meaning*, ed. Ruth Nanda Anshen, in *Harvard Law Review* 54 (June 1941): 1425.

52. Ibid., p. 1426. See also Cohen, *Reason and Nature*, pp. 392-95; and also Cohen, *Meaning of Human History*.

53. Cohen, "The Future of American Liberalism," p. 453.

54. See Cohen, *Reflections*, p. 7.

55. Cohen, *A Dreamer's Journey*, p. 47. On Cohen's liberalism, consult Herbert G. Reid, "Morris Cohen's Case for Liberalism," *Review of Politics* 33 (1971): 489-511.

56. Cohen, *A Dreamer's Journey*, p. 273. See also Cohen, *Reason and*

Nature, pp. 165-68.
57. Cohen, *Meaning of Human History*, p. 285.
58. Cohen, *A Dreamer's Journey*, p. 175.
59. Morris R. Cohen, *Studies in Philosophy and Science* (New York: Holt, 1949), p. 20. See also Morris R. Cohen, *Law and the Social Order* (New York: Harcourt, Brace, 1933).
60. Cohen, *American Thought*, p. 143. See also Cohen, *Law and the Social Order*.
61. See Cohen's essays on Holmes, Brandeis, and Cardozo in *Faith of a Liberal*, pp. 20-45.
62. Cohen, *American Thought*, p. 111.
63. Cohen, *A Dreamer's Journey*, p. 227.
64. Cohen, *Faith of a Liberal*, p. 437.
65. Ibid., p. 438.
66. Cohen, *A Dreamer's Journey*, p. 237.
67. Cohen, *Reflections*, p. 84.
68. Cohen once wrote that Jews should take their "proper part" in public life, since there is no safety in assuming a position of "permanent inferiority." Cohen to J. H. Berman (Jan. 11, 1937) in Rosenfield, *Portrait of a Philosopher*, p. 217.
69. Hollinger, *Morris R. Cohen and the Scientific Ideal*, p. 249.

CHAPTER 7

1. Daniel J. Elazar, "American Political Theory and the Political Notions of American Jews: Convergence and Contradictions," in Peter I. Rose, ed., *The Ghetto and Beyond* (New York: Random House, 1969), p. 217. For similar interpretations, see Lawrence Fuchs, "Sources of Jewish Internationalism and Liberalism," in Marshall Sklare, ed., *The Jews: Social Patterns of an American Group* (Glencoe, Ill.: Free Press, 1958); and Werner Cohn, "The Politics of American Jews," also in Sklare, *The Jews*. For different interpretations of Jewish liberalism, consult Charles Liebman, *The Ambivalent American Jew* (Philadelphia: Jewish Publication Society, 1973); and John M. Cuddihy, *The Ordeal of Civility* (New York: Basic Books, 1975).
2. Elazar, "American Political Theory," p. 215.
3. Ibid., p. 206.
4. See Arthur A. Cohen, *The Myth of the Judaeo-Christian Tradition* (New York: Harper & Row, 1969).
5. Irving Howe, *World of Our Fathers* (New York: Simon & Schuster, 1976), p. 626.
6. Stephen D. Isaacs, *Jews and American Politics* (Garden City, N.Y.:

Doubleday, 1974), pp. 1, 267.

7. There is almost no reliable data on the political participation of American ethnic groups. Isaacs substantiates his assertion of Jewish "hyperactivity" in politics with research done on *attitudes* toward politics, and his evidence is not persuasive. Andrew Greeley found that Jews, while more active than the norm (which is exceedingly low), are significantly less active than Irish-Americans and citizens of Scandinavian descent. Moreover, when social class was held constant, Jews were the *least* politically active of all ethnic groups. Greeley's research, it should be emphasized, was based on a very small sample. See Andrew Greeley, "Political Participation Among Ethnic Groups in the United States: A Preliminary Reconnaissance," *American Journal of Sociology* 80 (July 1974): 170-204.

8. Isaacs, *Jews and American Politics*, pp. 201-02.

9. Philip Roth, "The New Jewish Stereotypes," *American Judaism* (Winter 1961). For an excellent discussion of the relationship between Judaism and political attitudes, see Liebman, *Ambivalent American Jew*, pp. 139-44.

10. Georges Friedmann, *The End of the Jewish People?* (Garden City, N.Y.: Doubleday, 1967).

11. Burton J. Bledstein stresses the importance of "character" in his *The Culture of Professionalism* (New York: Norton, 1976), especially chapter 4.

12. The idea of "substitutes" is developed in Eugene Borowitz, *The Masks Jews Wear* (New York: Simon & Schuster, 1973).

13. Herman Melville, *Redburn* (Garden City, N.Y.: Doubleday Anchor, 1957), especially chapter 31.

14. Ahad Ha-Am (Asher Ginzberg), "Judaism and Nietzsche," in *Essays, Letters, Memoirs*, ed. Leon Simon (Oxford, Eng.: East and West Library, 1946), p. 81.

15. Randolph Bourne, "Trans-national America," in Van Wyck Brooks, ed., *The History of a Literary Radical* (New York: Russell, 1956); and Michael Novak, *The Rise of the Unmeltable Ethnics* (New York: Macmillan, 1972).

BIBLIOGRAPHIC ESSAY

Most of the sources for this study are referred to in the notes. In addition to the primary source material cited in this work, a growing body of memoirs and oral history is available to the scholar. The YIVO Institute in New York City and the Oral History Project of Columbia University are important repositories of this type of material.

Major secondary works begin with Irving Howe, *World of Our Fathers* (New York: Simon and Schuster, 1975), a massive and loving study of the experience of East European Jews in America. While it has its shortcomings, this work is so inclusive that it deserves to be a starting point for any student of the subject. It is also amply documented, especially in regard to Yiddish sources. Another valuable work on the early history of the East European Jew in America is Moses Rischin, *The Promised City* (Cambridge, Mass.: Harvard University Press, 1962). Other, more popular works of a general nature, include Ande Manners, *Poor Cousins* (New York: Coward-McCann, 1972) and Judd Teller, *Strangers and Natives* (New York: Delacorte Press, 1968). An early work of some value is Charles Bernheimer, ed., *The Russian Jew in the United States* (Philadelphia: J. C. Winston, 1905).

Very little has been written on Judaism and politics. As cited in the text, Part One of Hannah Arendt's *The Origins of Totalitarianism* (New York: Harcourt, Brace and World, 1966) provides an excellent

discussion of Jewish political inexperience in the context of the transformations of modern politics. Jacob Katz's works, particularly *Out
of the Ghetto* (Cambridge, Mass.: Harvard University Press, 1973),
are important sources for the medieval and early modern periods.
Charles Liebman's *The Ambivalent American Jew* (Philadelphia:
Jewish Publication Society of America, 1973) contains an intelligent
discussion of the relationship between Judaism and political liberalism. Various works of Michael Selzer, especially *The Wineskin and
the Wizard* (New York: Macmillan, 1970), echo the theme of Jewish
alienation from politics. The contrary view may be found in Daniel
Elazar's writings, including his recent *Community and Polity* (Philadelphia: Jewish Publication Society of America, 1976).

The role of Jews in American political life also deserves more attention than it has received. (For that matter, there are few good works on
the political experience of *any* ethnic group in America.) The two
major investigations of Jews in American politics are Lawrence H.
Fuchs, *The Political Behavior of American Jews* (Glencoe, Ill.: The
Free Press, 1956) and Stephen D. Isaacs, *Jews and American Politics*
(Garden City, N.Y.: Doubleday, 1974). Neither of these works is deep
in good analysis. Fuchs' book is an interesting narrative, but does not
penetrate into many significant issues. Isaacs' popular treatment is
very suggestive at certain points, but is marred by its "upbeat"
emphasis on proving that Jews have assimilated.

Other works which deal with immigrants and ethnic groups are
likewise useful in terms of Jews in American political life. Samuel
Lubell has always been sensitive to the political importance of ethnicity, and his *The Future of American Politics* (New York: Harper
and Row, 1952) remains a kind of classic in this respect. Nathan
Glazer and Daniel Patrick Moynihan's *Beyond the Melting Pot* (Cambridge, Mass.: MIT Press, 1963) is full of insight into the relationship
between Old and New World political behavior. Some of the essays in
Lawrence Fuchs, ed., *American Ethnic Politics* (New York: Harper
and Row, 1968) and Marshall Sklare, ed., *The Jews: Social Patterns of
an American Group* (Glencoe, Ill.: The Free Press, 1958) are also
quite useful.

A good book waits to be done on the political experience of German
Jews in America. A remarkable number of public men who shared
certain personal and political qualities emerged from this back-

ground around the turn of the century. Individual biographies some-times provide good perspectives on political attitudes. Robert Caro's critical study of Robert Moses, *The Power Broker* (New York: Knopf, 1974), Allan Nevins' *Herbert H. Lehman and His Era* (New York: Scribner, 1963) and Naomi W. Cohen's *A Dual Heritage, The Public Career of Oscar S. Straus* (Philadelphia: The Jewish Publication Society of America, 1969) are good biographical sources. Historical studies of early Zionist activity in America are also helpful, as in Naomi W. Cohen's study of the American Jewish Committee, *Not Free to Desist* (Philadelphia: Jewish Publication Society of America, 1972). The best sources, of course, remain the primary material.

On Louis Brandeis, the two major biographies by Alpheus Thomas Mason, both cited in the text, have preempted the field. Like most works on Brandeis, they are highly flattering. Melvin Urofsky, in *A Mind of One Piece: Louis Brandeis and American Reform* (New York: Scribner's 1971), takes a more analytic stance, although he generally accepts Brandeis on his own terms. Perhaps the most criti-cal study of the Justice appears in Yonathan Shapiro, *Leadership of the American Zionist Organization, 1897-1930* (Urbana: University of Illinois Press, 1971). Useful profiles of Brandeis also emerge out of the memoirs of Louis Lipsky, Felix Frankfurter, Dean Acheson, and Norman Hapgood.

The subject of Jews and modern America is discussed intelligently in various chapters of Howe's work. It is dealt with, of course, in the growing legion of books on the Jewish experience in America. Espe-cially stimulating is Milton Himmelfarb, *The Jews of Modernity* (New York: Basic Books, 1973). Two early classics on immigrant life should also be consulted: Robert E. Park and Herbert Miller, *Old World Traits Transplanted* (New York: Harper, 1921), and Florjan Zna-niecki and William I. Thomas, *The Polish Peasant in Europe and America* (New York: Knopf, 1927).

Secondary works on Isaac Bashevis Singer are cited in the notes. A recent book on Abraham Joshua Heschel is Franklin Sherman, *The Promise of Heschel* (Philadelphia: Lippincott, 1970).

The best general work on ethnic assimilation is Milton Gordon, *Assimilation in American Life* (New York: Oxford University Press, 1964). Michael Novak, *The Rise of the Unmeltable Ethnics* (New York: Macmillan, 1972) and Andrew Greeley, *Why Can't They Be*

Like Us? (New York: Dutton, 1971) are perceptive and controversial treatments of the issue. *The Immigrant Experience*, edited by Thomas Wheeler (Baltimore: Penguin, 1972), is an excellent collection of essays on this theme. Peter I. Rose, ed., *Nation of Nations: The Ethnic Experience and the Racial Crisis* (New York: Random House, 1972) is a useful source.

Discussions of Jewish assimilation approach infinity. Some of the better references include Georges Friedmann, *The End of the Jewish People?* (Garden City, N.Y.: Doubleday, 1967); Daniel Bell, "Reflections on Jewish Identity," *Commentary* 31 (June 1961); Stuart Rosenberg, *The Search for Jewish Identity in America* (Garden City, N.Y.: Doubleday, 1964). As implied in the text, the works of Ahad Ha-Am (Asher Ginzberg) are a must for any student of this subject.

Sentiment and ideology still influence many analyses of Jewish socialism. The works of Irving Howe and Will Herberg are most prominent in these respects. Ronald Sanders' *The Downtown Jews* (New York: Harper and Row, 1969) is a worthwhile analysis, which focuses on the life of Abraham Cahan. Melech Epstein, *Jewish Labor in the United States* (New York: Trade Union Sponsoring Committee, 1950-1953) and Elias Tcherikower, ed., *The Early Jewish Labor Movement in the United States* (New York: YIVO Institute for Jewish Research, 1961) are good overviews. Other secondary sources are indicated in the text.

Secondary material on Morris R. Cohen, Abraham Cahan, and the other individuals who were the subjects of this study has been cited within the notes.

ADDITIONAL BIBLIOGRAPHY

BOOKS

Aaron, Daniel. *Men of Good Hope*. New York: Oxford University Press, 1951.
———. *Writers on the Left*. New York: Harcourt, Brace and World, 1961.
Adamic, Louis. *Laughing in the Jungle*. New York: Harper, 1932.
Adler, Cyrus. *I Have Considered the Days*. Philadelphia: Jewish Publication Society, 1941.
———. *Jacob H. Schiff, His Life and Letters*, Vols. I and II. New York: Doubleday, Doran, 1928.
Adler, Felix. *Life and Destiny*. New York: McClure, Phillips and Co., 1905.
Allentuck, Marcia, ed. *The Achievement of Isaac Bashevis Singer*. Carbondale: Southern Illinois University Press, 1969.
Alter, Robert. *After the Tradition*. New York: Dutton, 1969.
Baeck, Leo. *This People Israel*. New York: Holt, Rinehart and Winston, 1964.
Baron, Salo W. *Modern Nationalism and Religion*. New York: Harper, 1947.
———. *The Russian Jew Under Tsars and Soviets*. New York: Macmillan, 1964.
———. *A Social and Religious History of the Jews*, 9 vols. New York: Columbia University Press, 1952-1973.
Baruch, Bernard. *Baruch: My Own Story*. New York: Holt, 1957.
———. *Baruch: The Public Years*. New York: Holt, Rinehart and Winston, 1960.
Bell, Daniel. *Marxian Socialism in the United States*. Princeton: Princeton University Press, 1967.

Blau, Joseph L., and Baron, Salo W., eds. *The Jews of the United States, 1790-1840, A Documentary History*. New York: Columbia University Press, 1963.

Bloom, Sol. *The Autobiography of Sol Bloom*. New York: G. P. Putnam's Sons, 1948.

Brandeis, Louis D. *The Curse of Bigness*, edited by Osmond K. Fraenkel. New York: The Viking Press, 1934.

Cantor, Eddie. *My Life Is in Your Hands*. New York: Harper and Brothers, 1928.

———. *The Way I See It*, edited by Phyllis Rosenteur. Englewood Cliffs, N.J.: Prentice-Hall, 1959.

Celler, Emanuel. *You Never Leave Brooklyn*. New York: J. Day Co., 1953.

Coleman, Terry, *Going to America*. New York: Pantheon, 1972.

Danish, Max D. *The World of David Dubinsky*. Cleveland: World Publishing Co., 1957.

Dawidowicz, Lucy S., ed. *The Golden Tradition: Jewish Life and Thought in Eastern Europe*. New York: Holt, Rinehart and Winston, 1967.

Delaney, Cornelius. *Mind and Nature: A Study of the Naturalistic Philosophies of Cohen, Woodbridge, and Sellars*. South Bend, Ind.: University of Notre Dame Press, 1969.

Drachsler, Julius. *Democracy and Assimilation*. New York: Macmillan, 1920.

Einbinder, Gershon (Chaver Paver). *Clinton Street and Other Stories*, Translated from the Yiddish by Henry Goodman. New York: YKUF Publishers, 1974.

Eisenstein, Louis, and Rosenberg, Elliot. *A Stripe of Tammany's Tiger*. New York: R. Speller, 1966.

Epstein, Melech. *The Jew and Communism*. New York: Trade Union Sponsoring Committee, 1959.

Ernst, Robert. *Immigrant Life in New York City*. New York: King's Crown Press, 1949.

Forcey, Charles. *The Crossroads of Liberalism*. New York: Oxford University Press, 1961.

Frankfurter, Felix. *Felix Frankfurter Reminisces*. New York: Reynal, 1960.

Glanz, Rudolf. *The German Jew in America*; an annotated bibliography. Cincinnati: Hebrew Union College Press, 1969.

———. *Studies in Judaica Americana*. New York: Ktav Publishing House, 1970.

Glazer, Nathan. *American Judaism*. Chicago: University of Chicago Press, 1957.

Goldmark, Josephine. *Pilgrims of '48*. New Haven: Yale University Press, 1930.

Goren, Arthur, *New York Jews and the Quest for Community: The Kehillah Experiment, 1908-1922*. New York: Columbia University Press, 1970.

Graetz, Heinrich H. *History of the Jews*, 6 vols. Philadelphia: Jewish Publication Society, 1891-1898.

Halpern, Ben. *The Idea of a Jewish State*. Cambridge: Harvard University Press, 1951.

Handlin, Oscar. *Adventure in Freedom*. New York: McGraw-Hill, 1954.

Harap, Louis. *The Image of the Jew in American Literature: From Early Republic to Mass Immigration*. Philadelphia: The Jewish Publication Society of America, 1974.

Herberg, Will. *Protestant, Catholic, Jew*. Garden City, N.Y.: Doubleday, 1955.

Horowitz, George. *The Spirit of Jewish Law*. New York: Central Book Co., 1953.

Hourwich, Isaac. *Immigration and Labor*. New York: G. P. Putnam's Sons, 1912.

Jones, Maldwyn A. *American Immigration*. Chicago: University of Chicago Press, 1960.

Josephson, Matthew. *Sidney Hillman, Statesman of American Labor*. Garden City: Doubleday, 1952.

Karp, Abraham J., ed. *The Jewish Experience in America*. Waltham, Mass.: American Jewish Historical Society, 1969.

Katcher, Leo. *The Big Bankroll: The Life and Times of Arnold Rothstein*. New York: Harper, 1959.

Katz, Irving. *August Belmont: A Political Biography*. New York: Columbia University Press, 1968.

Kaufmann, Yehezkel. *The Religion of Israel*. Translated and abridged by Moshe Greenberg. New York: Schocken, 1972.

Kazin, Alfred. *Starting Out in the Thirties*. Boston: Little, Brown, 1965.
———. *A Walker in the City*. New York: Harcourt, Brace, 1969.

Kessner, Thomas. *The Golden Door*. New York: Oxford University Press, 1977.

Kipnis, Ira. *The American Socialist Movement, 1897-1912*. New York: Columbia University Press, 1952.

Kisch, Guido. *The Jews in Medieval Germany*. Chicago: University of Chicago Press, 1949.

Klein, Henry. *My Last Fifty Years*. New York: Isaac Goldman Co., 1935.

Kriesberg, Bessie. *Hard Soil, Tough Roots: An Immigrant Woman's Story*. Jericho, N.Y.: Exposition Press, 1973.

Lasch, Christopher. *The Agony of the American Left*. New York: Vintage, 1969.

Lenski, Gerhard. *The Religious Factor: A Social Inquiry*. Garden City, N.Y.: Doubleday, 1961.

Levin, Meyer. *The Old Bunch*. New York: Viking Press, 1937.

Lewisohn, Ludwig. *The Island Within*. New York: Harper, 1928.

Moore, George Foot. *Judaism in the First Centuries of the Christian Era*, 3 vols. Cambridge: Harvard University Press, 1927-54.

Parkes, James W. *Antisemitism*. Chicago: Quadrangle Books, 1963.

———. *The Jew in the Medieval Community*. London: The Soncino Press, 1938.

Reik, Theodore. *Ritual.* Translated by Douglas Bryan. New York: International Universities Press, 1946.

Renan, Ernest. *History of the People of Israel*, 5 vols. Boston: Little, Brown, and Co., 1903-12.

Ribalow, Harold U., ed. *Autobiographies of American Jews*. Philadelphia: Jewish Publication Society of America, 1973.

Riis, Jacob. *How the Other Half Lives*. Introduction by Donald N. Bigelow. New York: Sagamore Press, 1957.

Rosenzweig, Franz. *On Jewish Learning*, edited by N. N. Glatzer. New York: Schocken Books, 1955.

———. *The Star of the Redemption*. Translated by William Hallo. New York: Holt, Rinehart and Winston, 1971.

Roskolenko, Harry. *When I Was Last on Cherry Street*. New York: Stein and Day, 1965.

Schwartz, Leo W., ed. *Great Ages and Ideas of the Jewish People*. New York: Random House, 1956.

Seidman, Joel. *The Needle Trades*. New York: Farrar, Rinehart, Inc., 1942.

Sherman, Charles B. *The Jew Within American Society*. Detroit: Wayne State University Press, 1960.

Sklare, Marshall. *Conservative Judaism*. Glencoe, Ill.: Free Press, 1955.

Stolberg, Benjamin. *Tailor's Progress*. Garden City, N.Y.: Doubleday, 1944.

Strauss, Leo. *Persecution and the Art of Writing*. Glencoe, Ill.: Free Press, 1952.

Szajkowski, Zosa. *Jews, War and Communism*. New York: Ktav Publishing House, 1972.

Todd, Alden. *Justice on Trial: The Case of Louis D. Brandeis*. New York: McGraw-Hill, 1964.

Waldman, Louis. *Labor Lawyer*. New York: Dutton, 1944.

Wiebe, Robert. *The Search for Order, 1877-1920*. New York: Hill and Wang, 1967.

Wise, Stephen. *Challenging Years*. New York: Putnam, 1946.

Yezierska, Anzia. *Breadgivers*. Garden City, N.Y.: Doubleday, Page, 1925.

———. *Children of Loneliness*. New York: Funk and Wagnalls, 1923.
———. *Hungry Hearts*. Boston and New York: Houghton Mifflin Co., 1920.

ARTICLES, ESSAYS

Berlin, William S. Review of *A Mind of One Piece* by Melvin Urofsky. *Worldview* 15 (February 1972).
Bloom, Bernard. "Yiddish-Speaking Socialists in America." *American Jewish Archives* 12 (April 1960).
Bourne, Randolph. "The Jew and Trans-National America." *The Menorah Journal* 2 (December 1916).
Cuddihy, John Murray. "Jews, Blacks, and the Cold War at the Top." *Worldview* 15 (February 1972).
Dreier, Peter. "Political Pluralism and Jewish Liberalism: Beyond the Cliches." *Journal of Ethnic Studies* 4 (Fall 1976).
Dubofsky, Melvyn. "Organized Labor and the Immigrant in New York City, 1900-1918." *Labor History* 2 (Spring 1961).
Geller, Stuart. "Why Did Louis D. Brandeis Choose Zionism?" *American Jewish Historical Quarterly* 62 (June 1973).
Gorenstein, Arthur. "A Portrait of Ethnic Politics." *American Jewish Historical Quarterly* 50 (March 1961).
Handlin, Oscar. "American Views of the Jew at the Opening of the Twentieth Century." *Publications of the American Jewish Historical Society* 40 (June 1951).
Helfgott, Roy B. "Trade Unionism Among the Jewish Garment Workers of Britain and the United States." *Labor History* 2 (Spring 1961).
Higham, John. "Anti-Semitism in the Gilded Age." *Mississippi Valley Historical Review* 43 (1957).
Liebman, Charles. "Orthodoxy in American Jewish Life." *American Jewish Yearbook* 66 (1965).
Litt, Edgar. "Status, Ethnicity, and Patterns of Jewish Behavior in Baltimore." *Jewish Social Studies* 22 (July 1960).
Mandel, Irving Aaron. "Attitude of the American Jewish Community Toward East European Immigration as Reflected in the Anglo-Jewish Press, 1880-1890." *American Jewish Archives* 3 (January 1951).
Nathanson, Nathaniel L. "Mr. Justice Brandeis: A Law Clerk's Recollections of the October Term, 1934." *American Jewish Archives* 15 (April 1963).
Pearlman, Selig. "Jewish-American Unionism, Its Birth Pangs and Contributions to the General American Labor Movement." *Publications of the American Jewish Historical Society* 41 (June 1952).
Rideout, Walter B. "'O Workers' Revolution . . . The True Messiah.' The Jew

as Author and Subject in the American Radical Novel." *American Jewish Archives* 11 (October 1959).

Singer, Isaac Bashevis. "If You Could Ask One Question About Life, What Would the Answer Be?" *Esquire* 82 (December 1974).

Spiro, Melford E. "The Acculturation of American Ethnic Groups." *American Anthropologist* 57 (December 1955).

Szajkowski, Zosa. "The Attitude of American Jews to East European Jewish Immigration, 1881-1883." *Publications of the American Jewish Historical Society* 40 (September 1950).

————. "The Jews and New York City's Mayoralty Election of 1917." *Jewish Social Studies* 32 (October 1970).

DISSERTATION

Cohn, Werner. *The Sources of Jewish Liberalism*, unpublished Ph.D. dissertation. New School for Social Research, 1956.

INDEX

Acheson, Dean, 29-30, 36
Aleichem, Sholom (Shalom
    Rabinowitz), 51-53, 55, 105,
    156, 163
Alienation: from Christian society, 5,
    9-20, 152; of Jewish socialists,
    105-109; and Morris R. Cohen,
    133, 137, 140, 149
American Jewish Committee, 24-25
Americanization: Berkson's critique
    of, 98-101; political conceptions
    involved in, 4, 6; in Ravage's
    thought, 86-87
Antin, Mary, 90-96, 101, 102, 152,
    155, 157, 161
Anti-Semitism: contributed to Jew-
    ish separatism, 10-12; in Ger-
    many and Austria, 9, 11, 59;
    Singer's views on, 74-75; in the
    United States, 44, 88
Arendt, Hannah, on Jews' political
    inexperience, 11-12
Asch, Shalom, 184 n.22
Assimilation: based on a creed, 3-4,

92-96, 155; tensions of, 4-5, 48-
    51, 77-103, 180 n.48
Auden, W. H., 57

Baron, Salo W., on Jewish commu-
    nity, 12-13
Benjamin, Judah, 169 n.18
Berkson, Isaac, 81, 98-101, 102,
    161
"Beth Din," 18
Bickel, Alexander, 33
Bisno, Abraham, 107, 108, 128, 129
Borowitz, Eugene, 165-166 n.8
Bourne, Randolph, 96, 159
Brandeis, Louis D., 21-45, 75-76, 96,
    109, 130-132, 144, 155; approach
    to reform, 32-36; conception of
    freedom, 30-32; stress on educa-
    tion, 33; and Zionism, 33, 35-36,
    37-42
Bride of the Sabbath (Ornitz), 114-
    118

Cahan, Abraham, 51, 77, 78, 98, 119-